THE SINO-SOVIET DISPUTE

Documented and Analyzed

by

G. F. HUDSON, RICHARD LOWENTHAL,
and RODERICK MacFARQUHAR

FREDERICK A. PRAEGER, *Publisher*
NEW YORK

BOOKS THAT MATTER

Published in the United States of America in 1961 by
Frederick A. Praeger, Inc., Publisher
64 University Place, New York 3, N. Y.

First published in Great Britain in 1961 as a special supplement
by *The China Quarterly*

© *The China Quarterly* 1961
Library of Congress Catalog Card Number: 61-15894

THE SINO-SOVIET DISPUTE is published in two editions:
A Praeger Paperback (PPS-58)
A clothbound edition

This book is Number 95 in the series of
Praeger Publications in Russian History and World Communism

Manufactured in the United States of America

PREFACE

THE object of this booklet is to document and analyse the dispute between Moscow and Peking over global policies that came into the open at the beginning of 1960 and was dramatically concluded, temporarily at any rate, at the Moscow conference of 81 Communist parties last November. Our examination commences with a general introduction by G. F. Hudson of the background to the dispute. Richard Lowenthal's analysis of the course of the dispute during 1960 is a revised and lengthier version of an article that originally appeared in *The China Quarterly* and has since been reproduced by *Commentary* in America and as a supplement to *Preuves* in France. A long note clarifies the economic issues that affect Sino-Soviet relations.

Finally, the bulk of the booklet is devoted to documenting the dispute in the hopes that it may serve as a useful and permanent work of reference. Mr. Lowenthal's article naturally deals with the major points raised by these documents; but since many of them are of formidable length, I have thought it worth while to analyse some in detail, describing their argument and delineating what seem to me their crucial passages. I have included as appendices two " inside " reports from the Indian magazine *Link*, the reliability of whose Indian Communist sources lends considerable credence to accounts which fit in well with what could be observed from the outside.

R. MacF.

CONTENTS

DATE SUMMARY

1956.	February 14	Khrushchev Addresses CPSU's Twentieth Congress.
1957.	November 22	Ruling Communist Parties Issue Declaration in Moscow.
1959.	January 27	Khrushchev Addresses CPSU's Twenty-first Congress.
	September 15	Khrushchev Arrives in Washington at Start of American Tour.
	September 30	Khrushchev Arrives in Peking for China's Tenth Anniversary Celebrations.
1960.	February 4	Meeting of Warsaw Treaty Powers in Moscow.
	March 23	Khrushchev Begins French Tour.
	April 19	Chou En-lai Arrives in Delhi to Discuss Sino-Indian Border Dispute.
	April 22	90th Anniversary of Birth of Lenin.
	May 5	Khrushchev Announces U-2 Shot Down over Soviet Territory.
	May 16	Opening of Summit Conference in Paris.
	June 5	WFTU Meeting Opens in Peking.
	June 16	Eisenhower Visit to Japan Cancelled due to Rioting in Tokyo.
	June 24	Bucharest Communiqué issued.
	July 11	Moscow Announces an American RB47 Plane Shot Down over Soviet Waters.
	August	Reports of Soviet Technicians Leaving China.
	August 30	Partial Blockade of West Berlin Initiated.
	September 19	Khrushchev arrives in New York with Satellite Leaders for UN General Assembly Session.
	November	Moscow Conference of World Communist Leaders.
	December 2	Liu Shao-ch'i Starts Goodwill Tour of Russia.
	December 6	81 Party Statement Published.
	December 29	Peking Reveals Severity of 1960 Natural Disasters.
1961.	January 6	Khrushchev Reports on Moscow Conference.
	January 18	Chinese Party Resolution on Moscow Conference Passed.

THE
SINO-SOVIET
DISPUTE

Introduction

By G. F. HUDSON

EVER since the Chinese Communists set up their government in Peking in 1949 and promptly concluded a treaty of military alliance with the Soviet Union, there has been speculation in the West about the reality and durability of the Sino-Soviet partnership. It was from the outset reasonable to assume that the Chinese Communists' heritage of national pride, their consciousness of the vast size and population of China and their sense of achievement in having carried through their revolution with a minimum of Russian aid would render them unwilling blindly to follow the lead of Moscow and inclined to formulate foreign as well as domestic policies of their own.

For the first six years, however, after the establishment of the Communist régime in China there was very little sign of dissension; on the contrary, Sino-Soviet relations were marked by a remarkable degree of harmony. The Chinese emphasised not only their devotion to the doctrine of Marxism-Leninism but their desire to learn from " the Soviet experience," and a well-organised Sino-Soviet Friendship Association expended much energy, with full Party backing, in glorifying the Soviet Union in general and Stalin in particular in propaganda to the Chinese people. Above all, the Korean war brought Russia and China together; both had the strongest common interest in preventing the overthrow of the Communist régime in North Korea after the failure of its attack on the South, and while China put in an army to fight against the United Nations forces, Russia provided arms and equipment and the threat of intervention if the war should be extended to Chinese territory.

The first serious trouble between Moscow and Peking occurred in connection with the Twentieth Congress of the Soviet Communist Party, and it was significant that it arose over Khrushchev's attack on the memory of Stalin. It was noticed at the time by some Western observers that the terms of eulogy in which mention of Stalin was made in Mao Tse-tung's message of greeting to the Congress were so contrary to the tenor of Khrushchev's speech to the secret session a few days later as to require the inference that the Chinese leader had either not been informed of what was about to be done or had disagreed with it. It has now been reported that one of the grievances brought by the Chinese in the Conference of the Eighty-one Parties last November was Khrushchev's failure to consult Peking before deciding on the demolition

1

of the Stalin myth. This was certainly no small matter, for whatever may have been the expediency of the action taken in relation to Soviet domestic politics, the discredit cast on the personality which Communists throughout the world had done their utmost to build up in propaganda over two and a half decades was clearly a concern of the whole international movement and not of the Soviet party alone.

It was the paradox of this extraordinary episode that Khrushchev in demanding that other Communist parties simply fall into line with a decision taken in Moscow to degrade Stalin was invoking precisely that supreme authority over the international movement which Stalin had acquired and which largely depended on his prestige as an almost superhuman being. Once the former " leader of progressive mankind " had been denounced as a tyrant and a fraud, the question was inevitably asked among Communists—and not only in Peking—whence Khrushchev could derive the right to issue instructions to the comrades of all lands.

The Chinese in particular questioned the wisdom of what had been done, but even more they resented the lack of consultation, and this was to be a permanent element in all subsequent policy conflicts; it raised the issue of " polycentrism " in the conditions of the post-Stalin era. In the days when Russia had been the only Communist-governed state and all other Communist parties had lacked any control of state-power, it had been natural enough for all non-Russian Communists to look to the Kremlin for a guidance which had been in practice words of command, but now that there were several other Communist parties with the powers and responsibilities of sovereign governments—and one of them ruled over the most populous nation in the world—it was no longer appropriate for a single party to lay down articles of faith and policy for all. The situation demanded some kind of new machinery for inter-party consultation, especially as the former organisation of the Comintern no longer existed. But the Soviet leadership was not at all disposed to give up the complete freedom of policy-making to which it had become accustomed, and outside the Soviet Union also there was a widespread recognition among zealous Communists of the need for a sort of international High Command if the Communist states were to maintain an effective coalition against the capitalist enemy..

The Chinese party about this time seems to have arrived at a view which sought to hold a balance between the claims of the non-Soviet Communist states to independence and acceptance of a Soviet " leadership " in the interest of the unity of the *bloc* as a whole. According to this view Communist-governed states should be free from Soviet interference in their internal affairs and should make their voices heard in matters of general concern, but should acknowledge the primacy of the

Soviet Union in the making and execution of a common policy. This attitude gained for China for a while the reputation of being the champion of " liberalism " within the *bloc,* for the Poles, in their struggle for a " Polish road to socialism," received moral support and encouragement from Peking.

On the other hand, the Chinese line also involved a most rigorous condemnation of Titoism as guilty of the unpardonable crime of neutrality between the two world camps, and by implication condemnation of those who were too tolerant of this heresy. The consequences of the Chinese view came out clearly in relation to the troubles in Eastern Europe in the autumn of 1956. In Poland the revolt was canalised within the Communist Party, the armed forces remained under party control and there was no question of breaking away from the Soviet alliance which alone guaranteed the Oder-Neisse frontier against German revisionism; China, therefore, backed Gomulka and is said to have intervened actively to restrain Khrushchev from military action against Poland after the rebuff he received from the central committee of the Polish party on his uninvited attendance at their deliberations on October 19.

In Hungary, on the other hand, the Communist Party had lost control of the armed forces, the insurgents demanded multi-party democracy and international neutrality, and only the Russian army could keep the country within the Communist camp; here China pressed for ruthless military intervention when Moscow was hesitating. The Chinese attitudes were opposite in the two cases, but each was judged on a consistent principle.

The line which Peking took on this upheaval in Eastern Europe was, however, less important than the fact that it took a line at all. Poland and Hungary were Russia's satellite states with which China hitherto had not been supposed to have any political concern. It was an epoch-making event when China claimed the right to have a say in what Russia should do about their affairs and sent Chou En-lai to assist in their settlement. The intervention appears not to have been entirely unwelcome to the Kremlin, for the sudden outbreaks had produced so much confusion and dissension in Moscow and had for the time being so lowered the prestige of the C.P.S.U. that the good offices of China were very useful in helping the Soviet Communist leadership to emerge from a dangerous and humiliating situation. The episode nevertheless gave China a new importance and sense of power. The Chinese position was that any counter-revolution in a Communist-ruled country or conflict between Communist states concerned all Communists everywhere and not Russia alone; there was an implicit challenge to the exclusive supreme authority which had belonged to the Kremlin under

Stalin and which Khrushchev in spite of his repudiation of " Stalinism " was in practice trying to preserve.

It was not, however, the aim of Mao Tse-tung at this stage to deny to the Soviet Union a special position in the Communist camp; on the contrary, the Chinese emphasis was on the unity of the camp as a military coalition standing in opposition to the camp of imperialism led by the United States, and this unity was held to require a joint command. At Moscow in November 1957, when a manifesto of ruling Communist parties was issued to mark the fortieth anniversary of the October Revolution, it was Mao Tse-tung who exerted himself to persuade Gomulka to acknowledge the " leadership " of the Soviet Union in the " socialist camp." But this leadership was conceived by the Chinese as a high command for carrying out agreed basic policies on behalf of all Communist parties and states, just as General Eisenhower in the invasion of France held command over both American and British forces in order to carry out the agreed aims of the two governments without any implication of American control over Britain.

The value of such formal recognition of Soviet primacy from the Chinese point of view was to check Titoist tendencies in the European satellite countries by ranging them definitively on the side of the Soviet Union in world affairs and excluding any deviations into neutralism. It was assumed that the Soviet Union itself would exercise its leadership in the right direction, that is to say against America, and that the ears which might listen to the siren voices of Washington would be found, not in Moscow, but in Warsaw.

In the following year, however, the Soviet government, evidently without consulting Peking, took a major initiative in world affairs which the Chinese regarded as injurious to themselves. In response to the American landing of troops in the Lebanon, Khrushchev demanded a summit conference of the three Western Powers and the Soviet Union together with India to discuss the problems of the Middle East. When the Western Powers demurred and countered with a proposal to hold a summit conference within the framework of a meeting of the United Nations Security Council, Khrushchev appeared at first willing to agree. Suddenly, however, he dashed off to Peking and in the end the whole project was dropped. Although the course of Russo-Chinese relations during this episode remains obscure, there is no need to doubt the inference that was drawn by diplomatic observers at the time—that Peking had protested strongly against a summit conference on the Middle East at which Communist China would not be represented, and that Khrushchev had called it off in response to Chinese pressure.

It was generally supposed that what had aroused the ire of Mao was the idea of such a meeting being held in the Security Council where

China would be represented by a nominee of Chiang Kai-shek. But the signs were that Peking objected no less to the inclusion of India instead of China to represent Asia in a Big Five summit conference. The Chinese stood firmly on their formal status as one of the five Great Powers recognised as such by permanent membership of the Security Council, and although in the circumstances of American non-recognition of Communist China they did not object to a Big Four meeting without China on European affairs, it was quite another matter to bring in India as a substitute for China in dealing with the affairs of Western Asia. It was indeed a piece of monumental tactlessness for Khrushchev ever to have supposed that the Chinese would put up with such an affront.

For their part, the Russians were offended by the claims put forward for the rural communes organised throughout China in the late summer of 1958. By asserting that with the advent of the communes, the achievement of Communism in China was no longer a distant prospect, the Chinese appeared to suggest that their society was overtaking the Soviet one, that it was jumping over whole " historic stages " as Moscow later put it. Both Khrushchev and Mikoyan went so far as to denigrate the communes in discussions with Americans, and it is doubtful whether the modification of the most extravagant Chinese claims at the end of 1958 wiped out Russian indignation over the affair.

The year 1959 saw the development in Soviet foreign policy of two trends both of which gave rise to increasing apprehension and resentment in Peking; the first was the policy of direct approach to the United States with the aim of reaching agreements *à deux* between Khrushchev and President Eisenhower, and the second the effort to cultivate close relations with India and Indonesia, with both of which countries Communist China had come into conflict. With the first of these policies Peking did not at first quarrel; negotiations of a sort had been going on for years over Germany and Berlin, and the invasion of the United States by the successive onsets of Mikoyan, Kozlov and Khrushchev himself seemed at first sight to be no more than a new move in the cold war.

But as the campaign showed signs of bringing about a genuine *détente* between Russia and America, the Chinese Communists naturally began to wonder what there would be for them in an agreement of the two super-Powers. It soon became evident that there would be very little. Khrushchev had a sufficiently difficult task in trying to persuade President Eisenhower to make concessions to Russia over Berlin; he was not going to jeopardise his chances of success by also pressing the claims of China, to which Washington was notoriously even more resistant. Mao Tse-tung was suddenly confronted with the prospect of

5

being left out in the cold while the leaders of the socialist and imperialist camps got together in a mutually advantageous deal.

By this time, after repeated manifestations of Khrushchev's disregard for the views and interests of his Chinese ally, Mao probably had a profound distrust of him. But how was he to be prevented from going ahead with his new policy? How was China to be safeguarded against the effects of the " Camp David spirit "? The Soviet Union was far too strong and self-confident, with its booming industrial production, its sputniks and its luniks, to be turned aside by any normal methods of persuasion or diplomatic pressure.

There was only one way for China to exert a compelling influence on Khrushchev, and that was by attacking him at his most vulnerable point—his standing as the supreme representative of the Marxist-Leninist cause. He was the leader of a party which based its claim to permanent and exclusive rule over Russia and to the loyalties of Communists throughout the world on an ideology of which it had been the first successful practical exponent. If it could now be shown that the First Secretary of the C.P.S.U. was betraying the principles for which not only Stalin but also Lenin had stood, that he had in fact fallen into heresy, then the very basis of his power would be undermined and he would have at least to compromise with the purists of Peking in order to save himself from the anathema.

Communist China was further goaded into launching such an attack on the Soviet leadership by the distinctly unfriendly attitude of Moscow towards China's conflicts with two of her Asian neutralist neighbours— India and Indonesia. These were disputes which had arisen not from any Chinese attempt to promote a Communist revolution in either country, but over issues concerning frontiers and rights of Chinese residents such as the most bourgeois of Chinese governments might have taken up; indeed, the quarrel with Indonesia was quite ludicrously out of keeping with the general Communist line, for by protesting against Indonesian legislation to exclude Chinese from the retail trade they had so efficiently engrossed, the Peking Government was making itself the champion abroad of those very interests of small private enterprise which in China it was doing its utmost to destroy.

But whatever the logic of their contentions with India and Indonesia the Chinese expected from the Russians at least a degree of moral support for them in accordance with the solidarity of the " socialist camp " against all outsiders. The Soviet Union, however, had been taking considerable trouble to cultivate friendly relations with the neutral nationalist governments of Asia, including those of India and Indonesia, and to influence their foreign policies to the advantage of

6

Soviet interests; this was a pattern of policy which was not to be discarded merely in order to please Mao Tse-tung. Khrushchev had already in 1958 sought to substitute India for China in a Big Five conference; he continued to woo and flatter India and carefully avoided taking China's side in the conflict which developed with India over the disputed frontier.

The friction between Moscow and Peking which developed from this Soviet courting of China's adversaries (in a region of the world which the Chinese regarded as geographically within their sphere of interest rather than Russia's) was brought to a head when at the beginning of 1960 Khrushchev in pursuit of his indefatigable personal diplomacy made a second tour of South and South-East Asia. He glorified the Soviet Union on every possible occasion and made the most extravagant professions of undying friendship for the peoples of India and Indonesia, but he did nothing to honour China or to present the Chinese case either in Delhi or Jakarta. The insult was symbolised by the fact that Khrushchev was in India on the occasion of the 10th Anniversary of the signing of the Sino-Soviet treaty. Chinese anger at this performance expressed itself in an almost complete news boycott; the tour was not mentioned in the Chinese press for a week and thereafter was treated as a matter of no importance. The impression produced by the Khrushchev tour was probably the last straw in causing Mao to lose patience with Khrushchev and embark on a systematic campaign against him.

As far as the Paris summit conference was concerned the Chinese campaign launched a month previously was almost certainly not a decisive factor in causing its breakdown; a deadlock at the conference was rendered in any case likely by the hardening of the American attitude over Berlin after American policy-makers had had time to repair the breaches effected in President Eisenhower's vulnerable personality by Khrushchev's personal assault tactics. When it became clear to Khrushchev that he was not going to get the great diplomatic triumph which he had hoped to obtain from the kindling of the Camp David spirit, he preferred that the summit conference should collapse at the outset in a blaze of Russian moral indignation at U.2 aggression over Russian territory rather than end in an anticlimax of agreement to disagree. But in thus for the time being raising rather than reducing international tension he may well have been influenced by the new pressure of Chinese ideological criticism which meant that any public setback in diplomacy would be used against him by the Maoist opposition.

The wrecking of the summit conference was not, however, the end of the affair; it was only the beginning. Within a few days of Khrushchev's theatrical display of intransigence, in which he showed himself to all appearances the implacable foe of the imperialist warmongers of Washington, he had given notice that he would again seek an agreement, if not any more with the Eisenhower administration, then with the President due to be elected in November.

Chinese suspicions were not allayed; it was clear that there was to be no fundamental change in the policy of direct approach to the United States, but only a postponement of it. The ideological conflict between Russia and China was thus not abated, but intensified, after the collapse of the summit conference. What China sought to get from the Kremlin was an admission that American imperialism was incorrigible and that nothing more than a temporary truce with it was possible; this was the real significance of the argument over the inevitability of war. The controversy was carried on with all the Communists of the world as audience and jury, and in the end the conference of the eighty-one parties had to be summoned to settle the dispute.

Since its manifesto was proclaimed to the world there has been discussion among Western commentators of the question whether Russia or China was the winner in the form of words that was adopted to restore the unity of the Communist camp. But the very fact that the conference had to be held was a success for Peking; it meant that the Kremlin, when subjected to criticism from China, could no longer ride roughshod over it and expect the international movement blindly to follow a Russian lead, but needed to put its case to a world assembly of Communist parties. This need arose from the fact that the Communist Party of China could not be silenced or suppressed by any " organisational " means; Khrushchev could not deal with the opposition of Mao as Stalin had dealt with Trotsky or Bukharin. Tito had already demonstrated that a Communist leader in control of a state could only be subjugated by Moscow through the use of military force across a frontier with all the international complications this might involve; in 1960 a state greater than Yugoslavia—indeed potentially the greatest on earth—was defying Moscow, and the only answer was reference to a Marxist-Leninist world parliament. In a manner that Khrushchev could not relish, the era of Stalin was over.

Diplomacy and Revolution:
The Dialectics of a Dispute

By RICHARD LOWENTHAL

THE policy declaration and the appeal to the peoples of the world adopted last December by the Moscow conference of eighty-one Communist parties mark the end of one phase in the dispute between the leaderships of the ruling parties of China and the Soviet Union—the phase in which the followers of Mao for the first time openly challenged the standing of the Soviet Communists as the fountain-head of ideological orthodoxy for the world movement. But the "ideological dispute" which began in April was neither a sudden nor a self-contained development: it grew out of acute differences between the two Communist Great Powers over concrete diplomatic issues, and it took its course in constant interaction with the changes in Soviet diplomatic tactics. Hence the total impact of that phase on Soviet foreign policy on one side, and on the ideology, organisation and strategy of international Communism on the other, cannot be evaluated from an interpretation of the Moscow documents alone, but only from a study of the process as a whole, as it developed during the past year on both planes.[1]

To say that the 1960 Chinese challenge to Soviet ideological authority grew out of pragmatic disagreements over foreign policy is not to take the view that the varieties of Communist ideology are a mere cloak for conflicts of national interest. The profound differences in the history of the Soviet and Chinese Communist parties, both in the strategy by which they conquered power and in the methods they used afterwards for transforming society, have clearly produced a different ideological climate,

---

[1] I have not attempted here to deal with the impact of the dispute on Chinese foreign policy, as distinct from Chinese ideology. Owing to the absence of diplomatic relations with the main enemy, the scope for Chinese diplomacy outside the *bloc* is somewhat limited. As experts on the subject have suggested in past issues of this review, the chief effect of the dispute in this field seems to have been to make the Chinese leaders try to mend some of their national quarrels with neutral Asian states, notably Burma, Nepal and Indonesia, and to reduce the temperature of their conflict with India: apparently they realised at some point that the multiplication of these quarrels made them needlessly vulnerable to Soviet criticism of their general views on war and peaceful co-existence—views that had, after all, been formulated primarily with an eye to relations with the "imperialist" West, and above all with the United States. On the main issue, the repetition of the proposal for an atom-free zone in the Pacific on August 1 may have been intended to stake out a Chinese negotiating position in case of Soviet-American agreement on a permanent ban on nuclear tests —a price to be exacted for agreement to be kept out of the nuclear club.

9

different forms of inner-party life and a different " style of work "; and the fact that Mao Tse-tung could only win control of the Chinese party and lead it to victory by repeatedly defying Stalin's advice has contributed to the formation of a Chinese Communist leadership which is highly conscious of those differences.

This is not the place either to discuss the origin and nature of the distinctive ideological climate of Chinese Communism in detail, or to trace its various manifestations from Mao's first " rectification " movement of 1941 to the methods adopted after his victory for the " re-education " of hostile classes, or from the reaction to Soviet " de-stalinisation " and the subsequent crisis in the Soviet *bloc* to the " Hundred Flowers " campaign and to the creation of the communes. Suffice it to say that while some of these manifestations of Chinese originality took an apparently " liberal " and others an apparently " extremist " form, their common characteristic is a historically conditioned tendency to believe that almost anything is possible to a revolutionary party armed with the right consciousness—an exaltation of faith and will over all " objective conditions " of the productive forces and all given class structures which exceeds that shown by the Bolshevik model, and is even more remote from the original Marxian doctrine than the latter.

A party leadership conditioned by this ideological climate will obviously perceive both the internal problems and the national interests of the state it governs in a peculiar way; to that extent, the ideological difference constitutes a kind of permanent potential for rivalry between the two Communist Great Powers. Yet it does not by itself explain the timing and content of any particular dispute between them. For given the manifestly overriding importance of their common interests, the potential rivalry can only become actual when concrete policy disagreements arise which cannot be settled by the ordinary means of intra-*bloc* diplomacy, and which the weaker and dependent ally regards as sufficiently vital to take recourse to the public use of the ideological weapon. This was done by China in muted hints during the 1958 disagreements, and much more openly in 1960.

THE CHINESE VIEW

In both cases, Chinese misgivings seem to have been based on a sense of insufficient Soviet diplomatic and military support in their long-standing conflict with the United States, and to have been acutely aggravated by Mr. Khrushchev's efforts to achieve a Soviet-American *détente* —by his repeated bids for a " summit conference " without Communist China, and by his visit to the U.S. in September 1959. The Chinese leaders apparently feared, probably not without reason, that such a *détente* would further diminish Soviet interest in taking serious risks on their behalf, and increase Soviet interest in preventing them from taking any such risks themselves.[1a] Above all, Soviet willingness to make disarmament one of the main items on any summit agenda, combined with the agreed temporary ban on nuclear test explosions and the continued negotiations for a permanent ban, must have given rise to Chinese anxiety lest the Russians might be willing on certain conditions to enter a commitment to close the " nuclear club." The mere fact of negotiation on that subject apparently precluded them from receiving Soviet aid in developing nuclear weapons of their own, and thus helped to delay their becoming a world power of the first rank; an actual Soviet commitment would have faced them with the choice of either accepting permanent inferiority in this field, or—if they went ahead successfully in developing and testing the weapon themselves—of defying an agreement of the world's leading powers in isolation.

Whatever the Chinese may have said in their private representations to Moscow, they did not think it advisable to spell out these fears in public. But during the winter of 1959–60—roughly from Khrushchev's visit to Peking, on his return from his talks with Eisenhower, at the beginning of October to the Moscow conference of the Warsaw Pact states in early February—they openly attacked the assumptions on which the effort to achieve a Soviet-American *détente* was officially based.[2] The core of their argument was that the policy of American " imperialism " and of Eisenhower, its " chieftain," could not change in substance even if it was temporarily disguised by peace-loving phrases; hence nothing could be gained by seeking an understanding with the U.S. in an atmosphere of *détente*, only by isolating this " main enemy " and putting maximum pressure on him. A period of quite visible, concrete disagreement on policy towards the Eisenhower administration thus preceded the Chinese Communists' generalised, ideological attack on Soviet authority.

The most striking characteristic of that period is the apparent unconcern with which the Soviet leaders pursued their preparations for a " summit conference," despite the increasingly outspoken Chinese protests. The impression that Mao Tse-tung had refused to approve the concept of a *détente* based on " mutual concessions " as advanced by Khrushchev was confirmed when the latter, addressing the Supreme Soviet on his return to Moscow, coupled his advocacy of that concept with blunt

---

[1a] Since this was written, a report based on unpublished Communist documents in the possession of Western governments has stated that a scheme for a joint Russo-Chinese Pacific naval command broke down owing to Soviet fears of being drawn by the Chinese into a war over Formosa. See Edward Crankshaw in the London *Observer*, February 12 and 19, 1961.

[2] For a full study of the development of the Chinese arguments during that phase, see A. M. Halpern, " Communist China and Peaceful Coexistence," *The China Quarterly*, No. 3, p. 16.

warnings against the "Trotskyite adventurism" of a policy of "neither peace nor war,"[3] and when the theoretical organ of the Chinese Communists developed an analysis of American foreign policy directly opposed to Khrushchev's optimism in the following months.[4] Nevertheless, Khrushchev announced to the Supreme Soviet in January 1960 a substantial reduction of Soviet conventional forces and military expenditures as his advance contribution to the ten-power disarmament negotiations, and also indicated willingness to help overcome the deadlock in the negotiations on an inspection system for a permanent ban on nuclear test explosions—a most sensitive issue from the Chinese point of view.

Within a week, the standing committee of the Chinese National People's Congress, in a resolution formally approving the Soviet disarmament proposals, solemnly announced to the world that China would not be bound by any agreements to which she was not a party; but when this stand, together with warnings against illusions about a change in the character of American policy, was repeated at the conference of Warsaw Treaty ministers in early February by the—possibly uninvited—Chinese observer, his speech was not published in any European member state of the Soviet *bloc*, and the declaration adopted by the conference showed virtually no concessions to his point of view.[5] To cap it all, Khrushchev spent most of the remainder of February, including the tenth anniversary of the Sino-Soviet alliance, in India and Indonesia, two countries with which China was involved in acute conflicts of national interest, and showed throughout the journey an almost ostentatious detachment from Chinese claims and actions.

All during the winter, the Chinese thus experienced the inherent weakness in the position of a dependent ally who urges the stronger partner to pay more heed to his interests, but is unable to switch sides if the latter turns a deaf ear: none of their objections, raised first in secret and then with increasing publicity, were able to deflect Khrushchev from his course. There remained to them one weapon—to interfere directly not with the Soviet policy of *détente*, but with the *détente* itself—by urging on Communist and revolutionary nationalist movements in the non-Communist world a bolder forward policy than was compatible with the plans of Soviet diplomacy. But this meant that the Chinese Communists must set themselves up as rivals to their Russian comrades in advising these movements—in other words, that they must generalise the dispute and raise the question of ideological authority.

3 Moscow Radio, October 31, 1959.
4 *e.g.* Yü Chao-li, "The Chinese People's Great Victory in the Fight against Imperialism," *Peking Review*, September 22, 1959, from *Red Flag*, No. 18, 1959; *idem*, "Excellent Situation for the Struggle for Peace," *Peking Review*, January 5, 1960, from *Red Flag*, No. 1, 1960; editorial, *People's Daily*, January 21, 1960.
5 See the text of both the declaration and K'ang Sheng's speech in *The China Quarterly*, No. 2, pp. 75–89.

During the later part of the winter 1959–60, a number of cases became known where Chinese representatives had opposed Soviet delegates in closed sessions of the directing organs of such international front organisations as the World Peace Council, the Afro-Asian Solidarity Committee, the World Federation of Trade Unions, etc.[5a] The central issue in these clashes was whether the "peace campaign" was the priority task to which all other forms of revolutionary struggle must be subordinated, as the Russians maintained, or whether it was only one among many forms of the struggle against imperialism, which must in no circumstances be isolated and "set in opposition" to more militant forms of revolutionary action, as the Chinese argued. It was as a platform for these discussions in the international movement that the Chinese Communists published in April their ideological statements on the teachings of Lenin —documents which, despite all later elaborations and modifications, have remained basic for that phase of the dispute.[6]

THE QUESTION OF WAR

It has been implied in subsequent Soviet polemics, against "dogmatists and sectarians," and innumerable times spelt out in Western comment, that the central thesis of those Chinese statements was the continued validity of Lenin's belief in the inevitability of world war. That is not so. Every one of the Chinese documents in question quoted with approval the sentence in the 1957 Moscow declaration (based in turn on the resolution of the Twentieth Congress of the CPSU) that, owing to the growth of the forces of peace, "it is now realistically possible to prevent war."[6a] What none of them approved, however, is the formula of the Twenty-first Congress on the emerging possibility "even before the full victory of Socialism in the world, while capitalism continues to exist in part of the world, to banish world war from the life of human society." The difference is that, in the Chinese view, the latter phrase implies the

---

[5a] e.g., at the Rome meeting of the Presidium of the World Peace Council and the sessions of the secretariat of the Afro-Asian Solidarity Committee in Cairo in January 1960. Chinese contributions had disappeared from *Problems of Peace and Socialism*, the Soviet-controlled international Communist monthly edited in Prague, since November 1959.

[6] Yü Chao-li, "On Imperialism as a Source of War in Modern Times," and "On the Way for all Peoples to struggle for Peace," NCNA, March 30, 1960, from *Red Flag*, No. 7, 1960; Editorial "Long Live Leninism," *Peking Review*, April 26, 1960, from *Red Flag*, No. 8, 1960; Editorial, *People's Daily*, April 22, 1960; Lu Ting-yi, "Get United under Lenin's Revolutionary Banner," speech at Lenin commemoration meeting in Peking, April 22, 1960 (NCNA same date).

[6a] This applies to all Chinese texts available for scrutiny. Mr. Crankshaw's summing up of a secret Communist report, referred to in Note 1a above, repeats the Soviet charge that the Chinese regard nuclear war as inevitable. (See particularly his second article in *Observer*, Feb. 19.) But he quotes no Chinese statements, and indicates that the report in question was rendered by the leader of a satellite Communist party favouring the Soviet view, and may have come into Western possession by a deliberate Soviet leak.

disappearance of any serious *danger* of world war while capitalism still exists; the Chinese Communists felt that this presupposed a change in the nature of imperialism—and that they had to deny such a possibility in order to contest the Khrushchevian hope of converting the ruling circles of the U.S. to a genuine acceptance of " peaceful coexistence " from realistic motives.

The picture drawn by the Chinese was that of an unchanged, though weakened, imperialism which would resort to war whenever it could to defend its sphere of exploitation, but might be prevented from doing so in any particular case by the " forces of peace." In practice, they agreed with the Soviets in regarding an all-out attack on the Soviet *bloc* as unlikely, but argued that inter-imperialist war was still possible, and insisted that colonial wars against national liberation movements were virtually inevitable: the latter could only be " stopped " by vigorous support for the revolutionary movements. But the Communists would fail to give support if they were " afraid " of another world war, if they " begged the imperialists for peace," or if they tolerated or even spread illusions about the warlike nature of imperialism, instead of mobilising the masses everywhere for an all-out struggle against it.

This analysis implied three charges of " muddle-headed concessions to revisionism " against Khrushchev's policy: exaggeration of the dangers of nuclear war, which might paralyse the will to resist imperialism or at any rate lead to excessive caution; illusions about the growth of a " realistic " tendency towards peaceful coexistence among such " chieftains of imperialism " as Eisenhower, which might lead to a relaxation of vigilance among the Communist governments and movements; and as a result, excessive reliance on diplomatic negotiation as a means to avert war, causing a desire to restrain revolutionary movements and " just wars " of liberation, instead of welcoming them as the best means to weaken the imperialists and stop *their* wars. Accordingly, the Chinese ideologists argued that it was all right for a Communist to seek a meeting with Eisenhower, but wrong to say that he believed in the latter's peaceful intentions; all right to propose " general and complete disarmament," but wrong to tell his own followers that there was a real chance of obtaining it; all right to propagate peaceful coexistence, but wrong to advise the Algerian nationalists to try and negotiate a cease-fire with President de Gaulle. They accepted peace *propaganda* as a means of revolutionary struggle against imperialism, but not peace *diplomacy* of a kind which might even temporarily mitigate the forms of that struggle.

THE SOVIET REPLY

The Russians, aware that there could be no serious negotiation without an atmosphere of *détente* and at least the pretence of believing in the peaceful intentions of the other side, recognised that this was an attack on their whole coexistence diplomacy; but they had to answer it on the ideological plane. Through the mouth of Otto Kuusinen, a member of the secretariat of the CC CPSU who had begun work in the Comintern in Lenin's time, they insisted [7] that Lenin had differentiated between militarist diehards and possible partners for peaceful coexistence in the imperialist camp, and had foreseen that changes in military technique might one day make war impossible. They argued that the growing strength of the " Socialist camp " and the destructive potential of nuclear weapons and long-range rockets had in fact provided a realistic basis for a diplomacy based on similar differentiation at the present time, and claimed as telling proof of their thesis the success of Khrushchev's personal diplomacy in general, and of his " historic visit " to the U.S. in particular, in largely dispersing the climate of the Cold War and restoring businesslike relations between the two different social systems. Yet only a few weeks later Khrushchev himself, even while maintaining this position in theory, reversed himself in practice to the extent of wrecking the summit conference on the ground that negotiation with Eisenhower had become impossible after his assumption of responsibility for the U 2 incident.

Western discussion of the causes of this *volte-face* has necessarily remained inconclusive in the absence of direct evidence of the motives of the Russian rulers and the course of their deliberations in the critical period. But a coherent analysis of the Sino-Soviet dispute is impossible without at least venturing a hypothesis. I have elsewhere stated my reasons for rejecting the theory that a decisive weakening of Khrushchev's position by some combination of " neo-Stalinist " or " pro-Chinese " elements in the Soviet leadership took place at that time [8]; indeed, I know of no convincing evidence for the assumption that such a grouping exists at all. On the other hand, Khrushchev's Baku speech of April 25 showed his anxieties, following a number of authorised American policy statements, lest the summit meeting might fail to yield the Western concessions on Berlin which he expected, and his desire to increase the pressure in that direction; and his initial reaction to the U 2 incident is consistent with the assumption that he regarded it not as a reason for evading the summit conference, but as an occasion for making the pressure more effective by driving a wedge between Eisenhower and his " diehard militarist " advisers.[9]

---

[7] Speech at Lenin commemoration meeting in Moscow, April 22, 1960: *Pravda*, April 23.

[8] " The Nature of Khrushchev's Power," *Problems of Communism*, July/August 1960.

[9] See Khrushchev's speeches to the Supreme Soviet on May 5 and 7, and at the reception of the Czechoslovak Embassy in Moscow on May 9.

By marking the complete failure of this crude attempt at differentiation, the President's assumption of personal responsibility for the spy-flights, whatever its other merits or demerits, must have been a double blow to Khrushchev: it deprived him of the last hope of obtaining substantial concessions at the summit, and it put him clearly in the wrong on one important part of his public argument with his Chinese allies. A failure to reach his summit objectives thus became certain at the very moment at which, from the viewpoint of his prestige in the "Socialist camp" and the Communist world movement, he could least afford such a failure: hence it seems natural that, with the full support of his colleagues, he decided rather to wreck the conference in advance unless he could still force a last-minute differentiation by obtaining a public apology from Eisenhower.

Within a few days, Khrushchev demonstrated by his refusal to go ahead with an East German peace treaty pending a possible summit conference with Eisenhower's successor that he had not abandoned the "general line" of his diplomacy but only intended to change the time schedule. But the Chinese Communists not only were not content with that, but felt that now they had been proved right by events, they were in a strong position to force a broad change of policy by pressing home their ideological attack.

PEKING PRESSES ITS ATTACK

The attempt was made officially and in fact publicly at the beginning of June at the Peking session of the General Council of the WFTU by the Chinese Vice-President of that body, Liu Chang-sheng, and there is reason to suppose that even more comprehensive and outspoken criticisms of Soviet policy were communicated non-publicly at the same time, at least to selected leaders of the Communist world movement. Liu's speech [10] went beyond the April documents in demanding a "clarification" of the Communist attitude towards war, denouncing "indiscriminate" opposition to war and calling for active support for "just wars" of liberation; in sharply opposing the formulation of the Soviet Twenty-first Congress about "eliminating war forever while imperialism still exists" as "entirely wrong" and leading to "evil consequences of a serious nature which, in fact, we already see at present," though he too admitted the possibility of preventing a new world war; and in condemning any belief that proposals for general and complete disarmament could be accepted, and that the funds formerly earmarked for war purposes could be used for the welfare of the masses and for assisting underdeveloped countries while imperialism still existed as "downright whitewashing and

[10] NCNA, June 8, 1960.

embellishing imperialism " and thus " helping imperialism headed by the U.S. to dupe the people."

Yet the Chinese had misjudged their chances of forcing a change of the Soviet line. At the WFTU session, they found themselves vigorously counter-attacked by both the Russian and the major European movements, and finally isolated with only the Indonesian trade unions on their side. Moreover, this seems to have been the point at which the Soviet leaders decided to give battle in defence of their ideological authority, and first of all to whip into line those European satellite parties which had in the past shown signs of sympathy for Chinese intransigence. They took the initiative in calling a conference of all ruling Communist parties to meet on the occasion of the Rumanian party congress later that month; and in the meantime the Soviet press began to publish warnings against the dangers of " dogmatism " and " sectarianism " in the international movement,[11] while the Italian delegates returning from Peking published the fact that the Chinese had been isolated and defeated in a major international discussion on the problems of the struggle for peace and disarmament.[12]

Now that the issue of authority was out in the open, the field of the dispute kept broadening. Already in April, the speaker at the Peking celebration of Lenin's birthday, Lu Ting-Yi, had claimed for Mao's creation of the communes the succession to Lenin's concept of " uninterrupted revolution," and had attacked people who in Socialist construction " rely only on technique and not on the masses " and deny the need for further revolutionary struggle in the transition to the higher stage of Communism.[13] Now *Pravda* quoted Engels and Lenin for their criticism of the Blanquist wish to " skip all the intermediate stages on the road to Communism " in the illusion that " if power were in their hands, communism could be introduced the day after tomorrow." [14] Yet the original Sino-Soviet disagreement about the communes had been ended in the winter of 1958–59 with the withdrawal of the Chinese claim that this institution constituted a short cut to the Communist stage, and an understanding that the Chinese would go on developing and the Soviets and their European satellites rejecting that institution without further debate. The revival of the issue now only made sense as part of the attempt by each side to throw doubt on the other's ideological orthodoxy.

[11] Articles on the fortieth anniversary of Lenin's "Leftwing Communism, an Infantile Disorder," by D. Shevlyagin in *Sovyetskaya Rossiya*, June 10, and by " N. Matkovsky " in *Pravda*, June 12, 1960; *Pravda* editorial " Full Support " on the Soviet disarmament proposals, June 13, 1960.

[12] Foa in *Avanti*, June 15; Novella in *Unita*, June 19, 1960.

[13] NCNA, April 22, 1960.

[14] N. Matkovsky on June 12.

THE BUCHAREST CONFERENCE

On the eve of the Bucharest conference, a *Pravda* editorial stated bluntly that " among Socialist countries, there cannot be two opinions on the question of peace or war. Socialists believe that in present conditions there is no necessity for war, that disarmament is not only needed but possible, and that peaceful coexistence between nations is a vital necessity."[15] Coupled with a quote from Khrushchev's December speech to the Hungarian party congress about the need for all Communist governments to " synchronise their watches," and his warning that " if the leaders of any one of the Socialist countries would set themselves up to be above the rest, that can only play into the hands of our enemies," this indicated the Soviet leaders' intention to force a clear decision that would be binding on all ruling parties.[15a]

But at Bucharest, this intention was at least partly foiled by the Chinese. Khrushchev's public attack[16] on people who quote the words of Lenin without looking at the realities of the present world, and whom Lenin would set right in no uncertain manner if he came back today, was plain enough for all the satellite leaders to understand that the time for manoeuvring between the two colossi was over, and for all but the Albanians to rally round. His account of how Soviet strength and Soviet skill had again and again foiled the war plans of the " imperialists," from Suez in 1956 to the Turkish-Syrian crisis of 1957 and the U.S. landing in the Lebanon after the Iraqi revolution of 1958, if historically dubious, was propagandistically effective as a demonstration of the meaning of his " peace policy " for a Communist audience. But the Chinese delegate P'eng Chen was clearly instructed neither to submit nor to carry the ideological debate to a conclusion at this point : he evaded a decision by a skilful withdrawal to prepared positions.

In public, P'eng Chen appeared as the advocate of Communist unity at almost any price, to be achieved on the basis of the 1957 Moscow declaration to which all but the Yugoslavs had agreed.[17] This committed the Chinese once more to recognition of the possibility of preventing or " checking " imperialist wars—a possibility that, P'eng claimed, could only be fulfilled by the united strength of the " Socialist camp " and the determined mobilisation of mass action against the imperialists. But it was also intended to commit the Russians once again to the 1957 thesis that the aggressive circles of the U.S. were the main enemy of peace and

15 June 20, 1960.
15a According to the secret Communist report referred to above, the internal correspondence between the Soviet and Chinese Central Committees reached a first climax at the same time with an 80-page all-round critique of the Chinese party by the Soviets dated June 21, the opening day of the Bucharest conference. The Chinese themselves are said to have communicated this document to the other parties present.
16 Speech at the Bucharest Congress on June 21, 1960, as carried by TASS.
17 Text in NCNA, June 22, 1960.

all popular aspirations, and that "revisionism" was the main danger within the ranks of the Communist movement. Having said that much, the Chinese representative spoke no word about *détente*, disarmament or the "elimination of war from the life of mankind" before the disappearance of capitalism.

Behind the scenes, he seems to have argued that the 1957 conference of ruling Communist parties had been called chiefly to settle problems of Communist power and "Socialist construction"; the questions now in dispute, being concerned with world-wide revolutionary strategy, could only be decided by a conference representing the whole Communist movement. Khrushchev might well complain about Chinese "factional" methods of carrying the quarrel into the ranks of other parties; in the end he had to agree to put up the dispute officially for worldwide inner-party discussion in preparation for a November conference in Moscow, and to content himself with a brief interim communiqué which, while stressing the primary importance of the "peace campaign," did not go beyond the 1957 declaration on any controversial point.

This fell far short of what the Soviet leaders had expected. The decisive showdown was not only postponed for several months, but it would take place before an audience of revolutionary parties many of whose members were less closely tied to Soviet control than the East European satellites, and might well regard the Chinese slogans of unconditional revolutionary solidarity as more attractive than the Soviet readiness to subordinate their struggle to the needs of co-existence diplomacy whenever that seemed expedient. Thus an Algerian Communist might prefer Chinese offers of aid for the F.L.N. to the repeated Russian advice favouring negotiation with de Gaulle; an Iraqi Communist might recall that neither Soviet support for Kassem's régime nor his own party's Soviet-ordered retreat from its earlier offensive policy had obtained for it a legal, let alone a dominating, position under that régime; an Indonesian Communist might resent the manner in which Khrushchev had ignored his party during his official visit, and the general Soviet wooing of the "bourgeois nationalist" régime of Soekarno that limited the democratic rights of the Communists as well as of other parties and favoured a neutralist *bloc* with the "renegade" Tito. And would not the Communists of Latin America be sensitive to the Chinese argument that as Yankee imperialism was the main enemy, any attempts to relax Soviet-American tension were bound to weaken Soviet support for them as well as for China?

Yet without the co-operation of these movements, Khrushchev's co-existence diplomacy could not be carried through: he needed their discipline, and the Chinese had launched their ideological attack on his authority precisely in order to undermine that. Now they had created a situation in which the objects of the struggle, the Communist movements *in partibus infidelium*, were to act to some extent as its arbiters. True, the Russians had still the advantage of the prestige and resources of a world Power as well as of older organisational ties: all the foreign Communists knew that the Soviets *could* help them more—financially, diplomatically, and ultimately militarily—than the Chinese, yet they were less certain that the Soviets *would* always help them to the limits of their ability. Hence Khrushchev seems to have felt that in preparation for the November meeting, not only the circulation of new Soviet documents and the dispatch of new emissaries to the wavering parties were needed, but above all new proofs of the spirit of revolutionary internationalism animating his foreign policy.

SOVIET FOREIGN POLICY HARDENS

The fact that he had already decided to postpone his new summit approach until after the U.S. presidential elections made it easier for him to furnish that proof: for he could now afford to increase rather than relax tension for a time without serious damage to his future diplomatic chances, and perhaps even in the hope to improve them by creating a dark backdrop for the next display of his sunny smile—provided only that he did not allow matters to get really out of hand. The weeks after Bucharest thus offered the strange spectacle of the Soviet leaders conducting themselves on the world stage in the very style which Peking's ideological theses had seemed to demand, while at the same time launching a vigorous campaign against those theses throughout the Communist world movement !

The Bucharest communiqué had not yet been published when Russia demonstratively walked out of the ten-power disarmament talks at Geneva, just before the Western counter-proposals for which she had been calling so insistently were officially submitted. There followed within a few days the shooting down of an American plane over the Arctic, the first Soviet note on the Congo accusing all the Western powers of backing Belgian military intervention as part of a plot to restore colonial rule, and as a climax Khrushchev's personal threat to use intercontinental rockets against the U.S. if the latter should attack Cuba. Yet during the same period, Khrushchev used his visit to Austria to insist again and again on the horrors of nuclear world war and on the need to avoid even local wars because of the risk that they might spread; and even in his most reckless gestures he took care not to do anything irrevocable. The Geneva test negotiations were *not* broken off; the Cuban rocket threat was soon " explained " as symbolic, while in the Congo the Russians refrained from backing their policy with force; and a proposal for taking the disarmament negotiations out of the U.N. and for calling instead for a disarmament conference of "all governments" including China, which the Chinese managed to get adopted by a Stockholm session of the World Peace Council in July, was promptly dropped down the memory hole by Moscow in favour of Khrushchev's suggestion that all heads of government of the member states should personally attend the next U.N. assembly session in order to discuss the Soviet plan for general and complete disarmament.

The same contradiction between the desire to keep the lines of negotiation open and the need to pose constantly as an uninhibited revolutionary agitator also dominated Khrushchev's subsequent behaviour at the U.N. assembly itself. He did not back the neutrals' initiative for a new summit meeting but left the onus of killing it to the West. He depreciated the importance of his own proposals for "general and complete disarmament," for the sake of which so many heads of government had come, by devoting far more energy to his attack on "colonialism" in general and on the U.N. secretariat in particular, and by choosing a language and style of behaviour more apt to inspire revolutionary movements outside than to influence delegates inside the assembly hall. He followed his attack on the secretariat by proposals for a reform of the latter and of the Security Council which appealed to the natural desire of the new African and Asian member states for stronger representation in the leading organs of the U.N., but then suggested that any such changes in the Charter should be postponed until the delegates of the Chinese People's Republic had been seated. These inconsistencies are incomprehensible unless the fact is borne in mind that during all that time Khrushchev was engaged in an effort to prove his revolutionary zeal and international solidarity in preparation for the Moscow conference.

Meanwhile the line for the ideological campaign itself had been laid down by a meeting of the central committee of the CPSU in mid-July, which had approved the conduct of its delegation at Bucharest, led by Khrushchev, oddly enough after a report by secretariat member F. R. Kozlov who had not been there. As developed during late July and August in the Soviet press and the statements of pro-Soviet leaders of foreign Communist parties, the campaign showed some significant changes of emphasis.[18] It was more uncompromising than ever on the need to avoid the horrors of nuclear war, and the rejection of all attempts to belittle them or to regard any kind of international war as desirable. It insisted that good Marxist-Leninist revolutionaries were entitled and indeed obliged to adopt on this matter conclusions different from Lenin, both because of the new techniques of destruction and because of the change

---

[18] F. Konstantinov and Kh. Momdzhan, "Dialectics and the Present," *Kommunist* No. 10, 1960; *Pravda* editorial, July 20; speech by M. A. Suslov, *Pravda*, July 30; Y. Frantsev, *Pravda*, August 7; B. Ponomarev, *Pravda*, August 12; Togliatti speech to Italian CC, *Pravda*, July 28; T. Zhivkov in August issue of *World Marxist Review*.

in the relation of world forces to the disadvantage of imperialism. It vigorously defended the possibility not only of stopping each particular war, but of altogether " eliminating war from the life of society " with the further growth of the strength of the " Socialist camp," even while capitalism still existed on part of the globe, as the Twenty-first Congress had laid down; and it claimed that the Soviet programme of general and complete disarmament was a realistic policy goal that could be achieved, even though this might require time, " mutual concessions " and compromises. Any opposition to this general line of peaceful coexistence was to be eliminated from the Communist movement as " Trotskyite adventurism."

Moscow and Peking Shift Their Ground

But the new campaign no longer laid stress on Khrushchev's differentiation between " realistic statesmen " and " diehard militarists " in the enemy camp, and no longer mentioned "relaxation of international tension " as a condition of coexistence diplomacy. Instead, the goals of peace and disarmament were now put forward, in language first used by the Chinese critics, as having to be " imposed " on the imperialists by the strength of the " Socialist camp " and the relentless struggle of the masses. Peaceful coexistence was now described as " the highest form of the class struggle," and justified as leading not to an even temporary weakening, but to an intensification of revolutionary movements everywhere, including civil wars and colonial revolts whenever the imperialists attempted to hold back the rising tide by force. It was only international wars, wars between states, that should be avoided by the policy of peaceful coexistence; and it was explicitly admitted that imperialist intervention against revolutionary movements might lead to " just wars of liberation," and that in that case the duty of the Socialist camp was to support the latter—though not necessarily with troops—and to seek to end the intervention. In short, it was now claimed that there was no contradiction at all between the diplomacy of coexistence and the policy of unconditional revolutionary solidarity: both had become compatible in an age where, owing to the growing strength of the " Socialist camp," the " dictatorship of the proletariat had become an international force " as once predicted by Lenin.

This interpretation of Soviet policy evidently placed its authors in a very strong position to meet the Chinese ideological challenge; yet as the Chinese had intended, and as Khrushchev's simultaneous actions illustrated, it was bound greatly to reduce the credibility and effectiveness of the coexistence campaign in non-Communist eyes. The Soviets could hope to succeed in restoring their international ideological authority to the exact extent to which they were prepared temporarily to weaken the political impact of their diplomacy. It was an expression of that dilemma that when the chief ideological spokesman of Yugoslav Communism, Vice-President Edvard Kardelj, published a pamphlet in defence of coexistence and against the Chinese cult of revolutionary war,[19] *Pravda* immediately turned against him and accused him of all the revisionist sins of which the Chinese had accused the Soviets [20]—not only because he had been so tactless as to name the Chinese as his target, which the Soviets had never done, but because he had taken a consistent position with which they could not afford to identify themselves. For Kardelj had argued that real peaceful coexistence between states with different social systems required that these systems should not become the basis of permanent " ideological *blocs* " in foreign policy; and this concept was, of course, as incompatible with Soviet practice as with the new definition of coexistence as " the highest form of the class struggle."

During the same period, the Chinese Communists were also shifting their ground. They stopped belittling the horrors of nuclear war and claiming that only cowards could fear them,[21] and repeatedly protested their willingness to fight for peaceful coexistence and the prevention or stopping of wars. But they kept rubbing in the formula of the Moscow declaration of 1957 about the role of the aggressive U.S. circles as the centre of world reaction and the need for vigilance against its war plans camouflaged by peace talk, which they felt had been borne out by Khrushchev's experience with Eisenhower; and they pictured peaceful coexistence and disarmament as goals which could be " imposed " on the enemy only " to some extent " and for limited periods, without the slightest assurance of permanence or completion before the final, worldwide victory of the Communist cause.[22] In other words, they remained adamant in their rejection of the thesis of the Twenty-first Congress about " eliminating war from the life of mankind " before that final victory.

THE QUESTION OF ROADS TO POWER

Parallel with that, the Chinese concentrated on extolling the importance of revolutionary violence, including revolutionary war. While the Russians now *admitted* that peaceful coexistence did not *exclude* colonial uprisings and civil wars, and that imperialist intervention in these cases *might lead* to " just wars of liberation," the Chinese stressed revolutionary

[19] " Socialism and War," first published in *Borba*, August 12–20, 1960.
[20] A. Arzumanyan and V. Koryonov, *Pravda*, September 2, 1960.
[21] The last Chinese statement on those lines seems to have been the article on the tenth anniversary of the outbreak of the Korean War by Gen. Li Chih-min, *People's Daily*, June 25, 1960.
[22] *People's Daily* editorial commenting on Bucharest communiqué, June 29 ; Liao Ch'eng-chih's speech to Bureau of World Peace Council in Stockholm, July 10 ; Ch'en Yi's speech in Peking, NCNA, July 15 ; Li Fu-ch'un's speech to the Vietnamese party congress, NCNA, September 6.

violence as the normal and classical road for the advance of the Communist cause, and support for just wars as the *criterion* of true internationalism. In fact, they abandoned the safe ground of the 1957 Moscow declaration (on which they were otherwise relying in that phase) to the extent of attacking its thesis, taken over from the Twentieth Congress of the CPSU, that the Communist seizure of power might take place in some countries without violent upheaval and civil war, as a peaceful revolution carried out with the help of the legal parliamentary institutions. Ignoring the examples given by the Russians at the time—such as the annexation of Esthonia and the Czechoslovak coup of February 1948—the Chinese now insisted that the bourgeoisie would never and nowhere abandon power without resorting to violence, and that it was " muddle-headed " at best to confuse the peaceful construction of Socialism *after* the seizure of power with the necessarily violent conquest of power itself.[23] To this, the Soviets replied with renewed charges of " Blanquism." [24]

Of all the differences raised in the 1960 dispute, this argument on the violent and non-violent roads to power seemed most artificial, at least in its generalised form. The Soviets had started talking about the " parliamentary road " in order to ease the tactical position of the Communist parties in the West, and it was chiefly the latter which made propagandist use of the formula. But in the weeks before the crucial Moscow meeting, the Chinese effort was chiefly directed at those Communist parties in underdeveloped countries for which the Chinese experience had long been regarded as a natural model; and most of these had developed alternately in co-operation or conflict with nationalist dictators, but had certainly no prospect of gaining power by " parliamentary " means. Only in the case of the faction-ridden Indian Communist Party—a party operating legally in an under-developed country with effective parliamentary institutions—was there a serious struggle going on between a " right wing " advocating and a " left wing " rejecting the " parliamentary road " to power; and it was primarily with an eye to the Indian " left wing " that the Chinese now engaged in a general denunciation of the Soviet concept of that road as " revisionist."

The Soviets replied to this twist by a similar piece of demagogy—accusing the Chinese of a sectarian refusal to work with broad nationalist movements against imperialism unless these movements subscribed in advance to Communist principles and leadership.[25] As a general

---

23 In public, this came out most clearly in the last weeks before the Moscow Conference, notably in comments on the publication of the fourth volume of the works of Mao, *e.g. People's Daily*, October 6, and above all *Red Flag* editorial, November 2. But it is clear from Soviet reaction that the point must have been raised internally before.
24 A. Belyakov and F. Burlatsky in *Kommunist* No. 13, 1960.
25 Y. Zhukov in *Pravda*, August 26.

charge, this was as untrue as the Chinese attack on the alleged "revisionism" of Moscow's "peaceful road"; the close contacts maintained by Peking with the Algerian and many African nationalists proved that daily. But Peking's conflicts with the Indian and Indonesian governments, due in fact not to doctrinaire prejudice but to Chinese chauvinism, and its support for leftish malcontents in several Asian Communist parties against Moscow's wooing of nationalist dictators gave to the charge a semblance of substance.

Soviet-Chinese relations seem to have reached their low point in August and early September. It was during that period that an unusually large number of Soviet technicians left China, while many Chinese students returned from Russia: that the organ of the Soviet-Chinese Friendship Society disappeared from the streets of Moscow; and that the expected Chinese scholars failed to turn up at the Orientalists' Congress there. It was then, too, that a number of Soviet provincial papers printed an article explaining that in contemporary conditions, not even a huge country like China could build Socialism in isolation and without the aid and backing of the Soviet Union,[26] while Peking's theoretical voice published a statement of the need for China to rely chiefly on her own resources for the fulfilment of her plans.[27] We do not know the inside story behind those visible symptoms—whether Moscow really tried to apply economic pressure and failed, or whether Peking made a gratuitous demonstration of her capacity for "going it alone."[27a] Chinese criticism, at any rate, had not been silenced by October 1st,[27b] when the Russians used the eleventh birthday of the CPR to make again a show of friendship; on the contrary, some of Peking's most polemical utterances came in the last weeks before the Moscow conference,[28] whereas the Soviet ideological campaign had rather abated since the middle of September. But by then the Soviets could afford to stop arguing in

[26] S. Titarenko in *Sovyetskaya Latviya, Bakunsky Rabochy et al.*, August 16, 1960.

[27] Li Fu-ch'un in *Red Flag*, No. 16, 1960.

[27a] Since the above was written, it has been reasonably well established that the Soviets took the initiative in withdrawing large numbers of technicians, giving as their reason Chinese attempts to influence them ideologically against official Soviet policy. Both the pro-Soviet secret report referred to by Crankshaw and a pro-Chinese account by the West Bengal Communist leader H. K. Konar, published in the Indian weekly *The Link* and quoted by B. Nikolayevsky in *The New Leader* of Jan. 16, 1961, agree on this.

[27b] According to the report summarised by Crankshaw, the Chinese CP circularised their systematic counter attack to the Soviet charges, going back to their disapproval of Mr. Khrushchev's 1956 "destalinisation" speech and to complaints of "unprincipled" Soviet behaviour in Poland and Hungary later that year, only on Sept. 10, 1960. Once again, the reported Chinese position is confirmed by the pro-Chinese account of Konar, referred to in the previous note, and based on Chinese statements made to the author at the North Vietnamese party congress at about the same time.

[28] *Cf.* the articles quoted in note 22 above; also Marshal Lo Jui-ch'ing's article for the (North) *Korean People's Forces Journal* on the tenth anniversary of Chinese intervention in Korea, NCNA, October 25, 1960.

public, for the Chinese had been largely, though not completely, isolated in the international movement: early in September, even the North Vietnamese party fell in line with the Soviet position.[29]

The mere duration of the Moscow conference—almost three weeks of argument behind closed doors—showed that agreement on a new common statement of principles was anything but easy. This time, the Chinese had sent the strongest possible team short of exposing Mao himself to the risk of defeat—a delegation led by Liu Shao-ch'i and the Party secretary Teng Hsiao-p'ing; and reports that he fought for every clause and comma, and finally yielded to the majority view on some crucial points only under the threat of an open ideological breach do not seem implausible. Halfway through the debates, the anniversary of the 1957 declaration was commented on by editorials in Moscow and Peking which still showed a marked difference of emphasis [30] on the primacy of revolutionary struggle in the *People's Daily*, on the " general line " of peaceful coexistence in *Pravda*; while at the same time a Chinese delegate to a session of the Afro-Asian Solidarity Committee threw off all restraint and claimed publicly that there could be no peaceful coexistence in those countries before the liquidation of colonialism, as the oppressed peoples would never accept " coexistence between the rider and the horse." [31] But it seems established that as the Moscow conclave wore on, the Chinese were only able to retain the support of a few Asian parties that were traditionally dependent on them or largely recruited from the Chinese minorities, of some rather weak Latin American parties, and of the faithful Albanians long tied to them by common enmity against the Yugoslav " revisionists."

THE MOSCOW STATEMENT

The long document on the strategy of international Communism that was agreed in the end thus marks a clear Soviet victory on almost all the points that had still been in dispute in the preceding three months. But the Soviet position as defended since the July session of the central committee of the CPSU already contained substantial concessions to the original Chinese criticism of Soviet policy.

The 1960 Moscow declaration starts from the Soviet analysis that Lenin's views are partly outdated because the present epoch is no longer primarily that of imperialism, but of the growing preponderance of the " Socialist world system " over the forces of imperialism. On this basis, it accepts not only the possibility of ending war forever with the worldwide victory of Socialism, but of " freeing mankind from the nightmare

---

29 See P. J. Honey's analysis of the North Vietnamese Party Congress in *The China Quarterly*, No. 4, p. 66.
30 *People's Daily*, November 21; *Pravda*, November 23.
31 NCNA, November 21.

of another world war even now "—of " banishing world war from the life of society even while capitalism still exists in part of the world." The thesis of the Twenty-first Congress of the CPSU which the Chinese had fought to the last has thus been reluctantly accepted by them,[31a] and so has the full description of the horrors of nuclear war. The declaration also proclaims the possibility not of preventing all local wars, but of " effectively fighting the local wars unleashed by the imperialists " and extinguishing them, and stresses the unanimity of all Communists in their support for " peaceful coexistence " and negotiation as the only alternative to destructive war. Finally, it recognises the " historic " importance which a fulfilment of the Soviet programme for general and complete disarmament would have, and states that its achievement, though difficult, may be accomplished in stages if the masses and the governments of the " Socialist camp " resolutely fight for it.

At the same time, " peaceful coexistence " is described as " a form of the class struggle " (not, as in some Soviet documents, as " the highest form," because in the Chinese party doctrine that rank remains reserved for revolutionary war). The hope of preserving peace is squarely based on the strength of the " Socialist camp," the revolutionary movements and their sympathisers; it is admitted that the latter may be found also in " certain strata of the bourgeoisie of the advanced countries " who realise the new relation of forces and the catastrophic consequences of a world war, but this appears as a marginal factor. Gone are Khrushchev's " realistic statesmen " and his successful goodwill visits; the emphasis is on the fact that the aggressive, warlike nature of imperialism has not changed, and that " American imperialism " as such—not only, as stated in 1957, " the aggressive imperialist *circles* of the United States "—has become the " main centre of world reaction, the international gendarme, the enemy of the peoples of the whole world." [31b] While condemning " the American doctrine of the Cold War," the document thus defines coexistence in rigid Cold War terms.

The declaration allots to the " peace campaign " pride of place as likely to unite the broadest possible fronts under Communist leadership, and rejects the " slander " that the Communists need war for extending their sway or believe in " exporting revolution." But it also calls for the most determined international support, both by the mass movement and by " the power of the Socialist world system," of revolutionary movements anywhere against " the imperialist export of counter-revolution." The statement that " the Socialist states . . . have become an international force exerting a powerful influence on world developments.

[31a] It has not, however, to my knowledge so far been quoted in Chinese comments on the Moscow declaration.
[31b] This formula in turn, has not been quoted in Mr. Khrushchev's report on the conference.

Hence real possibilities have appeared to settle the major problems of our age in a new manner, in the interest of peace, democracy and Socialism . . . " assumes a special meaning in this context: for the first time since Stalin's victory over Trotsky, active support for international revolution is proclaimed as an obligation of the Soviet Government and all other Communist governments. But the crucial question of whether that obligation includes the risk of war, of whether " peaceful coexistence " or " revolutionary solidarity " is to receive priority in case of conflict, is not settled explicitly—for the possibility of conflict between the two principles is not admitted.

On the question of violent or peaceful roads to power, the view of the Russians and of the 1957 declaration that both may be used according to circumstances is clearly upheld. Equally " broadminded " are the declaration's new directives for the policy of the Communists in underdeveloped countries towards their " national bourgeoisie "— *i.e.*, toward the nationalist, neutralist and non-Communist, though in fact hardly ever bourgeois régimes that have emerged from the struggle for national independence. The Communists are advised to aim at " national democratic " régimes, defined by their willingness to support the Soviet *bloc* against the " imperialists," to create the preconditions of progressive internal development by land reform, and to grant full freedom for the activity of the Communist Party and of Communist-controlled " mass organisations." They are told that those sections of the " national bourgeoisie " which oppose land reform and suppress the Communists, having taken a reactionary turn at home, will sooner or later also side with imperialism abroad. But again, the crucial question of a nationalist dictatorship that is willing to take Soviet aid and to vote anti-Western in the U.N., but gaols its own Communists is shirked [31c]; nor is there any clear indication of who is to interpret the ambiguous directives in case of conflict.

IDEOLOGICAL AUTHORITY

Thus matters come back to the ultimate issue of ideological authority —of the right to interpret ambiguous principles in a changing situation. Here, the Soviets score a clear but very limited victory: they emerge as the most successful, but not as the only orthodox interpreters of the true doctrine. The Soviet Union is hailed as the only country that, having completed " Socialist construction," is engaged in building the " higher stage " of Communism; the Chinese communes are not even mentioned, and the Soviet argument that Communist abundance is not

---

[31c] In practice, President Nasser's régime in the UAR continues to enjoy Soviet diplomatic backing while being vigorously attacked in Soviet-controlled organs of the Communist world movement.

possible short of the highest level of technical productivity, including automation, is hammered home. The CPSU is unanimously declared to be "the universally recognised vanguard of the world Communist movement," and its superior experience in conquering power and transforming society is stated to have fundamental lessons for all parties; the decisions of its Twentieth Congress in particular are said to have opened a new era for the whole international movement. But that new era now turns out to be an era of polycentric autonomy—just as the bolder spirits thought at the time.

For under the new declaration, the spiritual authority of the CPSU is not incarnated in the shape which all doctrinaire authority, and certainly all authority in the Bolshevik tradition, requires by its nature—the shape of hierarchical discipline. It is not only that the declaration repeats the ancient pious formula about the independence and equality of all Communist parties; it is that it fails to establish a visible, single centre for their dependence. It provides for irregular conferences, whether world-wide or regional, for mutual co-ordination, and for bipartite consultations betwen any two parties in case of differences. This may be intended to rule out the circulation of Chinese attacks on CPSU policy to third parties before they have raised the matter in Moscow directly; but it does not, on the face of it, prevent them from broadening the discussion again the next time they fail to get satisfaction in their direct contact with the "vanguard of the world movement." [31d] Clearly, the primacy of that vanguard is no longer that of an infallible Pope: the rule of *Moscow locuta, causa finita* is valid no more. For the first time in its forty years of history, international Communism is entering a "conciliary" period.

One phase of open ideological controversy between Moscow and Peking has thus ended. The Chinese have withdrawn their open challenge to the Marxist-Leninist orthodoxy of the Soviet Communists, but not before they had extracted from it as much advantage for their foreign policy as they could hope to gain without risking an open breach. The underlying differences of interest and viewpoint remain, though their public expression will now be muted for some time. But the phase that has now closed has not only had a considerable immediate impact on Soviet foreign policy; it is bound to produce lasting changes in the constellation of factors shaping that policy, in Soviet-Chinese relations, and in relations within the Communist world movement.

A measure of the immediate effect is the uncertainty of direction

---

[31d] According to the report summarised by Crankshaw, the Chinese explicitly affirmed their right to form factions in the international movement during the Moscow discussions, and finally accepted the declaration only on condition that another world conference should be called within two years.

shown by Soviet diplomacy from the wrecking of the summit conference in May to the end of 1960. Having set out to induce the U.S., by a mixture of pressure and courtship, to abandon some exposed positions and allies for the sake of a temporary understanding with their chief antagonist, the Kremlin did not indeed abandon that objective, but wavered visibly between it and the Chinese objective of isolating the U.S. as the one irreconcilable enemy. The oscillations were too fast, the conciliatory gestures too half-hearted, and the brinkmanship too risky to be explained merely as the conscious use of zig-zag tactics to " soften up " the opponent; even if the Soviets intended all the time to reserve the next serious offer of relaxation for the next American President, a cool calculation of diplomatic expediency would hardly have led them to commit themselves in the meantime to the point to which they have gone over, say, Laos or Cuba. By depriving them of the power automatically to subordinate all revolutionary movements everywhere to Soviet diplomatic needs, the Chinese forced Stalin's successors to compete for authority over those movements by playing up to them to some extent; and this meant that, while failing to impose on the Kremlin a policy made in Peking, the Chinese forced it to deviate from its own concepts to a significant extent.

Nor have they lost this power of interference as a result of the Moscow conference. True, they have failed to establish a power of veto over Soviet diplomacy in general and Soviet-American contacts in particular, as would have been the case if the Chinese theses of an unconditional priority of revolution over peace and of the hopelessness of any serious disarmament agreement with the " imperialists " had been adopted. There is nothing in the Moscow declaration that would make it *impossible* for the Soviets still to agree with the Western powers on a permanent ban on nuclear test explosions with proper guarantees of inspection, hence on an attempt to close the " atomic club." But there is much in it that will enable the Chinese to make it more difficult, and generally to raise suspicion against any direct Russo-American talks, and nothing that specifically endorses Mr. Khrushchev's methods of personal diplomacy, from his pursuit of summit meetings to his proposals for " reforming " the United Nations. In fact, if the text of the declaration is viewed in the context of the events leading up to it, it suggests that the Soviet Communist Party was only able to win on the controversial questions of principle by silently disavowing some of the more spectacular actions of its leader, and that the latter has emerged from the fight with his personal prestige noticeably impaired.

The declaration's approval of the " general line " of peaceful co-existence and of the aim to eliminate world war in our time permits the Soviets to go on pursuing their strategy of using both negotiation and violence short of world war as means to gain their ends; but it is not enough to assure them of tactical freedom to decide, in the light of their own interests alone, when and how far to use one or the other. To regain that freedom of manoeuvre, the Soviets would have either needed a plain and brutal statement that local revolutions may in certain circumstances have to be subordinated to the interest of preserving world peace and thus protecting the achievements of " Socialist construction " against a nuclear holocaust; or they would have required an equally plain recognition of their right to act as the only legitimate interpreters of revolutionary doctrine for the world movement, and to enforce the strategic and tactical consequences of their interpretation by means of centralised discipline. But either way of ensuring Soviet primacy, so natural in the Stalinist age when the Soviet Union alone was " the fatherland of all toilers," proved impossible in the post-Stalinist age of " the Socialist World System " proclaimed by Khrushchev himself.

On one side the doctrine that " the dictatorship of the proletariat has become an international factor," first announced in Russia by M. A. Suslov and now substantially incorporated in the declaration, amounts to a partial repeal of Stalin's " Socialism in a single country ": it does not, of course, deny what was achieved under the latter slogan, but it restores, in the new world situation, the idea of a duty of the Communist powers to aid the progress of world revolution for which Trotsky fought. Even if this principle of solidarity is not formulated as an absolute and unlimited obligation, it is enough to expose Soviet diplomacy to constant pressure to take bolder risks—pressure of the kind which the Chinese mobilised effectively during the past year, and are free to use again.

POLYCENTRIC COMMUNISM

On the other hand, the declaration's recognition of the Soviet Communist Party as the " vanguard " of the world movement falls far short of establishing a permanent and unchallengeable doctrinaire authority, let alone a single centre endowed with disciplinary powers. It even falls far short of the position conceded to the Soviet Union and the Soviet Communist Party at the time of the 1957 Moscow declaration—on Mao Tse-tung's initiative. Then, the Soviet Union was consistently described as being " at the head of the Socialist camp," and Mao publicly went out of his way to speak of the need for a single leader both among Communist states and parties, and to insist that only the Russians could fill both roles.

Now, the Chinese talk quite openly and naturally about the special responsibilities of " the two great Socialist powers," the Soviet Union and China; and in the declaration itself, the vanguard role of the Soviet party is balanced in part by the recognition of the " enormous influence " exerted by the Chinese revolution on the peoples of Asia, Africa and Latin America by its encouraging example to all movements of national liberation. In 1957, the failure to found a new formal international organisation only increased the influence of the large international liaison machinery developed within the secretariat of the central committee of the CPSU, compared with which all bilateral and regional contacts were bound to be of subordinate importance. Now, the failure formally to establish a single centre legitimates the *de facto* existence of two centres in Moscow and Peking, both with world-wide links and without any agreed division of labour, which will continue to cooperate on the basis of the declaration but also to give different advice on the questions it has left open and to compete for influence. And if Moscow is still the stronger power and the older authority, Peking is closer in its type of revolutionary experience and the emotional roots of its anti-colonialist ardour to those parts of the world where the chances of Communist revolution are most promising.

In a long-range view, the relative victory of the Soviets in the 1960 phase of the dispute thus appears less important than the fact that this phase has marked a new stage in their abdication of their former position of exclusive leadership. The reports that the Soviets themselves expressed during the Moscow conference a wish that they should no longer be described as being " at the head of the Socialist camp " may well be true : finding themselves unable any longer to exert effective control over the whole world movement, they may have preferred not to be held responsible for all its actions by their enemies. In a *bloc* containing two great powers, in an international movement based on two great revolutions, such a development was indeed to be expected as soon as important differences appeared between them. But while the two protagonists remain as determined to continue to co-operate as they are unable to settle their disagreements, the result is not a two-headed movement with neatly separated geographic spheres of control, but a truly polycentric one : many Communist parties outside the Soviet *bloc* may in future be able to gain increased tactical independence, based on their freedom of taking aid and advice from both Moscow and Peking, simultaneously or alternately—with all the risks that implies for the future unity of its doctrine and strategy.

The victory of Communism in China, and the subsequent growth of Communist China into a great power, thus appears in retrospect as the beginning of the end of the single-centred Communist movement that Lenin created, and the single-centred Soviet *bloc* that Stalin built. The process took a decisive step forward in 1956, when the Twentieth Congress of the CPSU recognised the existence of a " Socialist world system " and of different roads to power, and when the destruction of the Stalin cult inflicted an irreparable blow on the type of Soviet authority that had depended on the infallibility of the " father of nations." Mao's victory had killed the uniqueness of the Soviet Union; Khrushchev's speech buried the myth built around that uniqueness.

It was at that moment that the spectre of " polycentric Communism " first appeared. But when destalinisation was quickly followed by the crisis of Russia's East European empire, the façade of single-centred unity was restored in the following year with the help of China's prestige and Mao's authority. Now that China herself has brought back the spectre she helped to exorcise three years ago, the process is no longer reversible. This time, polycentric Communism has come to stay.

POSTSCRIPT

The above was written before the publication of Khrushchev's report on the Moscow conference,[32] given on January 6 to the party organisations of the Higher Party school, the Academy of Social Sciences and the Institute of Marxism-Leninism. Compared to the text of the Declaration, the report is distinguished by two diplomatic omissions and two theoretical elaborations.

Krushchev has made no mention of the role of U.S. imperialism as the gendarme of world reaction, etc., which would have embarrassed him in resuming diplomatic approaches to the new American administration; reactions to President Kennedy's first statements in Moscow and Peking have already confirmed that the original foreign policy difference the two great Communist Powers remains intact after the formal burial of the ideological dispute that arose from it.

The report also fails to define the new concept of " national democracy," created to designate the desirable type of régime in the under-developed, ex-colonial countries, by the criteria of land reform and freedom of Communist organisation given in the declaration. In view of the diplomatic importance of Soviet relations not only with Nasser's U.A.R. but with the traditionalist autocracy of Mohammed V of Morocco, this is understandable.

But Khrushchev is more precise than the declaration in his comment on " wars of national liberation." He goes further than any previous Soviet participant in the debate in agreeing with the Chinese that such just wars are " inevitable " so long as imperialism and colonialism exist, and he is emphatic about the need for all Communists to give them their fullest support. But he solves the apparent contradiction with his preceding condemnation of " local wars "—which might lead to the

[32] *Kommunist*, Nr. 1, 1961.

disaster of nuclear world war—by arguing that these wars of liberation are in their origin not " wars between states," but popular insurrections, and that the support which the Communist Powers must give them should consist not in taking the initiative to internationalise the conflict, but in preventing the intervention of the major imperialist Powers by the threat of their own counter-intervention—as in Vietnam and in the Cuban revolution—and thus assuring the victory of " the people." This is the most explicit formulation yet of the Soviet practice of " all aid by threats and indirect support short of war " for revolutionary movements.

Finally, Khrushchev confirms publicly that it was the Soviet delegation that asked for the omission of the flattering formula placing the Soviet Union " at the head of the Socialist Camp " and the CPSU " at the head of the Communist World movement," which Mao had bestowed on them at the 1957 conference; and he bluntly states his reason that this would have been a source of difficulties rather than advantages, as they are not in fact any longer in a position to act as a single centre giving directives. The polycentrism implicit in the declaration is thus made explicit for the first time through the mouth of the highest authority of Soviet Communism.

In the circumstances, Khrushchev's assurance that the Communist parties will in future be able to " synchronise their watches " without the help of a statute regulating their relations, merely by the light of their common ideology, amounts to little more than the hope that Russia and China will continue to be able to compromise their differences in the light of their common interests. Even assuming that this will still be true for a long time, nothing so far indicates that the achievement of compromise will in future be easier, or the effects on the world Communist movement less critical, than in the recent past.

Sino-Soviet Economic Relations

WHEN the Soviet delegation led by Kumykin, Deputy Minister of Foreign Trade, arrived in Peking early in February 1961 to hold preliminary talks on questions of mutual assistance and economic cooperation, the Chinese Foreign Minister referred to eternal, unbreakable, brotherly friendship and monolithic solidarity between the two countries. Marshal Ch'en Yi also praised the tremendous help received from the Soviet Union during the last decade and promised to remain for ever grateful for this assistance. A day or two earlier F. V. Konstantinov, Editor of *Kommunist*, arriving in Peking for the anniversary of the Sino-Soviet Treaty of Friendship had been greeted with equal warmth, in the name of a solidarity as firm as a rock and as hard as steel. As if to protect the newly forged bonds against assaults from hostile quarters, Radio Peking played the Soviet cantata "For ever we are together."

These manifestations seem to differ from others that have become known in the recent past. Chou En-lai when asked last year by Edgar Snow whether the Soviet Union had given China any aid without compensation was said to have replied: "Generally speaking, no; but in a specific sense, one can say yes." Blueprints came to the Chinese Prime Minister's mind, but no reference was made to capital equipment or technical expertise.

There had been cases of more generous acknowledgment of Soviet assistance, as in the *People's Daily* on February 14, 1959, when Soviet assistance was described as unprecedented in history. But on the whole, the emphasis has been on self-reliance rather than foreign aid. Li Fu-ch'un writing last autumn in the party journal Red Flag (August 1960) stressed that "the party has held consistently that we should mainly rely on our own efforts." In fact, this had been the general theme of public pronouncements at least as far back as the inauguration of the second Five Year Plan in 1956. Peking radio summarised thus the sentiments of the Communist leadership (29/5/57): "China should never rely on foreign aid for Socialist industrialisation."

It is sometimes argued that the apparently conflicting accounts of Sino-Soviet economic relations are merely the two sides of one and the same coin, the shining front facing the foreigner greedily looking at cash, but turned on its smudgy back becoming legal tender in China's indigenous bazaars. A more plausible explanation may be gauged from

Sino-Soviet ambivalence in the ever-changing relation between the two states. As to the facts of the case, even the magnitude of Soviet assistance to China is open to doubt. Only two loans of February 1950 and October 1954, providing the equivalent of $430 million, are among the few items known of Sino-Soviet relations. Thereafter the analyst enters the realm of the uncertain if not the fantastic.

After the fortieth anniversary of the October revolution the Soviet Union stated its aid to countries within the Communist camp to total some 28,000 million roubles or $7,000 million at the official rate of exchange. Li Hsien-nien, the Chinese Minister of Finance, quoted in his budget report of June 1957 the Chinese share in this gigantic programme of aid. The Soviet Union had extended to China economic assistance amounting to nearly 5,300 million yuan, or the same amount in roubles at the exchange rate apparently operating in Sino-Soviet transactions. If the " international " exchange rate of 1 yuan=1.70 roubles was applied, one-third of Soviet assistance to countries of the *bloc* would have been involved.

This sum included no doubt charges for the return to China of the Changchun Railway, the harbour of Port Arthur, the Soviet share in the joint-stock companies and the value of some fifty Manchurian plants first dismantled and then restored to China. This left large amounts unexplained since the two long term loans of 1950 and 1954 amounted to little more than 1,700 million roubles. Some observers have drawn the conclusion that large consignments of military aid granted during and after the Korean war or short term debts on trading accounts must have increased China's indebtedness to the Soviet Union. Others have dismissed Soviet claims of large scale assistance as phantoms since the agreements of mutual assistance of April 1956 and February 1959 excluded the possibility of long term credits and imposed repayment out of current production.

However this may be, sizeable short term debts did accumulate. Economic assistance is sometimes barely distinguishable from trade on deferred terms, and in fact Soviet trading practice allows for " technical credits," *i.e.*, swings which require payment of 2 per cent. interest if they surpass agreed ceilings. China made extensive use of this provision. Trading balances to the amount of almost $1,000 million accrued between 1950 and 1955 in favour of the Soviet Union providing China with substantial medium term credits. In 1956 she began to repay these and her trading deficit with the Soviet Union is likely to have declined by now to little more than $350 million. China began to repay her long term debts to the Soviet Union in 1954 and only two-fifths of these remain unpaid. The size of China's debts from invisible imports is unknown.

In 1956 when China was engaged in designing her second Five Year Plan, the Soviet leaders were preoccupied in Eastern Europe with political movements which were brought under control only at the expense of almost $1,000 million in short term credits. This unforeseen expenditure not only contributed to the premature termination of Soviet Russia's sixth Five Year Plan; it also prevented the Soviet Union from including in its foreign aid programme its most dependable ally China. Little wonder that the Chinese felt incensed to find that rebellion yielded better reward than loyalty. Much of the seed that has poisoned Sino-Soviet relations in recent years was sown in the autumn of 1956.

Whatever the causes of recent discord, there can be no doubt that Soviet economic assistance to China has been crucial for its industrialisation programme. This holds good in particular in case of her fuel and power economy, her iron and steel plants, and her chemical and engineering industries. Soviet Russia's share in China's foreign trade has increased from a mere 5 per cent. before the revolution to as much as 50 per cent. and more of a greatly increased volume from 1952 onwards. The Soviet Union has thus become China's main foreign supplier. Russia's exports to China are three times as large as those to all under-developed countries taken together. Since 1950 Sino-Soviet trade turnover has risen several times and it now amounts to about $2,000 million. A substantial part of Russia's exports consists of machinery and other capital goods. In 1959 half of all Soviet exports of machinery and nearly three of every four complete plants sent abroad went to China. During the last decade Soviet Russia has probably supplied complete plants and factory equipment to the tune of over $2,000 million.

At the same time China has found a wide open market for her surplus farm products, mineral ores and industrial consumer goods. She rivals with East Germany for first place among Soviet Russia's importers, supplying twice as much to the Soviet Union as all under-developed countries taken together. Whereas only five years ago foodstuffs provided the bulk of China's exports to Russia, by now they have been replaced largely by industrial consumer goods, particularly textiles.

Although probably no more than one-half of almost three hundred industrial projects undertaken under the auspices of Sino-Soviet agreements has been completed, Soviet Russia has contributed substantially to China's take-off from agrarian backwardness to semi-industrial development. Within the last decade China's share in the Soviet *bloc*'s industrial potential has doubled from 5 per cent. in 1950 to 10 per cent. in 1960. The provision of over 10,000 Soviet specialists has not been the least of Russia's contribution. The reduced rate of Soviet industrial supplies in 1957 and 1960 and the termination of service of certain

Soviet technicians last year caused dislocations in China's economy which provided a measure of her dependence upon continued Soviet economic assistance. Last year's rate of growth was probably no more than 5 per cent., a small increase by Chinese standards.

Two mediocre harvests aggravated the situation sufficiently to turn China from a food surplus producer to an importer of grain and sugar to the tune of $250 million or more. Since the temporary removal of political discord the Soviet Union has allowed China to spread the payment of last year's unpaid loan service over the next four or five years. Up to $200 million may be involved.

As a result of the disruptions of normal development, Chinese economic plans in spheres of potential influence may well have been delayed. Sino-Soviet friction in developing countries has thus been less in evidence than might have been the case otherwise. The economic ties of China have of course remained predominantly with the members of the Sino-Soviet *bloc*. She has so far offered to developing countries little more than $300 million in credits and grants and her trade with these countries amounts to a mere $400 million. Mongolia and some countries of South-East Asia seem to provide the only cases of economic rivalry, if not conflict, between China and the Soviet Union.

In view of her continued economic dependence on the Soviet Union China would seem unlikely to exploit fully, for some years to come, the possibilities of infiltration if this brings her into open conflict with the Soviet Union. The consequences of a lasting rift between the two chief Communist Powers would be serious to both; for China it could amount to a setback from which to recover it might take her the better part of a decade. However serious her dissent from Soviet Russia's political concepts, economic considerations would seem unlikely to allow friction to endanger monolithic solidarity within the *bloc*.

DOCUMENTATION

By RODERICK MACFARQUHAR

1. Points of Departure

THIS section contains the three important theoretical assessments of the world situation which form the background to the dispute during 1960: Khrushchev's assessment during the course of his report on February 14, 1956, to the Twentieth Congress of the Soviet Communist Party (CPSU), the assessment made by the ruling Communist Parties at their meeting in Moscow in November 1957 after the 40th anniversary celebrations of the Bolshevik revolution, and Khrushchev's further and, in Communist terms, even more optimistic assessment in his report to the CPSU's Twenty-first Congress on January 27, 1959.

That the assessments can be described as theoretical of course does not mean that they have no relevance to Soviet or Communist practice. In fact, ruling Communists normally feel obliged to justify important policies in Marxist-Leninist terms. Consequently theoretical innovations such as the two Khrushchev assessments represent invariably indicate major policy changes that have occurred or are about to take place.

Khrushchev's speech to the CPSU's Twentieth Congress contained two major modifications of Marxist-Leninist doctrine relevant to the dispute of 1960. First, he affirmed that the doctrine that war was inevitable so long as imperialism existed was no longer true. Lenin had argued that imperialist countries would quarrel among themselves over markets and exploitable underdeveloped territories with mounting bitterness. First one then another country would win a temporary advantage (the " law of uneven development ") and the resultant instability would lead inevitably to war.[1]

Khrushchev accepted Lenin's view that this instability would remain so long as imperialism persisted, and with it the " economic basis giving rise to wars." But he argued that the " epoch-making changes of the last decades " (*i.e.*, since the outbreak of World War II) entailed that " war is not fatalistically inevitable." These changes were: the growth of a powerful Communist *bloc*, the existence of a large number of non-

---

[1] For a discussion of Lenin's views see R. N. Carew Hunt, *The Theory and Practice of Communism* (London: Bles, 1950), pp. 161–167.

Communist countries with populations totalling hundreds of millions (*i.e.*, neutrals such as India and Indonesia) who were opposed to war (and, of course, were not allies of the West), the strength of the labour movement in capitalist countries, and the development of an international peace movement.

Khrushchev had only modified Lenin's views; war was still possible and Communists had to be careful lest it break out. But this modification was the basis for the whole diplomacy of " peaceful co-existence." This policy had two major aims. On the one hand it would reduce East-West tension so as to avert the danger of a thermo-nuclear holocaust which would devastate the Soviet Union as much as America.[2] This reduction of tension would also enable Moscow to soften up the West in order to gain its ends in Europe and in particular in Germany. This policy was already in operation. It will be remembered that by the time Khrushchev made this speech he had, with the then-Premier Bulganin, helped foster the " Geneva spirit " at the 1955 summit conference and that he and Bulganin had arranged to visit Britain in the spring of 1956.

The second aim of the peaceful co-existence policy was to allow the Russians to spread their influence throughout the neutralist world by trade, aid, glad-handing and the exploitation of anti-colonialism.[3] Since Khrushchev was clearly convinced that he could gradually oust the West this way, he doubtless needed to be sure that Soviet diplomatic victories would not frighten a militant West into attacking the Soviet Union. " Peaceful coexistence " diplomacy was designed partly to get the West to accept the march of world revolution.

Khrushchev's second major modification of Marxism-Leninism at the Twentieth Congress was his assertion that the weakening of capitalism relative to the growing power of the Communist *bloc* meant that it might be possible to introduce Communist rule in various countries by parliamentary means rather than by revolutionary violence. At the time it appeared that Khrushchev wished to help Western Communist Parties whose failure decisively to increase their influence was in many cases attributable to the popular image of them as bloodthirsty revolutionaries controlled from Moscow.

But in fact, Khrushchev talked of the possibility of " peaceful transition " in reference both to " capitalist *and former colonial countries* " (emphasis added). It would seem he was also concerned to assure men like Nehru and Sukarno that Soviet aid and friendship was not merely

---

[2] Malenkov had revealed in 1954 (*Pravda*, March 13) that he realised war would be as disastrous for Russia as the West though no Soviet leader has ever admitted to sharing this belief in such downright terms.

[3] Khrushchev's trip with Bulganin to India, Burma and Afghanistan late in 1955 was his first to the neutralist world. During it the Soviet Union made its first major aid agreements with the neutralist world.

a smoke screen behind which local Communist Parties were preparing *coups d'état*.

The Declaration issued in Moscow in 1957 by the leaders of the Communist *bloc* countries including China (Mao Tse-tung attended the conference in person) confirmed both of Khrushchev's theoretical innovations. But it contained important modifications of the Khrushchev presentation of those theses.

While war was stated not to be inevitable, there was no reference to those Western leaders on whose " sobering up " Khrushchev, in his Twentieth Congress speech, clearly relied in suggesting that deals with the West were possible. A major addition was made to the list of forces whose growing power could prevent war—the national liberation movement.[4] " Peaceful transition " to Communism was still regarded as possible, but only capitalist countries were referred to when the doctrine's applicability was discussed.

The " harder " tone of the Declaration as compared with Khrushchev's Twentieth Congress speech doubtless reflected the general worsening in the international situation between early 1956 and late 1957, a period which had seen the Hungarian revolt, the Suez war, and further tension in the Middle East. The disastrous effect of de-Stalinisation in Eastern Europe and of the " hundred flowers " and rectification in China meant that this was a time for reaffirming Communist principles in the strongest terms. Besides, the launching of the first sputnik shortly before the meeting made the most strident reassertion of the power of Communism almost inevitable.

But, with the benefit of hindsight, it can be suggested that Mao may have insisted on the insertion of the national liberation movement and on the exclusion of former colonies from the category of countries in which " peaceful transitions " might be engineered.

At the Twenty-first CPSU Congress, Khrushchev went beyond his original assertion that war was no longer inevitable. He said that when the Soviet Union had become the world's leading industrial power and with China and the other Communist countries produced over half the world's industrial output, there would be " an actual possibility of excluding *world* war from the life of society " (emphasis added). Clearly the new formulation was more optimistic than the old and could be made the basis of even greater reliance on " peaceful co-existence." This was the period of the Macmillan visit to Moscow and the Mikoyan visit to America and the slow march towards a summit conference. Before the end of the year, Nixon was to open the American exhibition in Moscow and Khrushchev, himself, was to tour the United States.

---

4 Khrushchev referred separately and at length to the national liberation movement, but did not accord it a role in helping maintain world peace.

Khrushchev's Twentieth Congress Speech

The peaceful co-existence of the two systems. The Leninist principle of peaceful co-existence of states with different social systems has always been and remains the general line of our country's foreign policy.

It has been alleged that the Soviet Union puts forward the principle of peaceful co-existence merely out of tactical considerations, considerations of expediency. Yet it is common knowledge that we have always, from the very first years of Soviet power, stood with equal firmness for peaceful co-existence. Hence, it is not a tactical move, but a fundamental principle of Soviet foreign policy.

This means that if there is indeed a threat to the peaceful co-existence of countries with differing social and political systems, it by no means comes from the Soviet Union or the rest of the socialist camp. Is there a single reason why a socialist state should want to unleash aggressive war ? Do we have classes and groups that are interested in war as a means of enrichment ? We do not. We abolished them long ago. Or perhaps, we do not have enough territory or natural wealth, and perhaps we lack sources of raw materials or markets for our goods ? No, we have enough and to spare of all those. Why then should we want war ? We do not want it, and as a matter of principle we renounce any policy that might lead to millions of people being plunged into war for the sake of the selfish interests of a handful of multi-millionaires. Do those who shout about the " aggressive intentions " of the U.S.S.R. know all this ? Of course they do. Why then do they keep up the old monotonous refrain about some imaginary " Communist aggression "? Only to stir up mud, to conceal their plans for world domination, a " crusade " against peace, democracy and socialism.

To this day the enemies of peace allege that the Soviet Union is out to overthrow capitalism in other countries by " exporting " revolution. It goes without saying that among us Communists there are no supporters of capitalism. But this does not mean that we have interfered, or plan to interfere, in the internal affairs of countries where capitalism still exists. Romain Rolland was right when he said that " freedom is not brought in from abroad in baggage trains like Bourbons ". It is ridiculous to think that revolutions are made to order. We often hear representatives of bourgeois countries reasoning thus : " The Soviet leaders claim that they are for peaceful co-existence between the two systems. At the same time they declare that they are fighting for communism, and say that communism is bound to win in all countries. Now if the Soviet Union is fighting for communism, how can there be any peaceful co-existence with it ? " This view is the result of bourgeois propaganda. The ideologists of the bourgeoisie distort the facts and deliberately confuse questions of ideological struggle with questions of relations between states, in order to make the Communists of the Soviet Union look like advocates of aggression.

When we say that the socialist system will win in the competition between the two systems—the capitalist and the socialist systems—this by no means signifies that its victory will be achieved through armed interference by the socialist countries in the internal affairs of the capitalist countries. Our certainty of the victory of communism is based on the fact that the socialist mode of production possesses decisive advantages over the capitalist mode of production. Precisely because of this, the ideas of Marxism-Leninism are more and more capturing the minds of the broad masses of the working people in the capitalist countries, just as they have captured the minds of millions of men and women in our country and the people's democracies. We believe that all working men in the world, once they have become convinced of the advantages communism brings, will sooner or later take the road of struggle for the construction of socialist society. Building communism in our country, we are resolutely against war. We have always held and continue to hold that the establishment of a new social system in this or that country is the internal affair of the peoples of the countries concerned. This is our attitude, based on the great Marxist-Leninist teaching.

The principle of peaceful co-existence is gaining ever wider international recognition. This principle is one of the cornerstones of the foreign policy of the Chinese People's Republic and the other people's democracies. It is being actively implemented by the Republic of India, the Union of Burma and a number of other countries. And this is natural, for in present-day conditions there is no other way out. Indeed, there are only two ways: either peaceful co-existence or the most destructive war in history. There is no third way.

We believe that countries with differing social systems can do more than exist side by side. It is necessary to proceed further, to improve relations, strengthen confidence between countries and co-operate. The historical significance of the famous five principles, put forward by the Chinese People's Republic and the Republic of India and supported by the Bandung Conference and the world public in general, lies in the fact that they provide the best form for relations between countries with differing social systems in present-day conditions. Why not make these principles the foundation for peaceful relations among all countries in all parts of the world? It would meet the vital interests and demands of the peoples if all countries subscribed to these five principles.

The Possibility of Preventing War in the Present Era

Millions of people all over the world are asking whether another war is really inevitable, whether mankind, which has already experienced two devastating world wars, must still go through a third one? Marxists must answer this question, taking into consideration the epoch-making changes of the last decades.

There is, of course, a Marxist-Leninist precept that wars are inevitable as long as imperialism exists. This precept was evolved at a time when (i) imperialism was an all-embracing world system, and (ii) the social and political forces which did not want war were weak, poorly organised, and hence unable to compel the imperialists to renounce war.

People usually take only one aspect of the question and examine only the economic basis of wars under imperialism. This is not enough. War is not only an economic phenomenon. Whether there is to be a war or not depends in large measure on the correlation of class, political forces, the degree of organisation and the awareness and determination of the people. Moreover, in certain conditions the struggle waged by progressive social and political forces may play a decisive role. Hitherto the state of affairs was such that the forces that did not want war and opposed it were poorly organised and lacked the means to check the schemes of the war-makers. Thus it was before the First World War, when the main force opposed to the threat of war—the world proletariat—was disorganised by the treachery of the leaders of the Second International. Thus it was on the eve of the Second World War, when the Soviet Union was the only country that pursued an active peace policy, when the other great powers to all intents and purposes encouraged the aggressors, and the right-wing Social-Democratic leaders had split the labour movement in the capitalist countries.

In that period this precept was absolutely correct. At the present time, however, the situation has changed radically. Now there is a world camp of socialism, which has become a mighty force. In this camp the peace forces find not only the moral, but also the material means to prevent aggression. Moreover, there is a large group of other countries with a population running into many hundreds of millions which are actively working to avert war. The labour movement in the capitalist countries has today become a tremendous force. The movement of peace supporters has sprung up and developed into a powerful factor.

In these circumstances certainly the Leninist precept that so long as imperialism exists, the economic basis giving rise to wars will also be preserved, remains in force. That is why we must display the greatest vigilance. As long as capitalism survives in the world, the reactionary forces representing the interests of the capitalist monopolies will continue their drive towards military gambles and aggression, and may try to unleash war. But war is not fatalistically inevitable. Today there are mighty social and political forces possessing formidable means to prevent the imperialists from unleashing war, and if they actually do try to start it, to give a smashing rebuff to the aggressors and frustrate their adventurist plans. In order to be able to do this, all the anti-war forces must be vigilant and prepared, they must act as a united front and never relax their efforts in the battle for peace. The more actively the peoples defend peace, the greater will be the guarantees that there will be no new war.

Forms of Transition to Socialism in Different Countries

In connection with the radical changes in the world arena new prospects are also opening up as regards the transition of countries and nations to socialism.

As long ago as the eve of the Great October Socialist Revolution, Lenin wrote: "All nations will arrive at socialism—this is inevitable, but not all will do so in exactly the same way, each will contribute something of its own in one or another form of democracy, one or another variety of the dictatorship of the proletariat, one or another rate at which socialist transformations will be effected in the various aspects of social life. There is nothing more primitive from the viewpoint of theory or more ridiculous from that of practice than to paint, ' in the name of historical materialism ', *this* aspect of the future in a monotonous grey. The result will be nothing more than Suzdal daubing " [*Works,* Russian edition, Vol. 23, p. 58].

The experience of history has fully confirmed Lenin's brilliant precept. Alongside the Soviet form of reconstructing society on socialist lines, we now have the form of people's democracy.

In Poland, Bulgaria, Czechoslovakia, Albania and the other European people's democracies this form sprang up and is being utilised in conformity with the concrete historical, social and economic conditions and peculiarities of each of these countries. It has been thoroughly tried and tested in the course of ten years and has fully proved its worth.

Much that is unique in socialist construction is being contributed by the People's Republic of China, whose economy prior to the victory of the revolution was exceedingly backward, semi-feudal and semi-colonial in character. Having taken over the decisive commanding positions, the people's democratic state is using them in the social revolution to implement a policy of peaceful reorganisation of private industry and trade and their gradual transformation into a component of socialist economy.

The leadership of the great cause of socialist reconstruction by the Communist Party of China and the Communist and Workers' Parties of the other people's democracies, exercised in keeping with the peculiarities and specific features of each country, is creative Marxism in action.

In the Federal People's Republic of Yugoslavia, where state power belongs to the working people, and society is founded on public ownership of the means of production, specific concrete forms of economic management and organisation of the state apparatus are arising in the process of socialist construction.

It is probable that more forms of transition to socialism will appear. Moreover, the implementation of these forms need not be associated with civil war under all circumstances. Our enemies like to depict us Leninists as advocates of violence always and everywhere. True, we recognise the need for the revolutionary transformation of capitalist society into socialist society. It is this that distinguishes the revolutionary Marxists from the reformists, the opportunists. There is no doubt that in a number of capitalist countries the violent overthrow of the dictatorship of the bourgeoisie and the sharp aggravation of class struggle connected with this are inevitable. But the forms of social revolution vary. It is not true that we regard violence and civil war as the only way to remake society.

It will be recalled that in the conditions that arose in April 1917 Lenin granted the possibility that the Russian Revolution might develop peacefully, and that in the spring of 1918, after the victory of the October Revolution, Lenin drew up his famous plan for peaceful socialist construction. It is not our fault that the Russian and international bourgeoisie organised counter-revolution, intervention and civil war against the young Soviet state and forced the workers and peasants to take to arms. It did not come to civil war in the European people's democracies, where the historical situation was different.

Leninism teaches us that the ruling classes will not surrender their power voluntarily. And the greater or lesser degree of intensity which the struggle may assume, the use or the non-use of violence in the transition to socialism, depends on the resistance of the exploiters, on whether the exploiting class itself resorts to violence, rather than on the proletariat.

In this connection the question arises of whether it is possible to go over to socialism by using parliamentary means. No such course was open to the Russian Bolsheviks, who were the first to effect this transition. Lenin showed us another road, that of the establishment of a republic of Soviets—the only correct road in those historical conditions. Following that course, we achieved a victory of world-wide historical significance.

Since then, however, the historical situation has undergone radical changes which make possible a new approach to the question. The forces of socialism and democracy have grown immeasurably throughout the world, and capitalism has become much weaker. The mighty camp of socialism with its population of over 900 million is growing and gaining in strength. Its gigantic internal forces, its decisive advantages over capitalism, are being increasingly revealed from day to day. Socialism has a great power of attraction for the workers, peasants and intellectuals of all countries. The ideas of socialism are indeed coming to dominate the minds of all working mankind.

At the same time the present situation offers the working class in a number of capitalist countries a real opportunity to unite the overwhelming majority of the people under its leadership and to secure the transfer of the basic means of production into the hands of the people. The right-wing bourgeois parties and their governments are suffering bankruptcy with increasing frequency. In these circumstances the working class, by rallying around itself the working peasantry, the intelligentsia, all patriotic forces, and resolutely repulsing the opportunist elements who are incapable of giving up the policy of compromise with the capitalists and landlords, is in a position to defeat the reactionary forces opposed to the interests of the people, to capture a stable majority in parliament, and transform the latter from an organ of bourgeois democracy into a genuine instrument of the people's will. In such an event this institution, traditional in many highly developed capitalist countries, may become an organ of genuine democracy—democracy for the working people.

The winning of a stable parliamentary majority backed by a mass revolutionary movement of the proletariat and of all the working people could create for the working class of a number of capitalist and former colonial countries the conditions needed to secure fundamental social changes.

In the countries where capitalism is still strong and has a huge military and police apparatus at its disposal, the reactionary forces will, of course, inevitably offer serious resistance. There the transition to socialism will be attended by a sharp class, revolutionary struggle.

Whatever the form of transition to socialism, the decisive and indispensable factor is the political leadership of the working class headed by its vanguard. Without this there can be no transition to socialism.

It must be strongly emphasised that the more favourable conditions for the victory of socialism created in other countries are due to the fact that socialism has won in the Soviet Union and is winning in the people's democracies. Its victory in our country would have been impossible had Lenin and the Bolshevik Party not upheld revolutionary Marxism in battle against the reformists, who broke with Marxism and took the path of opportunism.

Such are the considerations which the central committee of the Party considers it necessary to set out with regard to the forms of transition to socialism in present-day conditions. . . .

[From text in *Soviet News Booklet No. 4* (London: Soviet Embassy, 1956).]

✱

The 1957 Moscow Declaration

Representatives of the Albanian Party of Labour, the Bulgarian Communist Party, the Hungarian Socialist Workers' Party, the Vietnamese Working People's Party, the Socialist Unity Party of Germany, the Communist Party of China, the Korean Party of Labour, the Mongolian People's Revolutionary Party, the Polish United Workers' Party, the Rumanian Workers' Party, the Communist Party of the Soviet Union and the

Communist Party of Czechoslovakia discussed their relations, current problems of the international situation and the struggle for peace and socialism.

The exchange of opinions revealed identity of views of the parties on all the questions examined at the meeting and unanimity in their assessment of the international situation. In the course of discussion the meeting also touched upon general problems of the international Communist movement. In drafting the declaration the participants in the meeting consulted with representatives of the fraternal parties in the capitalist countries. The fraternal parties not present at this meeting will assess and themselves decide what action they should take on the considerations expressed in the declaration.

1. The main content of our epoch is the transition from capitalism to socialism which was begun by the great October socialist revolution in Russia. Today more than a third of the population of the world—over 950 million people—have taken the road of socialism and are building a new life. The tremendous growth of the forces of socialism has stimulated the rapid extension of the anti-imperialist national movement in the post-war period. During the last 12 years, besides the Chinese People's Republic, the Democratic Republic of Vietnam and the Korean People's Democratic Republic, over 700 million people have shaken off the colonial yoke and established national independent states. The peoples of the colonial and dependent countries, still languishing in slavery, are intensifying the struggle for national liberation. The progress of socialism and of the national-liberation movement has greatly accelerated the disintegration of imperialism. With regard to the greater part of mankind imperialism has lost its one-time domination. In the imperialist countries society is rent by deep-going class contradictions and by antagonisms between those countries, while the working class is putting up increasing resistance to the policy of imperialism and the monopolies, fighting for better conditions, democratic rights, for peace and socialism.

In our epoch world development is determined by the course and results of the competition between two diametrically opposed social systems. In the past 40 years socialism has demonstrated that it is a much higher social system than capitalism. It has ensured development of the productive forces at a rate unprecedented and impossible for capitalism, and the rise of the material and cultural levels of the working people. The Soviet Union's strides in economy, science and technology and the results achieved by the other socialist countries in socialist construction are conclusive evidence of the great vitality of socialism. In the socialist states the broad masses of the working people enjoy genuine freedom and democratic rights, people's power ensures political unity of the masses, equality and friendship among the nations and a foreign policy aimed at preserving universal peace and rendering assistance to the oppressed nations in their emancipation struggle. The world socialist system, which is growing and becoming stronger, is exerting ever greater influence upon the international situation in the interests of peace and progress and the freedom of the peoples.

While socialism is on the upgrade, imperialism is heading towards decline. The position of imperialism has been greatly weakened as a result of the disintegration of the colonial system. The countries that have shaken off the yoke of colonialism are defending their independence and fighting for economic sovereignty, for international peace. The existence of the socialist system and the aid rendered by the socialist nations to these countries on principles of equality and co-operation between them and the socialist nations in the struggle for peace and against aggression help them to uphold their national freedom and facilitate their social progress.

In the imperialist countries the contradictions between the productive forces and production relations have become acute. In many respects modern science and engineering are not being used in the interests of social progress for all mankind because capitalism fetters and deforms the development of the productive forces of society. The world capitalist economy remains shaky and unstable. The relatively good economic activity still observed in a number of capitalist countries is due in large measure to the arms drive and other transient factors.

However, the capitalist economy is bound to encounter deeper slumps and crises. The temporary high business activity helps to keep up the reformist illusions among part of the workers in the capitalist countries. In the post-war period some sections of the working class in the more advanced capitalist countries, fighting against increased exploitation and for a higher standard of living, have been able to win certain wage increases, though in a number of these countries real wages are below the pre-war level. However, in the greater part of the capitalist world, particularly in the colonial and dependent countries, millions of working people still live in poverty. The broad invasion of agriculture by the monopolies and the price policy dictated by them, the system of bank credits and loans and the increased taxation caused by the arms drive have resulted in the steady ruin and impoverishment of the main mass of the peasantry. There is a sharpening of contradictions not only between the bourgeoisie and the working class but also between the monopoly bourgeoisie and all sections of the people, between the United States monopoly bourgeoisie on the one hand and the peoples, and even the bourgeoisie of the other capitalist countries on the other. The working people of the capitalist countries live in such conditions that, increasingly, they realise that the only way out of their grave situation lies through socialism. Thus, increasingly favourable conditions are being created for bringing them into active struggle for socialism.

The aggressive imperialist circles of the United States, by pursuing the so-called " positions of strength " policy, seek to bring most countries of the world under their sway and to hamper the onward march of mankind in accordance with the laws of social development. On the pretext of " combating Communism " they are angling to bring more and more countries under their dominion, instigating destruction of democratic freedoms, threatening the national independence of the developed capitalist countries, trying to enmesh the liberated peoples in new forms of colonialism and systematically conducting subversive activities against the socialist countries. The policy of certain aggressive groups in the United States is aimed at rallying around them all the reactionary forces of the capitalist world. Acting in this way they are becoming the centre of world reaction, the sworn enemies of the people. By this policy these anti-popular, aggressive imperialist forces are courting their own ruin, creating their own grave-diggers.

So long as imperialism exists there will always be soil for aggressive wars. Throughout the post-war years the American, British, French and other imperialists and their stooges have conducted and are conducting wars in Indo-China, Indonesia, Korea, Malaya, Kenya, Guatemala, Egypt, Algeria,

Oman and Yemen. At the same time the aggressive imperialist forces flatly refuse to cut armaments, to prohibit the use and production of atomic and hydrogen weapons, to agree on immediate discontinuation of the tests of these weapons; they are continuing the " cold war " and arms drive, building more military bases and conducting the aggressive policy of undermining peace and creating the danger of a new war. Were a world war to break out before agreement on prohibition of nuclear weapons is reached it would inevitably become a nuclear war unprecedented in destructive force.

In West Germany militarism is being revived with United States help, giving rise to a hot-bed of war in the heart of Europe. Struggle against West German militarism and revanchism, which are now threatening peace, is a vital task facing the peace-loving forces of the German people and all the nations of Europe. An especially big role in this struggle belongs to the German Democratic Republic—the first workers—peasant state in German history with which the participants in the meeting express their solidarity and which they fully support.

Simultaneously the imperialists are trying to impose on the freedom-loving peoples of the Middle East the notorious " Eisenhower-Dulles doctrine " thereby creating the danger of war in this area. They are plotting conspiracies and provocations against independent Syria. The provocations against Syria and Egypt and other Arab countries pursue the aim of dividing and isolating the Arab countries in order to abolish their freedom and independence.

The S.E.A.T.O. aggressive bloc is a source of war danger in East Asia.

The question of war or peaceful co-existence is now the crucial question of world policy. All the nations must display the utmost vigilance in regard to the war danger created by imperialism.

At present the forces of peace have so grown that there is a real possibility of averting wars as was demonstrated by the collapse of the imperialist designs in Egypt. The imperialist plan to use the counter-revolutionary forces for the overthrow of the People's Democratic system in Hungary have failed as well.

The cause of peace is upheld by the powerful forces of our era: the invincible camp of socialist countries headed by the Soviet Union ; the peace-loving countries of Asia and Africa taking an anti-imperialist stand and forming, together with the socialist countries, a broad peace zone ; the international working class and above all its vanguard—the Communist Parties ; the liberation movement of the peoples of the colonies and semi-colonies ; the mass peace movement of the peoples ; the peoples of the European countries who have proclaimed neutrality, the peoples of Latin America and the masses in the imperialist countries are putting up increasing resistance to the plans for a new war. The unity of these powerful forces can prevent the outbreak of war. But should the bellicose imperialist maniacs venture, regardless of anything, to unleash a war, imperialism will doom itself to destruction, for the peoples will not tolerate a system that brings them so much suffering and exacts so many sacrifices.

The Communist and Workers' Parties taking part in the meeting declare that the Leninist principles of peaceful co-existence of the two systems, which has been further developed and brought up to date in the decisions of the 20th Congress of the C.P.S.U. is the sound basis of the foreign policy of the socialist countries and the dependable pillar of peace and friendship among the peoples. The idea of peaceful co-existence coincides with the 5 principles advanced jointly by the Chinese People's Republic and the Republic of India and with the programme adopted by the Bandung Conference of Afro-Asian countries. Peace and peaceful co-existence have now become the demands of the broad masses in all countries.

The Communist Parties regard the struggle for peace as their foremost task. They will do all in their power to prevent war.

2. The meeting considers that in the present situation the strengthening of the unity and fraternal co-operation of the socialist countries, the Communist and Workers' Parties and the solidarity of the international working-class, national liberation and democratic movements acquire special significance.

At bedrock of the relations of the world socialist system and all the Communist and Workers' Parties lie the principles of Marxism-Leninism, the principles of proletarian internationalism which have been tested by life. Today the vital interests of the working people of all countries call for their support of the Soviet Union and all the socialist countries who, pursuing a policy of preserving peace throughout the world, are the mainstay of peace and social progress. The working class, the democratic forces and the working people everywhere are interested in tirelessly strengthening fraternal contacts for the sake of the common cause, in safeguarding from enemy encroachments the historical, political and social gains effected in the Soviet Union—the first and mightiest socialist power—in the Chinese People's Republic and in all the socialist countries, in seeing these gains extended and consolidated.

The socialist countries base their relations on principles of complete equality, respect for territorial integrity, state independence and sovereignty and non-interference in one another's affairs. These are vital principles. However, they do not exhaust the essence of relations between them. Fraternal mutual aid is part and parcel of these relations. This aid is a striking expression of socialist internationalism.

On a basis of complete equality, mutual benefit and comradely mutual assistance, the socialist states have established between themselves extensive economic and cultural co-operation that plays an important part in promoting the economic and political independence of each socialist country and the socialist commonwealth as a whole. The socialist states will continue to extend and improve economic and cultural co-operation among themselves.

The socialist states also advocate all-round expansion of economic and cultural relations with all other countries, provided they desire it, on a basis of equality, mutual benefit and non-interference in each other's internal affairs. The solidarity of the socialist countries is not directed against any other country. On the contrary, it serves the interests of all the peace-loving peoples, restrains the aggressive strivings of the bellicose imperialist circles and supports and encourages the growing forces of peace. The socialist countries are against the division of the world into military blocs. But in view of the situation that has taken shape, with the western powers refusing to accept the proposals of the socialist countries for mutual abolition of military blocs, the Warsaw pact organisation, which is of a defensive nature, serves the security of the peoples of Europe and supports peace throughout the world, must be preserved and strengthened.

The socialist countries are united in a single community by the fact that they are taking the common socialist road, by the common class essence of the social and economic system and state authority, by the requirements of mutual aid and support, identity of interests and aims in the struggle against imperialism, for the victory of socialism and communism, by the ideology of Marxism-Leninism, which is common to all.

The solidarity and close unity of the socialist countries constitute a reliable guarantee of the sovereignty and independence of each. Stronger fraternal relations and friendship between the socialist countries call for a Marxist-Leninist internationalist policy on the part of the communist and workers parties, for educating all the working people in the spirit of combining internationalism with patriotism and for a determined effort to overcome the survivals of bourgeois nationalism and chauvinism. All issues pertaining to relations between the socialist countries can be fully settled through comradely discussion, with strict observance of the principles of socialist internationalism.

3. The victory of socialism in the U.S.S.R. and progress in socialist construction in the people's democracies find deep sympathy among the working class and the working people of all countries. The ideas of socialism are winning additional millions of people. In these conditions the imperialist bourgeoisie attaches increasing importance to the ideological moulding of the masses; it misrepresents socialism and smears Marxism-Leninism, misleads and confuses the masses. It is a prime task to intensify Marxist-Leninist education of the masses, combat bourgeois ideology, expose the lies and slanderous fabrications of imperialist propaganda against socialism and the Communist Movement and widely propagate in simple and convincing fashion the ideas of socialism, peace and friendship among nations.

The meeting confirmed the identity of views of the Communist and Workers Parties on the cardinal problems of the socialist revolution and socialist construction. The experience of the Soviet Union and the other socialist countries has fully borne out the correctness of the Marxist-Leninist proposition that the processes of the socialist revolution and the building of socialism are governed by a number of basic laws applicable in all countries embarking on a socialist course. These laws manifest themselves everywhere, alongside a great variety of historic national peculiarities and traditions which must by all means be taken into account.

These laws are: guidance of the working masses by the working class, the core of which is the Marxist-Leninist Party; in effecting a proletarian revolution in one form or another and establishing one form or other of the dictatorship of the proletariat; the alliance of the working class and the bulk of the peasantry and other sections of the working people; the abolition of capitalist ownership and the establishment of public ownership of the basic means of production; gradual socialist reconstruction of agriculture; planned development of the national economy aimed at building socialism and communism, at raising the standard of living of the working people; the carrying out of socialist revolution in the sphere of ideology and culture and the creation of a numerous intelligentsia devoted to the working class, the working people and the cause of socialism; the abolition of national oppression and the establishment of equality and fraternal friendship between the peoples; defence of the achievements of socialism against attacks by internal enemies; solidarity of the working class of the country in question with the working class of other countries, that is proletarian internationalism.

51

Marxism-Leninism calls for a creative application of the general principles of the socialist revolution and socialist construction depending on the concrete conditions of each country, and rejects mechanical imitation of the policies and tactics of the Communist Parties of other countries. Lenin repeatedly called attention to the necessity of correctly applying the basic principles of communism, in keeping with the specific features of the nation, of the national state concerned. Disregard of national pecularities by the proletarian party inevitably leads to its divorce from reality, from the masses and is bound to prejudice the cause of socialism and conversely, exaggeration of the role of these peculiarities or departure, under the pretext of national peculiarities, from the universal Marxist-Leninist truth on the socialist revolution and socialist construction is just as harmful to the socialist cause.

The participants in this meeting consider that both these tendencies should be combated simultaneously. The Communist and Workers' Parties of the socialist countries should firmly adhere to the principle of combining the above universal Marxist-Leninist truth with the specific revolutionary practice in their countries, creatively apply the general laws governing the socialist revolution and socialist construction in accordance with the concrete conditions of their countries, learn from each other and share experience. Creative application of the general laws of socialist construction tried and tested by experience and the variety of forms and methods of building socialism used in different countries, represent a collective contribution to Marxist-Leninist theory.

The theory of Marxism-Leninism derives from dialectical materialism. This world outlook reflects the universal law of development of nature, society and human thinking. It is valid for the past, the present and the future. Dialectical materialism is countered by metaphysics and idealism. Should the Marxist political party in its examination of questions base itself not on dialectics and materialism, the result will be one-sidedness and subjectivism, stagnation of thought, isolation from life and loss of ability to make the necessary analysis of things and phenomena, revisionist and dogmatist mistakes and mistakes in policy. Application of dialectical materialism in practical work and the education of the party functionaries and the broad masses in the spirit of Marxism-Leninism are urgent tasks of the Communist and Workers' Parties.

Of vital importance in the present stage is intensified struggle against opportunist trends in the working class and communist movement. The meeting underlines the necessity of resolutely overcoming revisionism and dogmatism in the ranks of the Communist and Workers' Parties. Revisionism and dogmatism in the working class and communist movement are today, as they have been in the past, international phenomena. Dogmatism and sectarianism hinder the development of Marxist-Leninist theory and its creative application in the changing conditions, replace the study of the concrete situation with merely quoting classics and sticking to books, and leads to the isolation of the party from the masses. A party that has withdrawn into the shell of sectarianism and that has lost contact with the masses cannot bring victory to the cause of the working class.

In condemning dogmatism, the Communist Parties believe that the main danger at present is revisionism or, in other words, right-wing opportunism, which as a manifestation of bourgeois ideology paralyses the revolutionary energy of the working class and demands the preservation or restoration of capitalism. However, dogmatism and sectarianism can also be the main danger at different phases of development in one party or another. It is for each Communist Party to decide what danger threatens it more at a given time.

It should be pointed out that the conquest of power by the proletariat is only the beginning of the revolution, not its conclusion. After the conquest of power the working class is faced with the serious tasks of effecting the socialist reconstruction of the national economy and laying the economic and technical foundation of socialism. At the same time the overthrown bourgeoisie always endeavours to make a comeback; the influence exerted on society by the bourgeoisie, the petty bourgeoisie and their intelligentsia, is still great. That is why a fairly long time is needed to resolve the issue of who will win—capitalism or socialism. The existence of bourgeois influence in an internal source of revisionism, while surrender to imperialist pressure is its external source.

Modern revisionism seeks to smear the great teachings of Marxism-Leninism, declares that it is " outmoded " and alleges that it has lost its significance for social progress. The revisionists try to exorcise the revolutionary spirit of Marxism, to undermine faith in socialism among the working class and the working people in general. They deny the historical necessity for a proletarian revolution and the dictatorship of the proletariat during the period of transition from capitalism to socialism, deny the leading role of the Marxist-Leninist party, reject the principles of proletarian internationalism and call for rejection of the Leninist principles of party organisation and, above all, of democratic centralism, for transforming the Communist Party from a militant revolutionary organisation into some kind of a debating society.

The experience of the international communist movement shows that resolute defence by the communist and workers' parties of the Marxist-Leninist unity of their ranks and the banning of factions and groups sapping unity guarantee the successful solution of the tasks of the socialist revolution, the establishment of socialism and communism.

4. The communist and workers' parties are faced with great historic tasks. The carrying out of these tasks necessitates closer unity not only of the communist and workers' parties, but of the entire working class, necessitates cementing the alliance of the working class and peasantry, rallying the working people and progressive mankind, the freedom and peace-loving forces of the world.

The defence of peace is the most important world-wide task of the day. The communist and workers' parties in all countries stand for joint action on the broadest possible scale with all forces favouring peace and opposed to war. The participants in the meeting declare that they support the efforts of all states, parties, organisations, movements and individuals who champion peace and oppose war, who want peaceful co-existence, collective security in Europe and Asia, reduction of armaments and prohibition of the use and tests of nuclear weapons.

The communist and workers' parties are loyal defenders of the national and democratic interests of the peoples of all countries. The working class and the peoples of many countries are still confronted with the historic tasks of struggle for national independence against colonial aggression and feudal oppression. What is needed here is a united anti-imperialism and anti-feudal front of the workers, peasants, urban petty bourgeoisie, national bourgeoisie and other patriotic democratic forces. Numerous facts show that the greater and stronger the unity of the various patriotic and democratic forces, the greater the guarantee of victory in the common struggle.

At present the struggle of the working class and the masses of the people against the war danger and for their vital interest is spearheaded against the big monopoly group of capital as those chiefly responsible for the arms race, as those who organise or inspire plans for preparing a new world war who are the bulwark of aggression and reaction. The interests and the policy of this handful of monopolies conflict increasingly not only with the interests of the working class but the other sections of capitalist society: the peasants, intellectuals, petty and middle urban bourgeoisie. In those capitalist countries where the American monopolies are out to establish their hegemony and in the countries already suffering from the United States' policy of economic and military expansion, the objective conditions are being created for uniting, under the leadership of the working class and its revolutionary parties, broad sections of the population to fight for peace, the defence of national independence and democratic freedoms, to raise the standard of living, to carry through radical land reforms and to overthrow the rule of the monopolies who betray the national interests.

The profound historic changes and the decisive switch in the balance of forces in the international sphere in favour of socialism and the tremendous growth of the power of attractions exerted by socialist ideas among the working class, working peasantry and working intelligentsia create more favourable conditions for the victory of socialism.

The forms of the transition of socialism may vary for different countries. The working class and its vanguard—the Marxist-Leninist Party—seek to achieve the socialist revolution by peaceful means. This would accord with the interests of the working class and the people as a whole as well as with the national interests of the country.

Today in a number of capitalist countries the working class led by its vanguard has the opportunity, given a united working-class and popular front or other workable forms of agreement and political co-operation between the different parties and public organisations, to unite a majority of the people, to win state power without civil war and ensure the transfer of the basic means of production to the hands of the people. Relying on the majority of the people and decisively rebuffing the opportunist elements incapable of relinquishing the policy of compromise with the capitalists and landlords, the working class can defeat the reactionary, anti-popular forces, secure a firm majority in parliament, transform parliament from an instrument serving the class interests of the bourgeoisie into an instrument serving the working people, launch a non-parliamentary mass struggle, smash the resistance of the reactionary forces and create the necessary conditions for peaceful realisation of the socialist revolution. All this will be possible only by broad and ceaseless development of the class struggle of the workers, peasant masses and the urban middle strata against big monopoly capital, against reaction, for profound social reforms, for peace and socialism.

In the event of the ruling classes resorting to violence against people, the possibility of non-peaceful transition to socialism should be borne in mind. Leninism teaches, and experience confirms, that the ruling classes never relinquish power voluntarily. In this case the degree of bitterness and the forms of the class struggle will depend not so much on the proletariat as on the resistance put up by the reactionary circles to the will of the overwhelming majority of the people, on these circles using force at one or another stage of the struggle for socialism.

The possibility of one or another way to socialism depends on the concrete conditions in each country.

In the struggle for better conditions for the working people, for preservation and extension of democratic rights, winning and maintaining national independence and peace among nations, and also in the struggle for winning power and building socialism, the communist parties seek co-operation with the socialist parties. Although the right-wing socialist party leaders are doing their best to hamper this co-operation there are increasing opportunities for co-operation between the communists and socialists on many issues. The ideological differences between the communist and the socialist parties should not keep them from establishing unity of action on the many pressing issues that confront the working-class movement.

In the socialist countries where the working class is in power the Communist and Workers' Parties which have the opportunity to establish close relations with the broad masses of the people should constantly rely on them and make the building and the defence of socialism the cause of millions who fully realise that they are masters of their own country. Of great importance for enhancing the activity and creative initiative of the broad masses and their solidarity, for consolidating the socialist system and stepping up socialist construction are the measures taken in recent years by the socialist countries to expand socialist democracy and encourage criticism and self-criticism.

To bring about real solidarity of the working class, of all working people and the whole of progressive mankind, of the freedom-loving and peace-loving forces of the world, it is necessary above all to promote the unity of the Communist and Workers' Parties and to foster solidarity between the Communist and Workers' Parties of all countries. This solidarity is the core of still greater solidarity, it is the main guarantee of the victory of the cause of the working class.

The Communist and Workers' Parties have a particularly important responsibility with regard to the destinies of the world socialist system and the international Communist movement. The Communist and Workers' Parties represented at the meeting declare that they will tirelessly promote their unity and comradely co-operation with a view to further consolidating the commonwealth of socialist states in the interests of the international working-class movement, of peace and socialism.

The meeting notes with satisfaction that the international Communist movement has grown, withstood numerous serious trials and won a number of major victories. By their deeds, the Communists have demonstrated to the working people on a world-wide scale the vitality of the Marxist-Leninist theory and their ability not only to propagate the great ideals of socialism but also to realise them in exceedingly strenuous conditions.

Like any progressive movement in human history, the Communist movement is bound to encounter difficulties and obstacles. However, as in the past, no difficulties or obstacles can change now, nor will they be able to change in the future, the objective laws governing historical progress or affect the determination of the working class to transform the old world and create a new one. Ever since they began their struggles the Communists have been baited and persecuted by the reactionary forces; but the Communist movement heroically repels all attacks, emerging from the trials stronger and more steeled. The Communists, by further consolidating their unity, counter attempts by the reactionary forces to prevent human society from marching towards a new era.

Contrary to the absurd assertions of imperialism about a so-called crisis of communism, the Communist movement is growing and gathering strength. The historic decisions of the 20th Congress of the C.P.S.U. are of tremendous importance not only to the C.P.S.U. and to the building of Communism in the U.S.S.R., they have opened a new stage in the world Communist movement and pushed ahead its further development along Marxist-Leninist lines. The results of the Congresses of the Communist Parties of China, France, Italy and other countries in recent times have clearly demonstrated the unity and solidarity of the party ranks and their loyalty to the principles of pro-letarian internationalism. This meeting of the representatives of Communist and Workers' Parties testifies to the international solidarity of the Communist movement.

After exchanging views, the participants in the meeting arrived at the conclusion that in present conditions it is expedient besides bilateral meetings of leading personnel and exchange of information, to hold, as the need arises, more representative conferences of Communist and Workers' Parties to dis-cuss current problems, share experience, study each other's views and attitudes and concert action in the joint struggle for the common goals—peace, a demo-cracy and socialism.

The participants in the meeting unanimously express their firm confidence that, by closing their ranks and thereby rallying the working class and the peoples of all countries, the Communist and Workers' Parties will surmount all obstacles in their onward movement and accelerate further big victories for the cause of peace, democracy and socialism.

[NCNA, November 22, 1957.]

*

Khrushchev's Twenty-first Congress Speech

The conclusion drawn by the Party's 20th Congress to the effect that war is not fatally inevitable has been fully justified. At present we have even more grounds for reaffirming the correctness of this deduction. There now exist enormous forces capable of rebuffing the imperialist aggressors and inflicting defeat upon them in the event of their unleashing world war.

What new things on the international arena will be introduced by the fulfilment of the economic plans of the Soviet Union and all the socialist countries of Europe and Asia? As a result of this, real possibilities will be created for doing away with war as a means of solving international issues. Indeed, when the U.S.S.R. becomes the world's foremost industrial power, when the C.P.R. becomes a mighty industrial power, while all socialist countries taken together will produce more than half the world's industrial output, the international situation will change radically. The successes of the countries of the socialist camp will undoubtedly exert a tremendous influence on the consolidation of the peace-loving forces throughout the world. One need not doubt that by that time the States championing the consolidation of peace will be joined by new countries, freed of colonial oppression.

The idea of the inadmissibility of war will take still deeper root in the consciousness of nations. The new correlation of power will be so obvious that even the most obdurate imperialists will clearly realise the hopelessness of any attempt to launch a war against the socialist camp. Relying on the might of the camp of socialism, the peace-loving peoples will then be able to force the bellicose imperialist circles to renounce plans for another world war.

Thus, even before the complete victory of socialism on earth, while capitalism still remains in part of the world, there will be an actual possibility of excluding world war from the life of society. Some people may say: " But capitalism will remain, and therefore adventurers who could start a war will remain also." This is correct and should not be forgotten. While capitalism exists, there will always be some people to be found who, contrary to reason, may want to plunge into a hopeless enterprise. But by this they will only speed up the downfall of the capitalist system. Any attempt at aggression will be cut short and the adventurers will find themselves where they should be. . . .

[Translated in *Supplement to the Summary of World Broadcasts (Part I)*, " Twenty-first Congress of the C.P.S.U.," No. 1: First Day's Proceedings, January 30, 1959, issued by the B.B.C., London.]

2. The Rival Views Propounded

THE feelings with which Mao Tse-tung and his colleagues greeted Khrushchev at Peking airport on September 30, 1959, can only be guessed at. The Soviet leader was gracing the Chinese Communist régime's tenth anniversary celebrations with his presence. But he had come to China, as he said in his speech at the airport, " immediately after my return to Moscow from my visit to the United States of America, literally speaking, by changing from one plane to another." From the fact that China's anti-American propaganda had not been modified during that trip, Peking's hostility to Khrushchev's peace diplomacy could be inferred. That night at the tenth anniversary banquet, Khrushchev told his Chinese hosts three things: that he believed Eisenhower wanted to relax East-West tension, that peaceful co-existence had been approved by Lenin, and that strong though the *bloc* was it must not test the stability of the capitalist system by force. That he felt compelled to make the latter point must be construed as indicating he felt some members of the *bloc* thought differently. That Mao chose neither to make any speeches welcoming Khrushchev nor to comment on his American trip is a negative item whose significance cannot be gauged; but it was surely odd that the leader of the Chinese revolution should not have made any official statements on this important anniversary.

Over the succeeding months, the Chinese were digesting what Khrushchev had told them and deciding, their comment on the international scene makes clear, against falling into line.[5] The inevitable clash between the two views finally occurred at the meeting of the Warsaw Treaty Powers in Moscow in February 1960.

It is worth noting that the circumstances surrounding the summoning of the meeting were mysterious enough to suggest that at first either the Chinese were not invited or they did not want to come. On January 28, Moscow Radio announced that the Communist Party and Government leaders of the European satellites would be coming to Moscow for an agricultural conference on February 2. Delegations of observers from North Korea and Outer Mongolia were to attend " by invitation." But then on February 3 it was revealed that the Foreign Ministers of the Warsaw Treaty countries had been meeting since February 1 in

[5] For an extended discussion see A. M. Halpern, " Communist China and Peaceful Co-existence," *The China Quarterly*, No. 3, 1960. Halpern suggests the Chinese had made up their minds by early December 1959.

58

preparation for a conference on February 4. On the same day, Peking Radio made its first announcement about the agricultural conference and simultaneously stated that Chinese observers would be attending the Warsaw Treaty meeting. By now Moscow Radio was saying that the Koreans and Mongolians were attending " at their own request," presumably to still questions as to why the Chinese and the North Vietnamese had not been invited.

An agricultural conference did meet, but the innocuous communiqué which it produced did not seem likely to have been sufficient justification for top-level delegations to come to Moscow. Presumably it had been intended all along to hold a Warsaw Treaty conference to discuss policy towards the West, but the probability of a clash with the Chinese in some form had made the Russians want to keep the conference secret. In any event the conference became the occasion for the public juxtaposition of the opposed viewpoints of Moscow and Peking in the form of the Declaration of the Warsaw Treaty Powers on the one side and the speech of the Chinese observer at the conference, K'ang Sheng, on the other.

It is worth noting that while the Chinese Press published both the Declaration and their observer's speech, the press of the Soviet Union and the East European satellites never even mentioned the latter document. Thus readers of the *People's Daily* were henceforth able to see clearly against whom China's subsequent polemics were directed, while Soviet newspaper readers always had to rely on inside information or intelligent if not over-difficult guesswork.

These two documents, unlike most of those issued during the subsequent course of the dispute, are couched in concrete rather than theoretical terms. Thus it is here possible to perceive some of the major policy considerations underlying the ideological stands later adopted.

The tone of the Warsaw Treaty Powers' Declaration is relatively mild and optimistic, while that of K'ang Sheng's speech is tough and pessimistic. The former does not mention " American imperialism "; the latter mentions it repeatedly. The former refers to N.A.T.O. strengthening of " German militarism " but adds that the conferees " express confidence that the plans of the West German revenge-seekers will not be supported by the present allies of the Federal Republic of Germany either "; K'ang Sheng's speech states that the " speeded-up revival of West German militarism " is " an important component part of the U.S. imperialist policy of war and aggression." Where K'ang condemns, the Declaration reproves more in sorrow than in anger.

The basis of the Declaration's optimistic assertion that the " world has now entered on a period of negotiations concerning a settlement of the principal international issues in dispute " is, predictably, the increasing power of the forces of peace. These forces it lists as the growing economic power of the Soviet camp; Soviet technical achievements, particularly in rocketry; and action for peace on the part of the Communist *bloc* and independent countries of Asia, Africa and Latin America.

The Declaration cites four pieces of concrete evidence to underpin its optimism: the creation of a permanent UN committee for the peaceful exploration of outer space; the East-West agreement of 1959 on the peaceful use of the Antarctic; the exchange of top-level visits between East and West; and the cessation of nuclear testing over a considerable period (this being just before the first French test).

K'ang Sheng admits that there " have appeared certain tendencies towards relaxation of the international tension created by imperialism." This he attributes to the " repeated struggles " of the Communist *bloc*, and in particular its strength and unity; the national revolutionary forces; and the " forces of peace and democracy." Thus at the very beginning of the dispute, the Chinese asserted the importance of the " national revolutionary movement " in the achievement of *bloc* aims.

But K'ang's speech implicitly rejects the suggestion that the time for negotiation has come—" the struggle for disarmament is a long-term and complicated " one. It affirms that the United States is only making " peace gestures "—" its imperialist nature will not change "—behind which arms expenditure is increased, disarmament proposals are sabotaged and more nuclear tests are prepared for—behind which, in effect, war is plotted. He does not make the Declaration's distinction between Western statesmen who want relaxation and those who want to continue the cold war; according to K'ang, the bellicose " U.S. ruling circles " are a monolithic group.

The speech ignores the Antarctic and outer space agreements cited in the Declaration as evidence that substantial negotiations are possible. There is no mention of the cessation of nuclear tests as such; one is left to infer it from the allusion to America's announcement that it felt free to resume testing at any time. As for Khrushchev's visit to the United States—this is explained away in terms of the general thesis as a meaningless gesture which Washington was compelled to make.

The major policy consideration shaping the Soviet analysis contained in the Declaration would seem to be the need to " rule out completely the possibility of a new war, which in the present conditions would lead to the death of hundreds of millions of people and the annihilation of whole states." Though elsewhere the Declaration talks in the habitual Communist manner of the routing of a violator of the peace (by implication the U.S.A.), it is more probable that the Declaration represents another acknowledgment by Moscow that the Soviet Union, too, would be devastated in a nuclear war—and that therefore agreements with the West on nuclear testing and disarmament are vital.

The key to the Chinese analysis is contained in the passage where K'ang Sheng argues that because "U.S. imperialism" has always adopted a " discriminatory attitude against our country in international relations," China had to declare that " any international disarmament agreement and all other international agreements which are arrived at without the formal participation of the Chinese People's Republic and the signature of its delegate cannot, of course, have any binding force on China." [6]

The implication was clear. In the absence of Soviet efforts to aid China in attaining its objective of removing American forces from the Far East in general and the Formosa Strait in particular, and in the absence of any voluntary abdication on the part of the United States, Peking would go its own way and would not collaborate in attempts to reduce East-West tension. The speech's linking of the German and Japanese menaces indicates a feeling that Moscow should not be content with achieving a *modus vivendi* with the West over Germany, but should not rest satisfied until it had helped China get rid of American troops from Japan. (The Soviet Union protested strongly to Japan about the signing of the new security treaty with America, but made no protest in Washington.)

The more intransigent Chinese attitude would seem to be the product also of another factor hinted at in K'ang's speech. Peking, recalling probably the warmth of Vice-President Nixon's reception in Poland in 1959, perhaps genuinely feared that the West might be able to use an easing of international tension to subvert the peoples of at least Eastern Europe—witness K'ang's warning that America was dreaming of " peaceful evolution " in the Communist *bloc*, albeit a warning that was coupled the obligatory assertion that the dream would not be realised.

Khrushchev's Speech in Peking

Comrades! Socialism brings to the people peace—that greatest blessing. The greater the strength of the camp of socialism grows, the greater will be its possibilities for successfully defending the cause of peace on this earth. The forces of socialism are already so great that real possibilities are being created for excluding war as a means of solving international disputes.

In our time the leaders of governments in some capitalist countries have begun to show a certain tendency towards a realistic understanding of the situation that has emerged in the world.

When I spoke with President Eisenhower—and I have just returned from the United States of America—I got the impression that the President of the U.S.A.—and not a few people support him—understands the need to relax international tension.

Perhaps not every bourgeois leader can pronounce the words " peaceful co-existence " well, but they cannot deny that two systems exist in the

---

[6] China had already made this point clear when it formally supported the Supreme Soviet's disarmament proposal. (See *Peking Review*, No. 4, 1960.)

world—the socialist and the capitalist. The recognition of this fact ran like a red thread through all the talks; this was repeatedly spoken about by the President and other leaders. Therefore we on our part must do all we can to exclude war as a means of settling disputed questions, and settle these questions by negotiations.

The leaders of the capitalist countries cannot but take account of such a decisive factor of modern times as the existence of the powerful world camp of socialism. There is only one way of preserving peace—that is the road of peaceful co-existence of states with different social systems. The question stands thus: either peaceful co-existence or war with its catastrophic consequences. Now, with the present relation of forces between socialism and capitalism being in favour of socialism, he who would continue the " cold war " is moving towards his own destruction. The " cold war " warriors are pushing the world towards a new world war in the fires of which those who light it will be the first to get burned.

Already in the first years of the Soviet power the great Lenin defined the general line of our foreign policy as being directed towards the peaceful co-existence of states with different social systems. For a long time, the ruling circles of the Western Powers rejected these truly humane principles. Nevertheless the principles of peaceful co-existence made their way into the hearts of the vast majority of mankind.

The leaders of many capitalist states are being forced more and more to take account of realities, and to recast their international relations because in our century it is impossible to resolve questions of relations between two systems successfully other than on the basis of the principles of peaceful co-existence. There is no other way.

We are convinced that the peaceful foreign policy of the socialist states, defending peace on earth, will continue to gain new victories. No small efforts will have to be exerted to achieve this. But it is well worth fighting for such a high aim with unsparing efforts.

Comrades! The socialist countries have achieved great successes in developing their economies and as a consequence have created mighty potential forces on the basis of which they can successfully continue their advance. They have the means to defend themselves from the attacks of the imperialist aggressors if these should attempt by interference in our countries' affairs to force them to leave the socialist path and return to capitalism. That old time has gone never to return.

But we must think realistically and understand the contemporary situation correctly. This, of course, does not by any means signify that if we are so strong, then we must test by force the stability of the capitalist system. This would be wrong: the peoples would not understand and would never support those who would think of acting in this way. We have always been against wars of conquest. Marxists have recognized, and recognize, only liberating, just wars; they have always condemned, and condemn, wars of conquest, imperialist wars. This is one of the characteristic features of Marxist-Leninist theory.

It is not at all because capitalism is still strong that the socialist countries speak out against war, and for peaceful co-existence. No, we have no need of war at all. If the people do not want it, even such a noble and progressive system as socialism cannot be imposed by force of arms. The socialist countries therefore, while carrying through a consistently peace-loving policy, concentrate their efforts on peaceful construction, they fire the hearts of men by the force of their example in building socialism, and thus lead them to follow in their footsteps. The question of when this or that country will take the path to socialism is decided by its own people. This, for us, is the holy of holies. . . .

[*Peking Review*, No. 40, 1959.]

*

Declaration of Member-States of the Warsaw Treaty

THE member-states of the Warsaw Treaty note with satisfaction that a definite change for the better has become noticeable in the international situation since the last conference of the Political Consultative Committee of the Warsaw Treaty Organisation in May 1958. For the first time after many years of the cold war, relations that are normal for peacetime are beginning to be established between the states belonging to the antagonistic groupings, tension has been markedly reduced and prospects are opening up for a strengthening of mutual confidence. The world has now entered on a period of negotiations concerning a settlement of the principal international issues in dispute, with the aim of establishing a lasting peace, and the advocates of the cold war are sustaining a defeat.

The important changes that have taken place in recent years in the correlation of forces in the world arena underlie this improvement in the international situation.

These have been years of rapid expansion of the economic power of the Soviet Union, the Chinese People's Republic and the other Socialist countries and of their further rallying within the framework of a united Socialist camp. These have been years marked by very great achievements of the Soviet Union in science and technology. The putting of the first artificial earth satellite into orbit, the launching of a rocket to the surface of the Moon and the fathoming of the mystery of the reverse side of the Moon, which is never seen from the Earth—such are the magnificent results of these achievements by the world's first Socialist state which have raised mankind to a new level in its struggle to understand and conquer the forces of nature.

And lastly, recent years have been marked by another upsurge in the activity of all countries of the Socialist camp aimed at consolidating peace, and also by the further enhancement of the international role of the peace-loving countries of Asia, Africa and Latin America which have liberated themselves from colonial and semi-colonial dependence.

As a result, the correlation of forces in the world is changing more and more in favour of those who are coming out for the discontinuance of the race in nuclear rockets and other armaments, for the ending of the cold war, and for peaceful co-existence among all states, irrespective of their social systems and ideologies. A situation has taken shape in which any attempt by any aggressive state to resort to arms in order to solve international disputes, to take the road of war, would lead to the immediate and complete routing of the violator of peace.

The opinion is increasingly gaining ground in the minds of the peoples, and in the minds of many political leaders and statesmen, including those in the West, that, given the present level of weapons of mass destruction and the means for their immediate delivery to any point on the Earth, war in general can no longer be a means of solving international disputes, that the only feasible way is to build relations between states on the basis of peaceful co-existence.

The participants in the conference note with profound satisfaction the increasing importance of such a form of contacts between states as meetings and discussions between the leading statesmen of various countries of the East and the West. These contacts, the development of which the member-states of the Warsaw Treaty have always advocated, are, as experience shows, of great positive significance.

The historic visit to the United States of Nikita Krushchov, the Chairman of the U.S.S.R. Council of Ministers, and his talks with Mr. Dwight D. Eisenhower, the President of the United States, have played an outstanding role in this respect. As a result of this visit the ice of the cold war was broken in the relations between the two strongest Powers in the world—the U.S.S.R. and the United States—and a new stage was opened in the development of international relations as a whole. An important contribution to the improvement in the international climate was also made, as is well known, by the discussions between the leaders of the Soviet and British Governments that were held at the time of the visit to Moscow by Mr. Harold Macmillan, the Prime Minister of the United Kingdom.

The participants in the conference expressed the hope that Nikita Khrushchov's forthcoming visit to France and the visit to the U.S.S.R. of Signor Gronchi, the President of the Italian Republic, will lead to a further strengthening of the mutual relations between states, and above all between the states of Europe, and will promote the strengthening of world peace.

It is the common and wholehearted desire of the participants in the conference that President Eisenhower's visit to the Soviet Union next summer should lead to a further development of the relations between the U.S.S.R. and the United States towards friendship and co-operation, which would be an important guarantee of the inviolability of peace throughout the world.

The exchange of visits between statesmen, which has been stepped up in recent years, has become a stable factor making for a *rapprochement* between the states of the Socialist camp and the peace-loving independent countries of Asia, Africa and Latin America.

The friendly meetings and talks of the leaders of the Soviet Union, the Polish People's Republic, the Czechoslovak Republic, the German Democratic Republic, the Rumanian People's Republic and other member-states of the Warsaw Treaty with the leaders of such countries as India, Indonesia, Burma, Cambodia, Afghanistan, the United Arab Republic, Ethiopia, Guinea and others, promote the concrete successful development of peaceful co-existence in vast regions of the world. All participants in the conference express their determination to continue strengthening and developing friendship with the peace-loving states of Asia, Africa and Latin America on the basis of equality and mutual respect, in the interests of peace.

The improvement in the international situation is already bearing fruit in many spheres of international relations.

Late in 1959 an important agreement on the peaceful uses of the Antarctic was concluded between twelve states, including the U.S.S.R., the United States, the United Kingdom and France, under which a vast though still uninhabited continent is completely removed from the sphere of war preparations in any form, including the staging of nuclear tests, and has been endorsed as a zone of peaceful exploration and scientific co-operation between states. Another useful step in the right direction is the decision taken by the United Nations General Assembly in December 1959, to set up a permanent United Nations committee for the peaceful exploration of outer space, among the members of which are seven Warsaw Treaty states: Albania, Bulgaria, Hungary, Poland, Rumania, the U.S.S.R. and Czechoslovakia.

At the same time, the participants in the conference note that the consolidation of peace is still being stubbornly resisted by influential forces in the Western countries. These are either circles which do not see behind the profits they are receiving from the manufacture of armaments the mortal danger that would threaten them in the event of war, or politicians so stuck in the ice of the cold war that they cannot conceive of normal peaceful relations between states.

The N.A.T.O. countries are not only continuing to maintain inflated armies, but are actually increasing the numerical strength of those armies, paying particular attention to the West German Bundeswehr, which is commanded by former Nazi generals and officers. The Bundeswehr has been equipped with rocket weapons. The Federal Republic of Germany has been enabled to start the manufacture of these weapons. Moreover, measures are being taken towards equipping the Bundeswehr with nuclear weapons. It is a fact that the session of the N.A.T.O. Council, held in December 1959, discussed plans for further increasing the size of the armed forces of the states belonging to that military *bloc*.

Parallel with the strengthening of West German militarism, there has been a marked revival of the militarist forces in Japan and the further involvement of that country in military preparations, as is shown by the recent signing of a new military treaty between Japan and the United States.

The continuation of the arms race by the members of N.A.T.O., and also S.E.A.T.O., Cento, and their allies, can in no way be justified by considerations of defence. It shows that the opponents of peaceful co-existence have not laid down their arms.

This is also borne out by the systematic propaganda of mistrust and hatred between states with different social systems which is still being conducted by influential political and military leaders in the West and by a section of the Press. The opponents of the consolidation of peace do not want talks on the settlement of international disputes and are seeking to prevent agreement from being reached even where possibilities for it have become apparent.

But no efforts by the advocates of the cold war can alter the fact that awareness of the need for peaceful co-existence is becoming the decisive factor in the development of international relations in our time. The balance of forces in the world is in favour of the peaceable states, and the forces of peace are greatly superior to the forces of war. All this provides favourable conditions for reaching the goals for which the Warsaw Treaty states have been striving consistently all along: the relaxation of international tension and the development of friendly co-operation between all countries.

Naturally, the greatest importance is attached to the problem of disarmament. This is the main problem of international life in our day. The question of whether it will be possible to rule out completely the possibility of a new war, which in the present conditions would lead to the death of hundreds of millions of people and the annihilation of whole states, depends on its solution.

The interests of mankind require that rocket nuclear weapons, with their tremendous destructive potential, should never be allowed to be used.

And the surest way to achieve this is the destruction of all types of armaments, of all weapons of war, that is to say, the general and complete disarmament of all states. That is why the proposal for such disarmament, submitted by the Soviet Union in the United Nations, is in keeping with the most vital interests of mankind. From this stems the great influence which this proposal of the U.S.S.R. is exerting on the peoples. Very significant is the unanimity with which the United Nations approved the idea of general and complete disarmament at the last, 14th session of the General Assembly. The fact that this decision was adopted on the basis of a draft resolution jointly prepared by two such powers as the U.S.S.R. and the United States is also gratifying.

In order to make agreement on disarmament a reality for the first time in history, it is necessary, above all, to proceed from words to practical deeds. This is the most important historical task of the present generation. The Warsaw Treaty countries, having exchanged views at the present conference concerning the prospects for the impending disarmament talks, have come to the conclusion that the situation at the present time is more favourable than ever before for fruitful disarmament talks between countries of the East and West.

The disarmament proposal submitted by the Soviet Government in the United Nations reflects the common position of the Warsaw Treaty countries, of all the Socialist states. All the countries belonging to the Warsaw Treaty Organisation declare their desire to become parties to the future agreement on general and complete disarmament.

The states represented at this meeting feel satisfaction that the first country to take practical steps towards implementing this United Nations resolution was a country belonging to the Warsaw Treaty Organisation, the Soviet Union, which has unilaterally decided to reduce its armed forces by 1,200,000 men. The strength of the Soviet armed forces will now be below the level which the Western Powers themselves suggested in 1956 for the Soviet Union and the United States, and also below the actual strength of the American armed forces, even though the United States has a much smaller territory and much shorter frontiers than the U.S.S.R. The reduction of the Soviet armed forces by one-third in conditions in which Western military *blocs* are proceeding with the arms race is an act of good will which should impel the other states to take reciprocal steps in the sphere of disarmament and to reply to trust by trust.

Some people in the West are always ready to misconstrue, to misrepresent any good deed, any good initiative in international relations. This is what the opponents of disarmament are doing now when they allege that the new reduction of the Soviet armed forces is not a step towards disarmament, but rearmament. Only deliberate bad faith can explain such irresponsible contentions in face of practical steps in the sphere of disarmament.

Who does not realise that only states which have no aggressive intentions can unilaterally reduce their armed forces?

In present conditions there is no need for big armies and military bases on foreign soil for the defence of a country. Would a state harbouring predatory plans voluntarily carry out a reduction in its armed forces? It is clear that even if those armed forces were reorganised with the aim of increasing their combat power, it would not be in its interests to cut their numerical strength.

The states represented at the conference regard the Soviet Union's decision on another big reduction of its armed forces, taken in agreement with the other countries of the Socialist camp, as a common contribution by the Warsaw Treaty Organisation to the cause of disarmament, as an initiative facilitating agreement between the states of the East and West on general and complete disarmament.

The states united in the Warsaw Treaty Organisation are consistently and unswervingly carrying through a policy aimed at ending the arms race. Since its inception, the Warsaw Treaty Organisation has cut the total strength of the armed forces of its member-states by 2,596,500 men, and the present unilateral reduction of the strength of the Soviet armed forces will bring this figure up to 3,796,500 men.

Can the N.A.T.O. states claim the credit for similar measures, the importance of which for strengthening peace is obvious to all? Unfortunately, N.A.T.O. measures up to the present time have been directed towards stepping up war preparations and accumulating armed forces and armaments.

The member-states of the Warsaw Treaty consider it necessary to emphasise the positive example set by the German Democratic Republic, which has voluntarily reduced the strength of its armed forces to 90,000 men and refrained from introducing compulsory military service. This attitude which has been adopted by the German Democratic Republic and is prompted by a desire to do its utmost to facilitate a relaxation of tension, has the full support of all states of the Warsaw Treaty Organisation. Of great importance for the cause of peace and the national future of Germany is the fact that the German Democratic Republic is proving by its policy that Germany, if she renounces nuclear arming and the policy of revenge, revision of frontiers and militarism, can live in peace and prosperity and have a worthy place in the family of nations.

The states represented at the conference call upon the member-states of the North Atlantic Treaty Organisation, and especially on those among them who have the greatest military strength, to respond to the unilateral reduction of the armed forces of the U.S.S.R. by reducing their own armed forces, and to follow the example set by the Soviet Union.

The participants in the conference are proceeding on the basis of the assumption that the Soviet Union's disarmament proposals should be thoroughly examined in the 10-Power committee which is to begin its work on March 15 this year. In this connection they agreed that the Governments of the U.S.S.R., Poland, Czechoslovakia, Rumania and Bulgaria, that is to say the member-states of the Warsaw Treaty Organisation which belong to the 10-power committee, shall instruct their representatives on that committee to facilitate in every way fruitful work by the committee and press for the early drafting of a treaty on general and complete disarmament.

Of course, a successful and speedy solution to the problem of general and complete disarmament calls for efforts not only on the part of the member-states of the Warsaw Treaty Organisation. Such efforts are also called for on the part of the Western Powers. The participants in the conference express the hope that the Western Powers will also make their contribution to an early solution of the disarmament problem.

A mutual and honest desire for agreement will make it possible to avoid the repetition of a situation in which efforts to agree on disarmament are drowned in floods of speeches and resolutions.

An effective system of international control over general and complete disarmament is necessary for the successful implementation of such disarmament. Control, divorced from practical steps in the sphere of disarmament, could be used in the present situation for purposes diametrically opposed to disarmament: to search for a breach in the defence systems of other countries and to collect information facilitating the drawing up of plans for an attack on this or that country. That is why the states which have no aggressive intentions show a natural concern for the amount of international control to correspond to the real extent of the disarmament of the states. In conditions of general and complete disarmament the states will have no reason to fear each other. Every possibility will exist there for any check, for any inspection. If disarmament is general and complete, control will also be all-embracing and complete.

The states represented at the conference consider it necessary to re-emphasise their interest in an agreement on disarmament such as would provide complete confidence that no side would violate disarmament commitments or would have the possibility of rearming in secret.

The member-states of the Warsaw Treaty note it as a positive fact that for a long time not a single atomic or hydrogen bomb has been exploded in any part of the world. However, though nuclear explosions are not being staged for the time being, there is no international agreement banning them. The peoples do not want just a truce on the nuclear test front; they expect that such tests will be ended once and for all. Anxiety is also created by certain attempts to go back on the positive practical achievements towards the discontinuance of nuclear tests.

If the tests were really resumed by one of the sides, that might set off a kind of chain reaction as a result of which our planet would again become the arena for competition in holding nuclear weapon tests, with all the hazardous consequences this would entail. It would also be difficult to reconcile this with the resolution of the United Nations, which unanimously urged the parties to the Geneva talks—the U.S.S.R., the United States and the United Kingdom—not to resume nuclear weapon tests and to expedite the conclusion of an international agreement on this question.

The Soviet Government's decision not to resume nuclear tests in the future, if only the Western Powers do not resume such test explosions, provides favourable conditions for concluding a treaty on the discontinuance of nuclear weapon tests. The states represented at this conference express the hope that all parties to the Geneva talks will exert the greatest possible efforts to secure in the near future the cessation of all kinds of nuclear weapon tests in the atmosphere, on the surface, underground and under water.

The participants in the conference had a thorough exchange of views on the German question.

The states represented in the Warsaw Treaty Organisation have experienced more than once what German aggression brings to the peoples.

It is the common concern of all these states that German militarism should never again imperil the security of Germany's neighbours and world peace, and this makes them determined to come out in favour of signing a peace treaty with Germany. The liquidation of the remnants of the Second World War and the conclusion of a peace treaty are imperative for the peaceful development of the whole of Germany and for making the peoples confident that firm barriers have been set up against the outbreak of another war in Europe.

At a time when the German Democratic Republic is expressing its complete readiness to enter into negotiations and conclude a peace treaty at any moment, the other German state—the Federal Republic of Germany—is opposing the conclusion of such a treaty. An abnormal and unprecedented situation has emerged in which the conclusion of a peace treaty is refused by a state which is a successor of the defeated side—the aggressor who surrendered unconditionally fifteen years ago.

The policy of the Federal Republic of Germany is designed to obstruct successful talks between the powers and a settlement of outstanding international problems. Attempts are also being made to cancel out the results which have already been achieved during the negotiations, for instance, the narrowing of the gap in the views of the sides on some questions which was achieved by the parties to the Geneva Foreign Ministers' conference in 1959.

Why does the Government of the Federal Republic of Germany so stubbornly resist the conclusion of a peace treaty? It does so above all because the peace treaty is called upon to consolidate the situation that has arisen as a result of the war, including the German state frontiers, and the Government of the Federal Republic is against this. Only one conclusion is possible: The Government of the Federal Republic of Germany expects that an opportune moment may arise for altering the frontiers established in Europe as a result of the defeat of Nazi Germany. In the present conditions, however, this means a policy of preparing a new war, for none of the states on whom the Federal Republic is attempting to make territorial claims will ever surrender its lands, as the Government of the Federal Republic should realise. All reasonable people understand that these frontiers are inviolable.

The Warsaw Treaty states declare with the utmost determination that these calculations of the West German Government are doomed to failure. The German Democratic Republic, as an impregnable bastion of peace, is barring to German militarists the road to new aggressive gambles. The Warsaw Treaty states declare that they support the measures taken by the Government of the German Democratic Republic to safeguard peace against the revenge-seeking policy of the Adenauer government. The joint might of the Socialist camp is a firm guarantee against encroachment on the independence of the German Democratic Republic, or a new seizure of Poland's western lands, or a violation of the integrity of the Czechoslovak frontiers.

The participants in the conference express confidence that the plans of the West German revenge-seekers will not be supported by the present allies of the Federal Republic of Germany either.

It is the deep conviction of the participants in the conference that the population of the Federal Republic, too, thirsting as they are for peace, cannot and will not support the plans of the West German revenge-seekers. The participants in the conference are convinced that the population of

Western Germany deserves a better fate than that of being a tool in the hands of the violators of peace. In the past, the Germans were driven repeatedly to this by the greedy imperialist policy of their rulers, and time and time again the German people had to pay a heavy price.

The conclusion of a peace treaty, the renunciation of all ideas of revenge or revision of frontiers, the renunciation of the policy of Germany's re-militarisation and atomic arming—such is the best road towards ensuring the security of all European nations and the peaceful future of the German nation. This road is being consistently followed by the German Democratic Republic. If the Federal Republic of Germany, too, were to take to this road, that would be its most convincing contribution to the cause of strengthening peace and facilitating general and complete disarmament.

The Government of the Federal Republic of Germany is turning down the proposal for a peace treaty because it does not want to allow the question of West Berlin to be settled on the basis of it being transformed into a free city. The Government of the Federal Republic is going so far as to demand that West Berlin, which lies within the territory of the German Democratic Republic, be incorporated in Western Germany, and since this cannot be done, it prefers to preserve there the occupation régime which enables it to use West Berlin as a seat of unrest and military danger.

The Government of the Federal Republic of Germany opposes a peaceful settlement with Germany because it does not want the question of Germany's unity to be settled peacefully by means of talks between the two German states and the conclusion of a peace treaty.

Going in the face of all common sense, it does not want to see that for over ten years there have existed two German states which have chosen different paths of development. Disregarding the vital interests of the German people, the Government of the Federal Republic of Germany is rejecting the only possible way to the reunification of the country—that of talks with the G.D.R., which has been repeatedly offered by the Government of the German Democratic Republic. The Government of the Federal Republic is thereby demonstrating its hostility to the cause of German unity.

The Government of the Federal Republic of Germany does not want to hear of a peace treaty because it is afraid lest the conclusion of that treaty might put an end to the present situation in Western Germany which enables it to bring people to trial merely for having the courage to stand by their progressive convictions and come out in defence of the national rights of the German people and the interests of peace. All the actions of the Government of the Federal Republic of Germany show that it is clearing the way, step by step, for the establishment in Western Germany of a régime that should look like a democratic régime but which, in actual fact, would be close to the régime which plunged the world into a murderous war and led the German people to an unparalleled national catastrophe. Could the brazen Nazi and anti-Semitic outrages of the Fascist elements in Western Germany, which the world has recently witnessed, have occurred if conditions were different? Recently the Government of the Federal Republic of Germany did not scruple to take under its wing the organisers of those disgraceful demonstrations, and some West German officials, in the best Nazi tradition, have tried to lay the blame for those demonstrations on the Communists.

All this can only increase the people's mistrust of the policy of the

Federal Republic. Under these circumstances, an even more active struggle for the conclusion of a peace treaty with Germany becomes a necessity.

The countries represented at the present conference stand for peaceful co-operation and good-neighbourly relations with all states, including the Federal Republic of Germany, and they are sparing no efforts to achieve such co-operation in practice.

The Warsaw Treaty states are striving for a peaceful settlement with Germany, together with the other allied and associated Powers which took part in the war against Germany. This means the conclusion of a peace treaty which, in the existing conditions, can only be signed by both German states. At the same time, they cannot agree that the solution of these questions be postponed indefinitely, which can only encourage the militarist and revenge-seeking forces of Western Germany.

If the efforts towards the conclusion of a peace treaty with both German states do not meet with support and if the solution of this question comes up against attempts at procrastination, the states represented at the present conference will have no alternative but to conclude a peace treaty with the German Democratic Republic, together with the other states that are ready for this, and solve on this basis the question of West Berlin as well.

The states represented at the present conference reaffirm their inflexible desire for an improvement in the relations between countries of the East and West, for the strengthening of confidence between them, and for the development of all forms of international co-operation.

They continue to stand for the unhampered development of international trade, for the strengthening of contacts between statesmen, public leaders and organisations, and for exchanges of achievements in the fields of culture, science and technology, which enrich the peoples of all countries.

The ending of war propaganda, subversive appeals and attempts to threaten by the use of force would be of great importance for improving the international climate and eliminating suspicion in international relations.

As regards the Warsaw Treaty countries, war propaganda has been outlawed on their territories, and they are ready, for their part, to take further measures to have the atmosphere of mutual suspicion and sharp polemics in the relations between states superseded by good will and trust.

With the present noticeable relaxation of international tension, the proposal for the conclusion of a non-aggression pact between the two groups of states, the Warsaw Treaty and the North Atlantic Treaty Organisations, which has still not met with a positive solution, acquires even greater importance than in the past years. Convinced that the task of concluding a non-aggression pact between N.A.T.O. and the Warsaw Treaty Organisation, far from losing its topicality, is becoming steadily more important, the participants in the conference consider it necessary to declare that this offer still stands and that they are ready at any time to sign a non-aggression pact with the N.A.T.O. states.

The conclusion of bilateral non-aggression pacts between states belonging to different military groupings and the establishment in Europe of zones free from atomic and hydrogen weapons could also play a not inconsiderable part in improving the international situation.

The participants in the conference welcome with great satisfaction the agreement between the Soviet Union, the United States, Great Britain and France to hold a summit meeting in Paris in May this year. The governments of the Warsaw Treaty countries have long pressed for such a meeting to be held, regarding it—as was pointed out in their Declaration of May 24, 1958—as "the most important means in the existing situation of safeguarding mankind against a military calamity and turning the course of international developments towards the consolidation of peace."

The Warsaw Treaty states consider that the forthcoming meeting of the heads of government should discuss such important and urgent questions as the problem of general and complete disarmament; the question of a German peace treaty, including the establishment of a free city of West Berlin; the prohibition of atomic and hydrogen weapon tests; and East-West relations. Proceeding on the basis of the conviction that any international problem, however complex it may seem, can be settled given reasonable consideration for the interests of the parties and a general desire for peace, the participants in the conference express the hope that the heads of government will succeed in finding the correct ways to a successful solution of the aforementioned questions in the interests of strengthening universal peace, and that the forthcoming summit meeting will be a turning point in East-West relations.

Now, on the eve of crucial talks between statesmen of the East and the West, on the eve of a meeting at the summit, it is especially important, in the opinion of the Warsaw Treaty countries, that all states should do everything in their power to create a situation facilitating the success of the coming talks. The states represented at the present conference declare that they will act precisely in this direction and urge all other countries to promote the success of East-West talks and to refrain from any steps capable of complicating these negotiations.

The governments of the Warsaw Treaty countries note with satisfaction that their untiring efforts aimed at the termination of the arms race, the elimination of dangerous seats of international conflicts, and the ending of the cold war, are meeting with ever wider support from the peoples of the world and are yielding positive results. They are unanimous in believing that in our time the states do not and cannot have any greater or nobler task than that of contributing to the establishment of lasting peace on earth. Moscow, February 4, 1960.

[Text as published in *Soviet News* (London: Soviet Embassy), No. 4207, February 5.]

K'ang Sheng's Speech to the Warsaw Treaty Meeting

Comrade Chairman, Dear Comrades:

In the capacity of an observer of the People's Republic of China, I have the honour to attend this regular conference of the Political Consultative Committee of member states of the Warsaw Treaty. We are convinced that the convening of this conference will make new contributions to further relaxing the international situation and encouraging the people of the world in their struggle against the expansion of armaments and war preparations and for a lasting peace. We wish the conference success.

The current international situation continues to develop in a direction favourable to peace. There have appeared certain tendencies towards relaxation of the international tension created by imperialism. Comrade Nikita Khrushchov made a successful visit to the United States. Prompted by the Soviet Union's foreign policy of peace and the peace-loving people and countries of the world, an East-West summit conference will soon be convened. As to the disarmament question, a certain measure of agreement has also been reached on procedural matters. The Chinese people and all other peace-loving people and countries the world over rejoice at this. The emergence of such a situation is not accidental. This is the result of repeated struggles waged by the Socialist forces, the national revolutionary forces and the forces of peace and democracy against the imperialist war forces, the result of the East wind prevailing over the West wind.

The incomparable strength and the firm unity of the Socialist camp headed by the Soviet Union and its outstanding and effective efforts in the cause of peace are the decisive factors in this tendency towards easing the international situation. We are happy to see that construction in all the Socialist countries is gathering speed and their material strength greatly enhanced. The Soviet Union, particularly, has scored brilliant achievements in carrying out its enormous Seven-Year Plan. The Soviet success in successive launchings of man-made earth satellites and cosmic rockets marks the fact that in the most important fields of science and technology, the Soviet Union has left the United States far behind. The balance of world forces has undergone a further, huge change favourable to peace and Socialism thereby greatly fortifying the will to struggle, and confidence in victory, of the people throughout the world.

The unswerving struggle carried out by the powerful world forces of peace has caused repeated setbacks to the U.S. imperialists' " position of strength " and " brink of war " policies. Not only is the United States becoming increasingly isolated politically as the days go by, but militarily, its forces are dispersed and it is lagging behind in new weapons; economically, too, its situation is becoming increasingly difficult. In these circumstances, and particularly under pressure of the strong desire for peace of the people everywhere, the U.S. ruling circles were obliged to make some peace gestures. Of course it is better to talk peace than to talk war. Nevertheless, even the U.S. ruling circles themselves do not try to hide the fact that the change in their way of doing things is aimed at numbing the fighting spirit of the people of the world by means of the " strategy to win victory by peace," wrecking the unity of the peace forces of the world and disintegrating the Socialist camp; they are even dreaming of a so-called " peaceful evolution " in the Socialist countries. These wild ambitions of the U.S. ruling circles will, of course, not be realised. While being obliged to make certain peace gestures, the U.S. ruling circles are still pushing ahead vigorously with their arms expansion and war preparations, making a strenuous effort to develop inter-continental ballistic missiles, setting up and expanding missile bases in various places, claiming to be ready at any time to resume nuclear weapons tests, and actively trying to strengthen and patch up military *blocs* in an attempt to gain time to improve their inferior military position.

U.S. President Eisenhower's State of the Union Message recently gave the clearest indication that the new tricks of the United States are designed to gain precisely what it failed to obtain by its old tricks. The actions of the United States prove fully that its imperialist nature will not change. American imperialism still remains the arch enemy of world peace. All those throughout the world who are working sincerely for peace must maintain their vigilance against U.S. double-dealing. If our Socialist camp and the people of all countries in the world continue to strengthen unity, continue to fortify our strength and thoroughly smash all the intrigues and schemes of the enemy of peace, U.S. war plans can be set back even further and even checked, and the cause of defence of peace will certainly win still greater victories.

At the present time universal disarmament is an important question relating to the defence of world peace. Since World War II, the Soviet Union has time and again made positive proposals for disarmament, the banning of atomic weapons and the ending of nuclear weapons tests. The Soviet Union and other Socialist countries have, on their own initiative, reduced their armed forces. Not long ago, the Soviet Union proposed general and complete disarmament at the U.N. General Assembly. It later adopted a law at the Supreme Soviet session, again slashing its armed forces unilaterally by 1·2 million men. These facts convincingly demonstrate the sincerity of the Soviet Union and other Socialist countries for peace and their confidence in their own strength.

Although U.S. imperialism dare not oppose disarmament in so many words, it has always in fact sabotaged universal disarmament. Whenever certain U.S. proposals were accepted by the Soviet Union, the United States always concocted new pretexts for a retreat from its original position, creating all kinds of difficulties and preventing by every means the reaching of agreement on the disarmament question. U.S. actions prove that it will not abandon its policy of the arms race. Therefore, the struggle for universal disarmament is a long-term and complicated struggle between us and imperialism.

The Chinese Government and the Chinese people have always stood for universal disarmament, and actively supported the proposals concerning disarmament made by the Soviet Union and other Socialist countries. Since 1951, the Chinese Government has on its own initiative again and again reduced its armed forces. The present Chinese armed forces are less than half their original size. We shall continue to work tirelessly for universal disarmament together with the Soviet Union and other Socialist countries. We hope that the countries concerned will reach agreement on this question of universal disarmament. The Chinese Government has never hesitated to commit itself to all international obligations with which it agrees. But U.S. imperialism, hostile to the Chinese people, has always adopted a discriminatory attitude against our country in international relations. Therefore, the Chinese Government has to declare to the world that any international disarmament agreement and all other international agreements which are arrived at without the formal participation of the Chinese People's Republic and the signature of its delegate cannot, of course, have any binding force on China.

The German question has a particularly important place among outstanding international issues. Its solution has a bearing not only on the security of Europe but also on the peace of the world. The permanent division of Germany and the speeded-up revival of West German militarism are an important component part of the U.S. imperialist policy of war and aggression. The recent frenzied war cries of Adenauer and the rampant anti-semitic activities started by the West German Fascist forces are the outcome of U.S. instigation and support. The Governments of the Soviet Union and the German Democratic Republic have time and again put forward reasonable proposals for settlement of the German question. But all these proposals have been rejected by the United States and West Germany. In its efforts to come to agreement with the Western Powers on the conclusion of a German peace treaty and on ending the occupation régime in West Berlin, the Soviet Union has made many concessions, whereas the Western Powers have to date made no appropriate response. The Chinese Government and people will steadfastly support the basic stand taken by the Soviet Union and the German Democratic Republic on the solution of the German question, and the struggle of the German people for the reunification of their motherland on the basis of peace and democracy.

While intensifying its efforts to re-arm West Germany, U.S. imperialism is reviving Japanese militarism in the East, and has signed a Japan-U.S. treaty of military alliance with the Kishi Government, its close follower. The Chinese Government has issued a statement strongly condemning this act of the U.S. and Japanese reactionaries which threatens the peace and security of Asia. The Soviet Government, too, has sent a memorandum to the Japanese Government, pointing out that the treaty seriously endangers the interests of the Soviet Union, China and many other countries in the Asian and Pacific regions. The people of all lands, including the Japanese people, are unanimous in their firm opposition to this further step of military collusion between the U.S. and Japanese reactionaries.

The Chinese Government and people hold that West Germany and Japan, which are supported energetically by U.S. imperialism, have become two sources of serious war danger. All peace-loving peoples and countries of the world must maintain a high state of vigilance against this, and exert every effort to prevent the militarism of these two countries from violating world peace.

In other parts of Asia, U.S. imperialism also continues to create international tension. The Chinese People's Volunteers withdrew from Korea on their own initiative long ago, but U.S. forces are still hanging on in South Korea and are trying hard to obstruct Korea's peaceful reunification. The United States, supporting the reactionary forces in Laos, undermined the Geneva agreements and the Vientiane agreements and provoked civil war in Laos. At the Sino-American ambassadorial talks, China has persistently advocated the principle of settling disputes between China and the United States by means of peaceful negotiation and without resort to force or threat of force. But the United States has all along refused to reach agreement with China in accordance with this principle and up till now is occupying our territory of Taiwan. The U.S. navy and air force have been constantly making military provocations against our country despite our repeated warnings. Therefore, the Chinese people and all the people of the world must unite still more closely and resolutely smash U.S. schemes for new wars and aggression in Asia.

The foreign policy of our Socialist countries has always firmly adhered to the principle of peaceful coexistence among countries with different social systems. We Socialist countries will never encroach upon others, but neither will we tolerate encroachment by others. Lenin said that to achieve peaceful coexistence, no obstacle would come from the Soviet side. Obstacles could come only from imperialism, from the side of American (as well as any other) capitalists. We will continue to adhere to Lenin's principle of peaceful coexistence. Our efforts to carry out this principle have won the support of increasing numbers of people. But if the imperialist reactionaries mistake this for a sign of weakness and dare to impose war on us, then they will only be inviting their own destruction.

The Chinese people have always sympathised with and supported the national and democratic movements of the peoples of Asia, Africa, and Latin America and striven for long-term, friendly relations with the nationalist countries in Asia and Africa on the basis of the Five Principles of Peaceful Coexistence jointly initiated by our country with India and Burma. To realise their ulterior aims, the imperialists have tried by every means to undermine our country's unity with these countries. One of their chief tricks to undermine this unity is to use the border issue and the overseas Chinese issue, which are legacies of history, to sow discord and cook up anti-Chinese plots in a vain attempt to isolate China. The reactionary forces in certain Asian countries also make use of these issues to try to undermine the friendship between the people of their countries and the Chinese people. They attempt to use the anti-Chinese campaign to divert the attention of the people of their countries from domestic issues and to create pretexts for suppressing the democratic, progressive forces in their own countries. In our relations with certain Asian nationalist countries, there once appeared small patches of dark cloud, but the sun cannot be overshadowed for long and friendship between our people and the people of these countries will certainly be maintained and developed.

Recently the Indonesian Government and our Government have exchanged the instruments of ratification of the treaty concerning the question of dual nationality, set up a joint committee to implement the treaty and started talks on questions relating to the return of overseas Chinese to their homeland. A certain period of time is needed for an overall settlement of the overseas Chinese question and there may still be some twists and turns. But, if both sides treasure their friendship, persist in peaceful consultations and seriously carry out the agreements already reached, the overseas Chinese question can be solved justly and reasonably.

China and Burma have always had friendly relations. Recently, the Prime Minister of Burma Ne Win visited our country and signed with the Chinese Premier the Sino-Burmese Treaty of Friendship and Mutual Non-Aggression and an agreement between the two Governments on the boundary question. This not only signifies that friendly relations of the two countries have entered a new stage, but also sets a new example for friendship and solidarity among the Afro-Asian countries. The Sino-Burmese border question is a complicated one left over by history. The imperialist reactionaries used this question to sow dissension and cause division. But both Chinese and Burmese Governments sincerely desire peace and friendship, so the two parties were able to reach agreement in principle speedily and pave the way for an overall, thorough settlement of this question. The Sino-Burmese Treaty of Friendship and Mutual Non-Aggression offers striking proof that the Five Principles of Peaceful Coexistence have certainly not "outlived themselves" or "become defunct" as certain reactionary elements and instigators of war allege, but, on the contrary, are showing their great vitality with increasing clarity. These facts thoroughly give the lie to the slanders of the imperialists and all reactionaries about China's "aggression." They amply prove that China's sincerity in abiding by the Five Principles of Peaceful Coexistence can stand the test of time and history. Those who attempt to isolate China have failed to do so. On the contrary, they have isolated themselves.

Strengthening the unity of the countries of the Socialist camp is a matter of the utmost importance. Our unity is built on the ideological basis of Marxism-Leninism, on the basis of proletarian internationalism. The

Moscow meetings of the Communist and Workers' Parties of the Socialist countries held in 1957 ushered in a new historic period in our unity. The Declaration adopted at this meeting is the charter of solidarity of our Socialist camp. The imperialists, the modern revisionists and the reactionaries in all countries are always dreaming that changes in their favour will occur within our countries and splits will occur in the unity between our countries. The greater the difficulties they come up against, the more they hope to save themselves from their doom by sabotage within our countries and by undermining the unity between our countries. However, in face of our great unity, their futile calculations can never be realised. The Chinese Communist Party and the Chinese people have always taken the safeguarding of the unity of the Socialist camp headed by the Soviet Union as their sacred international duty. They have always regarded an attack against any Socialist country by the imperialists and all reactionaries as an attack against China. They have always considered that the modern revisionists of Yugoslavia are renegades to the Communist movement, that revisionism is the main danger in the present Communist movement and that it is necessary to wage a resolute struggle against revisionism. This stand of ours is firm and unshakable. Working for the cause of peace and Socialism, we Socialist countries will certainly extend further support and help to each other. As long as the Socialist camp is united, the unity of the peoples of the world has a firm nucleus and the victory of our cause has a reliable guarantee.

The present situation is extremely favourable to us. Let us hold aloft the banner of peace, the banner of Socialism and Communism and march victoriously towards our great goal!

[*Peking Review*, No. 6, 1960.]

3. The Conflict Raised to the Ideological Plane

THE publication of the article "Long Live Leninism!" in the Chinese Communist Party's theoretical journal *Red Flag* (No. 8, 1960) on April 16, marked the start of the most important and bitter stage of the dispute. The opening shots had already been fired in the previous issue of *Red Flag*[7]; but "Long Live Leninism!" must rank as the major statement of the four issued by Peking on the occasion of the ninetieth anniversary of the birth of Lenin[8] because of its comprehensive nature and its translation of the most recent Sino-Soviet policy disagreements into ideological terms.

By stating their position in theoretical language, by asserting their orthodoxy in Leninist terms, the Chinese were doing two things. They were challenging the right of Moscow to act as supreme arbiter of *bloc* policy by alleging Khrushchev to be guilty of doctrinal deviations; and they were affirming their determination to persist in their own views. Such a challenge to his leadership and his policies by the second power of the *bloc* Khrushchev had to reject in the strongest terms.

The first section of "Long Live Leninism" outlines the scope of the problems to be discussed. A series of "irrefutable truths" which Lenin revealed are first listed: as long as imperialism exists the possibility of war remains; the liberation of the proletariat must be through revolution not reformism; the struggle between Communism and capitalism will embrace a whole historical epoch; the fundamental question concerning the proletarian revolution is the establishment of the proletarian dictatorship by smashing the bougeois state machine; the proletariat must have its own genuinely revolutionary party.

Since the Bolshevik revolution there had been a number of important changes in the world situation—tremendous economic and technological progress in the Soviet Union, the establishment of the Communist *bloc*, the continuing disintegration of the colonial system, the increasing instability of capitalism. The forces of Communism had surpassed those

---

[7] See "Imperialism—Source of War in Modern Times—and the Path of the Peoples' Struggle for Peace" by Yü Chao-li, reproduced in *Peking Review*, No. 15, 1960.

[8] The other two were the *People's Daily* editorial on the actual anniversary, April 22, entitled "Forward Along the Path of the Great Lenin," and the speech made by Lu Ting-yi, Chairman of the Communist Party's Propaganda Department, at the Lenin anniversary meeting in Peking on the same day. Both statements and "Long Live Leninism!" are reproduced in *Peking Review*, No. 17, 1960.

of capitalism. Did this mean that the aforementioned teachings of Lenin had lost some or all of their validity?

The second section discusses the question of epochs, refuting Tito's assertion that the world had entered upon a new epoch of tranquillity in which nations could devote themselves to internal construction and consider problems of international economic co-operation rather than those of war and peace. The main concern of this section is to tackle the question of rockets and nuclear weapons, in effect to reject the idea that the invention of these weapons necessitates both *blocs* seeking a *modus vivendi* in order to avoid joint suicide. That the argument is aimed at Khrushchev and not just Tito is indicated by the statement that besides the Yugoslav dictator " there are people who hold incorrect views because they are not able to approach the question from the materialist standpoint of history."

The importance of the new weapons is minimised by a reference to them as " specific details of technological progress " and it is stated categorically that " it is not technique but man, the masses of the people, that determine the fate of mankind." Even if the " imperialists " were to launch a war, it would only mean their destruction, " the result will certainly not be the annihilation of mankind." Here the Chinese were of course on the solid ground of orthodoxy, an orthodoxy which for all his hints Khrushchev had not yet had the desire or, perhaps, the courage to reject in the way Malenkov had.

The question of war and peace is considered in detail in section three though the Chinese attitude has already been made clear in the preceding argument. It is allowed that " some new questions have now arisen concerning peaceful co-existence," that due to the power of the Communist *bloc* the West would have to consider whether an attack on it would not result in its own extinction—a roundabout admission that nuclear weapons had made war more dangerous and therefore less likely. The 1957 Declaration's assertion that the forces of peace could prevent war is quoted; even the possibility of a nuclear test ban agreement is mentioned.

But yet the article goes on to assert: " War is an inevitable outcome of systems of exploitation and the source of modern wars is the imperialist system. Until the imperialist system and the exploiting classes come to an end, wars of one kind or another will always occur." The wars might be inter-imperialist wars, attacks by imperialist nations on " oppressed nations " (*i.e.*, neutralists such as Egypt), revolutionary civil wars, or East-West wars.

What is quite clear from this categorical statement is that the Chinese refused to accept the optimistic analysis made by Khrushchev at the CPSU's Twenty-first Congress which is nowhere referred to. What is not so clear is how the Chinese reconciled their acceptance of Khrushchev's revision of Leninism at the Twentieth Congress, embodied in the 1957 Declaration, with their assertion that some form of war was inevitable.

Clearly there is a contradiction here. A possible explanation of it that would jibe with what seem to be the main policy considerations of the Chinese would be that in signing the 1957 Declaration, Mao Tse-tung committed himself to too imprecise a definition of " war." The section from the Declaration quoted in " Long Live Leninism! " almost certainly means *world* war though it only refers to " war." Khrushchev, himself, in his Twenty-first Congress speech, referred to *world* war as we emphasised in the discussion of his remarks.

Certainly the Chinese do not concede much by agreeing *world* war is not inevitable; for even so, other wars must occur and so peace must be struggled for, and this means that international tension will be maintained. But an admission that war in general was not inevitable would imply an overall easing of the international situation and a dampening of the national revolutionary movement in particular. Now the Chinese, as we have seen, consider the latter a vital component in the struggle for peace, *i.e.*, a major method of sapping the strength of the West. And any general easing of international tension would, we have suggested, result in the freezing of what is for China a basically unfavourable situation in the Far East.

The next two sections are concerned with the problem of " peaceful transition " and the attitude towards parliament in bourgeois countries to be adopted by local Communist Parties. The argument would seem designed to undermine the position adopted by Khrushchev at the Twentieth Congress. " Peaceful transition " is described in Lenin's words as an " extraordinarily rare opportunity "; the general rule remains that civil war must be the road to power for Communists. The use of parliament is to enhance the political consciousness of the masses; it would be " difficult to imagine " that a Communist Party could introduce a Communist programme by this method. The article continues:

> A series of experiences in the capitalist countries long ago proved this point fully and the experience in various European *and Asian countries* after the Second World War provide additional proof of it (emphasis added).

It is reasonable to suppose that while the Chinese mention Western Europe, their primary concern here is with Asia, and probably with India in particular. Certainly the reference to the bourgeoisie's ability to dissolve parliament when necessary, or to use various open and underhand tricks to turn a working-class party which is the biggest party in parliament into a minority, or to reduce its seats in parliament, even when it has polled more votes in an election would apply neatly, from a Communist point of view, to the events in Kerala over the previous nine months.

Clearly the general aim of the Chinese is to prevent the sapping of the revolutionary vigour of Asian Communist Parties. They allude to the disastrous results for the Chinese Communist Party when it lowered its revolutionary standards. But doubtless national considerations played a considerable role in determining the Chinese to put forward their analysis. China was involved in major disputes with India and Indonesia, and the attitude adopted by Peking had considerably lessened the friendliness of those two powers towards Mao's régime. The Bandung " spirit " had disappeared. The benefit to China of cultivating Mr. Nehru and President Sukarno must have seemed extremely marginal; while if the Communist Parties in those leaders' countries were to adopt more revolutionary tactics, China might well expect to benefit from any internal weakening that ensued.

Besides, a prominent aspect of Soviet friendship for the neutralist countries was the granting to them of considerable quantities of aid. The Chinese could well feel aggrieved at the comparatively niggardly treatment they had received bearing in mind their relationship to the Soviet Union; they might hope that a new and more jaundiced view of the neutralists would result in the diversion of more aid to themselves.

The national liberation movement is mentioned only in passing in these two sections (which are followed by a final call for supporting Leninism and combating " revisionism "). It is treated at somewhat greater length in Yü Chao-li's article mentioned above. The not unexpected conclusion is that the

> masses of the oppressed fighting for complete national independence . . . form an important and indispensable force in the peace movement. . . . To achieve world peace, people everywhere should give their support to national liberation movements in the colonial and semi-colonial countries, to the anti-imperialist struggles of countries which have already won national independence and to the righteous wars for national liberation and against imperialist aggression.

From the point of view of the dispute, the main interest in the *People's Daily* editorial of April 22 is its extended documentation of the Chinese case propounded at the Warsaw Treaty meeting, namely that the United States is not really interested in peace and only makes " peace gestures " to hide its preparations for war. The thirty-seven items of documentation, which range from America's support of the Tibet resolution in the UN to Under-secretary of State Dillon's analysis of Soviet foreign policy, are all drawn from the period succeeding Khrushchev's talks with Eisenhower at Camp David. They are used to support the conclusion that even after the Camp David talks and even on the eve of the East-West summit conference, we see no change at all in substance in U.S. imperialist war policy, in the policy carried out by the U.S. Government and by Eisenhower personally.

This passage strongly suggests that this editorial together with all the other Chinese pronouncements issued at this juncture were issued with the imminent summit conference in mind, perhaps in a last attempt to sway Khrushchev, certainly with a view to emphasising Peking's continuing rejection of his policy towards the West. The passage is a firm rejection of Soviet propaganda claiming valuable gains were achieved by the Camp David meeting and Khrushchev's personal vouching for Eisenhower as a man of peace as distinct from the advocates of the cold war among his advisers.[9]

There is a hint in the editorial that Khrushchev may have asked Mao Tse-tung without success to display moderation on the eve of the summit, for the editorial asks of no one in particular:

> Can it be bad for peace, can it aggravate tension if we explain the true state of affairs to the Chinese and world public, or can concealing the truth help peace and help relax tension?

"Long Live Leninism!"

I

APRIL 22 of this year is the ninetieth anniversary of the birth of Lenin.

1871, the year after Lenin's birth, saw the heroic uprising of the Paris Commune. The Paris Commune was a great, epoch-making revolution, the first dress rehearsal of universal significance in the proletariat's attempt to overthrow the capitalist system. When the Commune was on the verge of defeat as a result of the counter-revolutionary attack from Versailles, Marx said:

> If the Commune should be destroyed, the struggle would only be postponed. The principles of the Commune are perpetual and indestructible; they will present themselves again and again until the working class is liberated. ("Speech on the Paris Commune," *Collected Works of Marx and Engels*, 1st Russ. ed., Vol. XIII, part 2, p. 655.)

What is the most important principle of the Commune? According to Marx, it is that the working class cannot simply take hold of the existing state machine, and use it for its own purposes. In other words, the proletariat should use revolutionary means to seize state power, smash the military and bureaucratic machine of the bourgeoisie and establish the proletarian dictatorship to replace the bourgeois dictatorship. Anyone familiar with the history of proletarian struggle knows that it is precisely this fundamental question which forms the dividing line between Marxists on the one hand and opportunists and revisionists on the other, and that after the death of Marx and Engels it was none other than Lenin who waged a thoroughly uncompromising struggle against the opportunists and revisionists in order to safeguard the principles of the Commune.

---

[9] See Khrushchev's speech in Peking on p. 61, above.

The cause in which the Paris Commune did not succeed finally triumphed forty-six years later in the Great October Revolution under Lenin's direct leadership. The experience of the Russian Soviets was a continuation and development of the experience of the Paris Commune. The principles of the Commune continually expounded by Marx and Engels and enriched by Lenin in the light of the new experience of the Russian revolution, became a living reality for the first time on one-sixth of the earth. Marx was perfectly correct in saying that the principles of the Commune are perpetual and indestructible.

In their attempt to strangle the new-born Soviet State, the imperialist jackals carried out armed intervention against it, in league with the Russian counter-revolutionary forces of that time. But the heroic Russian working class and the people of the various nationalities of the Soviet Union drove off the foreign bandits, wiped out the counter-revolutionary rebellion within the country and thus consolidated the world's first great Socialist Republic.

Under the banner of Lenin, under the banner of the October Revolution, a new world revolution began, with the proletarian revolution playing the leading role. A new era dawned in human history.

Through the October Revolution, the voice of Lenin quickly resounded throughout the world. The Chinese people's anti-imperialist, anti-feudal May 4 Movement in 1919, as Comrade Mao Tse-tung put it, " came into being at the call of the world revolution of that time, of the Russian Revolution and of Lenin." (" On New Democracy," *Selected Works of Mao Tse-tung*, Lawrence and Wishart, London, 1954, Vol. III, p. 146.)

Lenin's call is powerful because it is correct. Under the historical conditions of the imperialist era, Lenin revealed a series of irrefutable truths concerning the proletarian revolution and the proletarian dictatorship.

Lenin pointed out that the oligarchs of finance capital in a small number of capitalist powers, that is, imperialists, not only exploit the masses of people in their own countries, but oppress and plunder the whole world, turning most countries into their colonies and dependencies. Imperialist war is a continuation of imperialist policy. World wars are started by the imperialists because of their insatiable greed in struggling for world markets, sources of raw materials and fields for investment, and to redivide the world. So long as capitalist imperialism exists in the world, the sources and possibility of war will remain. The proletariat should guide the masses of people to an understanding of the sources of war and to struggle for peace and against imperialism.

Lenin asserted that imperialism is monopolistic, parasitic or decaying, moribund capitalism, that it is the final stage in the development of capitalism and therefore is the eve of the proletarian revolution. The emancipation of the proletariat can only be arrived at by the road of revolution, and certainly not by the road of reformism. The liberation movement of the proletariat in the capitalist countries should ally itself with the national liberation movements in the colonies and dependent countries; this alliance can smash the alliance of the imperialists with the feudal and comprador reactionary forces in the colonies and dependent countries, and will therefore inevitably put a final end to the imperialist system throughout the world.

In the light of the law of the uneven economic and political development of capitalism, Lenin came to the conclusion that, because capitalism developed extremely unevenly in different countries, socialism would achieve victory first in one or several countries but could not achieve victory simultaneously in all countries. Therefore, in spite of the victory of socialism in one or several countries, other capitalist countries will still exist, and this will give rise not only to friction but also to imperialist subversive activities against the socialist states. Hence the struggle will be protracted. The struggle between socialism and capitalism will embrace a whole historical epoch. The socialist countries should maintain constant vigilance against the danger of imperialist attack and do their best to guard against this danger.

The fundamental question of all revolutions is the question of state power. Lenin showed in a comprehensive and penetrating way that the fundamental question of the proletarian revolution is the proletarian dictatorship. The proletarian dictatorship, established by smashing the state machine of the bourgeois dictatorship by revolutionary means, is an alliance of a special type between the proletariat and the peasantry and all other working people; it is a continuation of the class struggle in another form under new conditions; it involves a persistent struggle, both sanguinary and bloodless, violent and peaceful, military and economic, educational and administrative, against the resistance of the exploiting classes, against foreign aggression and against the forces and traditions of the old society. Without the proletarian dictatorship, without its full mobilization of the working people on these fronts to wage these unavoidable struggles stubbornly and persistently, there can be no socialism, nor can there be any victory for socialism.

Lenin considered it of prime importance for the proletariat to establish its own genuinely revolutionary political party which completely breaks with opportunism, that is, a Communist Party, if the proletarian revolution is is to be carried through and the proletarian dictatorship established and consolidated. This political party is armed with the theory of Marxist dialectical materialism and historical materialism. Its programme is to organize the proletariat and all oppressed working people for class struggle, to set up proletarian rule and passing through socialism to reach the final goal of communism. This political party must identify itself with the masses and attach great importance to their creative initiative in the making of history; it must closely rely on the masses in revolution and must do the same in socialist and communist construction.

These truths were constantly set forth by Lenin before and after the October Revolution. The world reactionaries and philistines of the time thought these truths of Lenin terrifying. But we see these truths winning victory after victory in the practical life of the world.

In the forty years and more since the October Revolution, tremendous new changes have taken place in the world.

Through its great achievements in socialist and communist construction, the Soviet Union has transformed itself from an economically and technically very backward country in the days of imperial Russia into a first-rate world power with the most advanced technology. By its economic and technological leaps the Soviet Union has left the European capitalist countries far behind and left the United States behind, too, in technology.

The great victory of the anti-fascist war in which the Soviet Union was the main force broke the chain of imperialism in Central and Eastern Europe. The great victory of the Chinese people's revolution broke the chain of imperialism on the Chinese mainland. A new group of socialist countries was born. The whole socialist camp headed by the Soviet Union has one-quarter of the earth's land space and over one-third of the world's population. The socialist camp has now become an independent world economic system, standing opposite the capitalist world economic system. The gross industrial output value of the socialist countries now accounts for nearly 40 per cent. of the world total, and it will not be long before it surpasses the gross industrial output value of all the capitalist countries put together.

The imperialist colonial system has disintegrated and is disintegrating further. The struggle naturally has its twists and turns, but on the whole the storm of the national liberation movement is sweeping over Asia, Africa and Latin America on a daily increasing scale. Things are developing towards their opposites: There the imperialists are going step by step from strength to weakness, while the people are going step by step from weakness to strength.

The relative stability of capitalism, which existed for a time after the First World War, ended long ago. With the formation of the socialist world economic system after the Second World War, the capitalist world market has greatly shrunk. The contradiction between the productive forces and production relations in capitalist society has become more acute. The periodic economic crises of capitalism no longer come as before once every ten years or so, but occur almost every three or four years. Recently, some representatives of the U.S. bourgeoisie have admitted that the United States has suffered three " economic recessions " in ten years, and they now have premonitions of a new " economic recession " after just having pulled through the one in 1957–58. The shortening of the interval between capitalist economic crises is a new phenomenon. It is a further sign that the world capitalist system is drawing nearer and nearer to its inevitable doom.

The unevenness in the development of the capitalist countries is worse than ever before. The domain of the imperialists has shrunk more and more, so that they collide with one another. U.S. imperialism is constantly grabbing markets and spheres of influence away from the British, French and other imperialists. The imperialist countries headed by the United States have been expanding armaments and making war preparations for more than ten years, while West German and Japanese militarists, defeated in the Second World War, have risen again with the help of their former enemy— U.S. imperialism. The imperialists of these two countries have come out to join in the scramble for the capitalist world market, are now once again talking long and loudly about their " traditional friendship " and are engaging in new activities for a so-called " Bonn-Tokyo axis with Washington as the starting point." West German imperialism is looking brazenly around for military bases abroad. This aggravates the bitter conflicts within imperialism and at the same time heightens the threat to the socialist camp and all peace-loving countries. The present situation is very much like that after the First World War when the U.S. and British imperialists fostered the resurgence of German militarism, and the outcome will again be their " picking up a rock only to drop it on their own feet." The U.S. imperialists' creation of world tension after the Second World War is a sign not of their strength but of their weakness and precisely reflects the unprecedented instability of the capitalist system.

The U.S. imperialists, in order to realize their ambition for world domination, not only carry out all kinds of premeditated sabotage and subversion against the socialist countries, but also, under the pretext of opposing " the communist menace," in their self-appointed role of world gendarme for suppressing the revolution in various countries, deploy their military bases all around the world, seize the intermediate areas and carry out military provocations. Like a rat running across the street while everyone shouts " Throw something at it!" the U.S. imperialists run into bumps and bruises everywhere and, contrary to their intentions, everywhere arouse a new upsurge of the people's revolutionary struggle. Now, they themselves are becoming aware that, in contrast with the growing prosperity of the socialist world headed by the Soviet Union, " the influence of the United States as a world power is declining." In them, one " can only see the decline and fall of ancient Rome."

The changes taking place in the world in the past forty years and more indicate that imperialism rots with every passing day while for socialism things are daily getting better. It is a great, new epoch that we are facing, and its main characteristic is that the forces of socialism have surpassed those of imperialism, that the forces of the awakening people of the world have surpassed those of reaction.

The present world situation has obviously undergone tremendous changes since Lenin's lifetime, but these changes have not proved the obsoleteness of Leninism; on the contrary, they have more and more clearly confirmed the truths revealed by Lenin and all the theories he advanced during the struggle to defend revolutionary Marxism and develop Marxism.

In the historical conditions of the epoch of imperialism and proletarian revolution, Lenin carried Marxism forward to a new stage and showed all the oppressed classes and people the path along which they could really shake off capitalist-imperialist enslavement and poverty. These forty years have been forty years of victory for Leninism in the world, forty years in which Leninism has found its way deeper into the hearts of the world's people. Leninism has not only won and will continue to win great victories in countries where the socialist system has been established, but is also constantly achieving new victories in the struggles of all oppressed peoples.

The victory of Leninism is acclaimed by the people of the whole world, and at the same time cannot but incur the enmity of the imperialists and all reactionaries. The imperialists, to weaken the influence of Leninism and paralyse the revolutionary will of the masses, launch the most barbarous and despicable attacks and slanders against Leninism, and, moreover, put up and utilize the vacillators and renegades within the workers' movement to distort and emasculate the teachings of Lenin. At the end of the nineteenth century when Marxism was putting various anti-Marxist trends to rout, spreading widely throughout the workers' movement and gaining a predominant position, the revisionists represented by Bernstein proposed to revise the teachings of Marx, in keeping with the needs of the bourgeoisie. Now, when Leninism is guiding the working class and all oppressed classes and nations of the world to great victories in the march against imperialism and all kinds of reactionaries, the modern revisionists represented by Tito propose to revise the teachings of Lenin (that is, modern Marxist teachings), in keeping with the needs of the imperialists. As pointed out in the Declaration of the meeting of representatives of the Communist and Workers' Parties of the socialist countries held in Moscow in November 1957, " The existence of bourgeois influence is an internal source of revisionism, while surrender to imperialist pressure is its external source." Old revisionism attempted to prove that Marxism was outmoded, while modern revisionism attempts to prove that Leninism is outmoded. The Moscow Declaration said:

> Modern revisionism seeks to smear the great teaching of Marxism-Leninism, declares that it is " outmoded " and alleges that it has lost its significance for social progress. The revisionists try to kill the revolutionary spirit of Marxism, to undermine faith in socialism among the working class and the working people in general.

This passage of the Declaration has put it correctly; such is exactly the situation.

Are the teachings of Marxism-Leninism now " outmoded "? Does the whole, integrated teaching of Lenin on imperialism, on proletarian revolution and proletarian dictatorship, on war and peace, and on the building of socialism and communism still retain its vigorous vitality? If it is still valid and does retain vigorous vitality, does this refer only to a certain portion of it or to the whole? We usually say that Leninism is Marxism in the epoch of imperialism and proletarian revolution, Marxism in the epoch of the victory of socialism and communism. Does this view remain correct? Can it be said that Lenin's original conclusions and our usual conception of Leninism have lost their validity and correctness, and that therefore we should turn back and accept those revisionist and opportunist conclusions which Lenin long ago smashed to smithereens and which have gone disgracefully bankrupt in actual life? These questions now confront us and must be answered. Marxist-Leninists must thoroughly expose the absurdities of the imperialists and modern revisionists on these questions, eradicate their influence among the masses, awaken those they have temporarily hoodwinked and further arouse the revolutionary will of the masses.

II

THE U.S. imperialists, open representatives of the bourgeosie in many countries, the modern revisionists represented by the Tito clique, and the right-wing social democrats, in order to mislead the people of the world, do all they can to paint an utterly distorted picture of the contemporary world situation in an attempt to confirm their ravings on how " Marxism is outmoded," and " Leninism is outmoded too."

Tito's speech at the end of last year referred repeatedly to the so-called " new epoch " of the modern revisionists. He said, " Today the world has entered an epoch in which nations can relax and tranquilly devote themselves to their internal construction tasks." Then he added, " We have entered an epoch when new questions are on the agenda, not questions of war and peace but questions of co-operation, economic and otherwise, and when economic co-operation is concerned, there is also the question of economic competition." (From Tito's speech in Zagreb, December 12, 1959.) This renegade completely writes off the question of class contradictions and class struggle in the world, in an attempt to negate the consistent interpretation of Marxist-Leninists that our epoch is the epoch of imperialism and proletarian revolution, the epoch of the victory of socialism and communism.

But how do things really stand in the world?

Can the exploited and oppressed people in the imperialist countries " relax "? Can the peoples of all the colonies and semi-colonies still under imperialist oppression " relax "?

Has the armed intervention led by the U.S. imperialists in Asia, Africa and Latin America become " tranquil "? Is there " tranquillity " in our

Taiwan Straits when the U.S. imperialists are still occupying our country's Taiwan? Is there "tranquillity" on the African continent when the people of Algeria and many other parts of Africa are subjected to armed repressions by the French, British and other imperialists? Is there any "tranquillity" in Latin America when the U.S. imperialists are trying to wreck the people's revolution in Cuba by means of bombing, assassination and subversion?

What kind of "construction" is meant in saying "(they) devote themselves to their internal construction tasks"? Everyone knows that there are different types of countries in the world today, and principally two types of countries with social systems fundamentally different in nature. One type belongs to the socialist world system, the other to the capitalist world system. Is Tito referring to the "internal construction tasks" of arms expansion which the imperialists are carrying out in order to oppress the peoples of their own countries and oppress the whole world? Or is it the "internal construction" carried out by socialism for the promotion of the people's happiness and in the pursuit of lasting world peace?

Is the question of war and peace no longer an issue? Is it that imperialism no longer exists, the system of exploitation no longer exists, and therefore the question of war no longer exists? Or is it that there can be no question of war even if imperialism and the system of exploitation are allowed to survive for ever? The fact is that since the Second World War there has been continuous and unbroken warfare. Do not the imperialist wars to suppress national liberation movements and the imperialist wars of armed intervention against revolutions in various countries count as wars? Even though these wars have not developed into world wars, still do not these local wars count as wars? Even though these wars were not fought with nuclear weapons, still do not wars using so-called conventional weapons count as wars? Does not the U.S. imperialists' allocation of nearly 60 per cent. of the 1960 budget outlay to arms expansion and war preparations count as a bellicose policy on the part of U.S. imperialism? Will the revival of West German and Japanese militarisms not confront mankind with the danger of a new big war?

What kind of "co-operation" is meant? Is it "co-operation" of the proletariat with the bourgeoisie to protect capitalism? Is it "co-operation" of the colonial and semi-colonial peoples with the imperialists to protect colonialism? Is it "co-operation" of socialist countries with capitalist countries to protect the imperialist system in its oppression of the peoples in these countries and suppression of national liberation wars?

In a word, the assertions of the modern revisionists about their so-called "epoch" are so many challenges to Leninism on the foregoing issues. It is their aim to obliterate the contradiction between the masses of people and the monopoly capitalist class in the imperialist countries, the contradiction between the colonial and semi-colonial peoples and the imperialist aggressors, the contradiction between the socialist system and the imperialist system, and the contradiction between the peace-loving people of the world and the warlike imperialist bloc.

There have been different ways of describing the distinctions between different "epochs." Generally speaking, there is one way which is merely drivel, concocting and playing around with vague, ambiguous phrases to cover up the essence of the epoch. This is the old trick of the imperialists, the bourgeoisie and the revisionists in the workers' movement. Then there is another way, which is to make a concrete analysis of the concrete situation with regard to the overall class contradictions and class struggle, putting forward strictly scientific definitions, and thus bringing the essence of the epoch thoroughly to light. This is the work of every serious Marxist.

On the features that distinguish an epoch, Lenin said:

> . . . We are speaking here of big historical epochs; in every epoch there are and there will be, separate, partial movements sometimes forward, at other times backwards, there are, and there will be, various deviations from the average type and average tempo of the movements.
>
> We cannot know how fast and how successfully certain historical movements of the given epoch will develop. But we can and do know *which class* occupies a central position in this or that epoch and determines its main content, the main direction of its development, the main characteristics of the historical situation in the given epoch, etc.
>
> Only on this basis, *i.e.*, by taking into consideration first and foremost the fundamental distinctive features of different " epochs " (and not of individual episodes in the history of different countries) can we correctly work out our tactics. . . . (" Under a False Flag," *Collected Works*, 4th Russ. ed., Vol. XXI, p. 125.)

An epoch, as referred to here by Lenin, presents the question of which class holds the central position in an epoch and determines its main content and main direction of development.

Faithful to Marx's dialectics, Lenin never for a single moment departed from the standpoint of analysing class relations. He held that: " Marxism judges ' interests ' by the class antagonisms and the class struggles which manifest themselves in millions of facts of everyday life." (" Collapse of the Second International," *Selected Works*, International Publishers, New York, 1943, Vol. V, p. 189.) He stated:

> The method of Marx consists, first of all, in taking into consideration the *objective* content of the historical process at the given concrete moment, in the given concrete situation, in understanding first of all *which* class it is whose movement constitutes the mainspring of possible progress in this concrete situation. . . . (" Under a False Flag," *Collected Works*, 4th Russ. ed., Vol. XXI, p. 123.)

Lenin always demanded that we examine the concrete process of historical development on the basis of class analysis, instead of talking vaguely about " society in general " or " progress in general." We Marxists must not base proletarian policy merely on certain passing events or minute political changes, but on the overall class contradictions and class struggle of a whole historical epoch. This is a basic theoretical position of Marxists. It was by taking a firm stand on this position that Lenin, in the new period of class changes, in the new historical period, came to the conclusion that the hope of humanity lay entirely with the victory of the proletariat and that the proletariat must prepare itself to win victory in this great revolutionary battle and establish a proletarian dictatorship. After the October Revolution, at the Seventh Congress of the Russian Communist Party (Bolsheviks) in 1918, Lenin stated:

> We must begin with the general basis of the development of commodity production, the transition to capitalism and the transformation of capitalism into imperialism. Thereby we shall be theoretically taking up and consolidating a position from which nobody who has not betrayed socialism can dislodge us. From this follows an equally inevitable conclusion: the era of social revolution is beginning. (" Report on Revising the Programme and Name of the Party," *Selected Works*, International Publishers, New York, 1943, Vol. VIII, p. 317.)

This is Lenin's conclusion, a conclusion which up to the present still requires deep consideration by all Marxists.

The formulation of revolutionary Marxists that ours is the epoch of imperialism and proletarian revolution, the epoch of the victory of socialism and communism is irrefutable, because it grasps with complete correctness the basic features of our present great epoch. The formulation that Leninism is the continuation and development of revolutionary Marxism in this great epoch and that it is the theory and policy of proletarian revolution and proletarian dictatorship is also irrefutable, because it is precisely Leninism that exposed the contradictions in our great epoch—the contradictions between the working class and monopoly capital, the contradictions among the imperialist countries, the contradictions between the colonial and semi-colonial peoples and imperialism, and the contradictions between the socialist countries, where the proletariat has triumphed, and the imperialist countries. Leninism has, therefore, become our banner of victory. Contrary, however, to this series of revolutionary Marxist formulation, in the so-called "new epoch" of the Titos, there is actually no imperialism, no proletarian revolution and, needless to say, no theory and policy of the proletarian revolution and proletarian dictatorship. In short, with them, the fundamental focal points of the class contradictions and class struggles of our epoch are nowhere to be seen, the fundamental questions of Leninism are missing and there is no Leninism.

The modern revisionists assert that in their so-called "new epoch," because of the progress of science and technology, the "old conceptions" of Marx and Lenin are no longer applicable. Tito made the following assertion: "We are not dogmatists, for Marx and Lenin did not predict the rocket on the moon, atomic bombs and the great technical progress." (From Tito's speech in Zagreb, December 12, 1959.) Not dogmatists, that's fine. Who wants them to be dogmatists? But one can oppose dogmatism to defend Marxism-Leninism or one can actually oppose Marxism-Leninism in the name of opposing dogmatism. The Titos belong to the latter category. On the question of what effect scientific and technological progress has on social development, there are people who hold incorrect views because they are not able to approach the question from the materialist viewpoint of history. This is understandable. But the modern revisionists, on the other hand, are deliberately creating confusion on this question in a vain attempt to make use of the progress in science and technology to throw Marxism-Leninism to the winds.

In the past few years, the achievements of the Soviet Union in science and technology have been foremost in the world. These Soviet achievements are products of the Great October Revolution. These outstanding achievements mark a new era in man's conquest of nature and at the same time play a very important role in defending world peace. But, in the new conditions brought about by the development of modern technology, has the ideological system of Marxism-Leninism been shaken, as Tito says, by the "rocket on the moon, atomic bombs and the great technical progress" which Marx and Lenin "did not predict"? Can it be said that the Marxist-Leninist world outlook, social-historical outlook, moral outlook and other basic concepts have therefore become what they call stale "dogmas" and that the law of class struggle henceforth no longer holds good?

Marx and Lenin did not live to the present day, and of course could not see certain specific details of technological progress in the present-day world. But what, after all, does the development of natural science and the advance of technology augur for the capitalist system? Marx and Lenin held that this could only augur a new social revolution, but could certainly not augur the fading away of social revolution.

We know that both Marx and Lenin rejoiced in the new discoveries and progress of natural science and technology in the conquest of nature. Engels said in his " Speech at the Graveside of Karl Marx ":

> Science was for Marx a historically dynamic, revolutionary force. However great the joy with which he welcomed a new discovery in some theoretical science whose practical application perhaps it was as yet quite impossible to envisage, he experienced quite another kind of joy when the discovery involved immediate revolutionary changes in industry, and in historical development in general. (*Selected Works of Marx and Engels*, Foreign Languages Publishing House, Moscow, 1955, Vol. II, p. 168.)

Engels added: " For Marx was before all else a revolutionist." Well said! Marx always regarded all new discoveries in the conquest of nature from the viewpoint of a proletarian revolutionist, not from the viewpoint of one who holds that the proletarian revolution will fade away.

Wilhelm Liebknecht wrote in his *Reminiscences of Marx*:

> Marx made fun of the victorious European reaction which imagined that it had stifled the revolution and did not suspect that natural science was preparing a new revolution. King Steam, who had revolutionized the world in the previous century, was coming to the end of his reign and another incomparably greater revolutionary would take his place, the electric spark.
> . . . The consequences are unpredictable. The economic revolution must be followed by a political one, for the latter is only the expression of the former.
> In the manner in which Marx discussed this progress of science and mechanics, his conception of the world, and especially what has been termed the materialist conception of history, was so clearly expressed that certain doubts which I had hitherto still maintained melted away like snow in the sunshine of spring. (Wilhelm Liebknecht and Paul Lafarge's *Reminiscences of Marx*, Lawrence & Wishart, p. 15.)

This is how Marx felt the breath of revolution in the progress of science and technology. Marx held that the new progress of science and technology would lead to a social revolution to overthrow the capitalist system. To Marx, the progress of natural science and technology further strengthens the whole position of the Marxist world outlook and the materialist conception of history, and certainly does not shake it. The progress of natural science and technology further strengthens the position of the proletarian revolution, and of the oppressed nations in their fight against imperialism, and certainly does not weaken it.

Like Marx, Lenin also viewed technological progress in connection with the question of revolution in the social system. Thus Lenin held that:

> The age of steam is the age of the bourgeoisie, the age of electricity is the age of socialism. (" Report on Work of All-Russia Central Executive Committee and People's Council," *Collected Works*, 4th Russ. ed., Vol. XXX, p. 310.)

Please note the contrast between the revolutionary spirit of Marx and Lenin and the modern revisionists' shameful attitude of betraying the revolution!

In class society, in the epoch of imperialism, Marxist-Leninists can only approach the question of the development and use of technology from the viewpoint of class analysis.

Inasmuch as the socialist system is progressive and represents the interests of the people, the socialist countries want to utilize such new techniques as atomic energy and rocketry to serve peaceful domestic construction and the conquest of nature. The more the socialist countries master such new techniques and the more rapidly they develop them, the better will they attain the aim of high-speed development of the social productive forces to meet the needs of the people, and the more will they strengthen the forces for checking imperialist war and increase the possibility of defending world peace. Therefore, for the welfare of their peoples and in the interest of peace for people the world over, the socialist countries should, wherever possible, master more and more of such new techniques serving the well-being of the people.

At the present time, the socialist Soviet Union clearly holds the upper hand in the development of new techniques. Everybody knows that the rocket that hit the moon was launched by the Soviet Union and not by the United States, the country where capitalism is most developed. This shows that only in the socialist countries can there be unlimited prospects for the large-scale development of new techniques.

On the contrary, inasmuch as the imperialist system is reactionary and against the people, the imperialist powers want to use such new techniques for military purposes of aggression against foreign countries, to intimidate the people within their own countries, to make weapons for human slaughter. To the imperialist powers, the emergence of such new techniques only means pushing to a new stage the contradiction between the development of the social productive forces and the capitalist relations of production. What this will bring about is not by any means the perpetuation of capitalism but the further rousing of the revolution of the people in those countries and the destruction of the old, criminal, cannibalistic system of capitalism.

The U.S. imperialists and their partners use weapons like atom bombs to threaten war and blackmail the whole world. They declare that anyone who does not submit to the domination of U.S. imperialism will be destroyed. The Tito clique echoes this line, it takes up the U.S. imperialist refrain to spread terror of atomic warfare among the masses. U.S. imperialist blackmail and the chiming in of the Tito clique can only temporarily dupe those who do not understand the real situation, but cannot cow the people who have awakened. Even those who for the time being do not understand the real situation will gradually come to understand it with the help of the advanced elements.

Marxist-Leninists have always maintained that in world history it is not technique but man, the masses of people, that determine the fate of mankind. There was a theory current for a time among some people in China before and during the War of Resistance to Japanese Aggression, which was known as the " weapons-mean-everything theory "; from this theory they concluded that since Japan's weapons were new and its techniques advanced while China's weapons were old and its techniques backward, " China would inevitably be subjugated." Comrade Mao Tse-tung in his work *On the Protracted War* published at that time refuted such nonsense. He made the following analysis : The Japanese imperialists' war of aggression against China was bound to fail because it was reactionary, unjust, and being unjust lacked popular support; the Chinese people's war of resistance against Japan would certainly win because it was progressive, just, and being just enjoyed abundant support. Comrade Mao Tse-tung pointed out that the most abundant source of strength in war lay in the masses, and that a people's army organized by awakened and united masses of people would be invincible throughout the world. This is a Marxist-Leninist thesis. And what was the outcome? The outcome was that the Marxist-Leninist thesis triumphed and the " theory of national subjugation " ended in defeat. During the Korean war after the Second World War, the triumph of the Korean and Chinese peoples over U.S. aggressors far superior in weapons and equipment again bore out this Marxist-Leninist thesis.

An awakened people will always find new ways to counteract a reactionary superiority in arms and win victory for themselves. This was so in past history, it is so at present, and it will still be so in the future. Because the socialist Soviet Union has gained supremacy in military techniques, the U.S. imperialists have lost their monopoly of atomic and nuclear weapons; at the same time, as a result of the awakening of the people the world over and the awakening of the people in the United States itself, there is now in the world the possibility of concluding an agreement for the banning of atomic and nuclear weapons. We are striving for the conclusion of such an agreement. Unlike the bellicose imperialists, the socialist countries and peace-loving people the world over actively and firmly stand for the banning and destruction of atomic and nuclear weapons. We are always struggling against imperialist war, for the banning of atomic and nuclear weapons and for the defence of world peace. The more broadly and profoundly this struggle is waged and the more fully and thoroughly exposed are the brutish faces of the bellicose U.S. and other imperialists, the more will we be able to isolate these imperialists before the people of the world, the greater will be the possibility of tying their hands and the better it will be for the cause of world peace. If, on the contrary, we lose our vigilance against the danger of the imperialists launching a war, do not work to arouse the people of all countries to rise up against imperialism but tie the hands of the people, then imperialism can prepare for war just as it pleases and the inevitable result will be an increase in the danger of the imperialists launching a war and, once war breaks out, the people may not be able quickly to adopt a correct attitude towards it because of complete lack of preparation or in-adequate preparation, thus being unable to vigorously check the war. Of course, whether or not the imperialists will unleash a war is not determined by us; we are, after all, not chiefs-of-staff to the imperialists. As long as the people of all countries enhance their awareness and are fully prepared, with the socialist camp also mastering modern weapons, it is certain that if the U.S. or other imperialists refuse to reach an agreement on the banning of atomic and nuclear weapons and should dare to fly in the face of the will of all humanity by launching a war using atomic and nuclear weapons, the result will be the very speedy destruction of these monsters encircled by the peoples of the world, and the result will certainly not be the annihilation of mankind. We consistently oppose the launching of criminal wars by imperialism, because imperialist war would impose enormous sacrifices upon the peoples of various countries (including the peoples of the United States and other imperialist countries). But should the imperialists impose such sacrifices on the peoples of various countries, we believe that, just as the experience of the Russian revolution and the Chinese revolution shows, those sacrifices would be repaid. On the débris of a dead imperialism, the victorious people would create very swiftly a civilization thousands of times higher than the capitalist system and a truly beautiful future for themselves.

The conclusion can only be this: whichever way you look at it, none of the new techniques like atomic energy, rocketry and so on has changed, as alleged by the modern revisionists, the basic characteristics of the epoch of imperialism and proletarian revolution pointed out by Lenin. The capitalist-imperialist system absolutely will not crumble of itself. It will be overthrown by the proletarian revolution within the imperialist country concerned, and the national revolution in the colonies and semi-colonies. Contemporary technological progress cannot save the capitalist-imperialist system from its doom but only rings a new death knell for it.

III

THE modern revisionists, proceeding from their absurd arguments on the current world situation and from their absurd argument that the Marxist-Leninist theory of class analysis and class struggle is obsolete, attempt to totally overthrow the fundamental theories of Marxism-Leninism on a series of questions like violence, war, peaceful coexistence, etc.

There are also some people who are not revisionists, but well-intentioned persons who sincerely want to be Marxists, but get confused in the face of certain new historical phenomena and thus have some incorrect ideas. For example, some of them say that the failure of the U.S. imperialists' policy of atomic blackmail marks the end of violence. While thoroughly refuting the absurdities of the modern revisionists, we should also help these well-intentioned people to correct their erroneous ideas.

What is violence? Lenin had a lot to say on this question in his book *The State and Revolution*. The emergence and existence of the state is in itself a kind of violence. Lenin introduced the following elucidation by Engels:

> . . . it (this public power) consists not merely of armed men, but of material appendages, prisons and coercive institutions of all kinds. . . . (*Selected Works*, International Publishers, New York, Vol. VII, p. 10.)

Lenin tells us that we must draw a distinction between two types of states different in nature, the state of bourgeois dictatorship and the state of proletarian dictatorship, and between two types of violence different in nature, counter-revolutionary violence and revolutionary violence; as long as there is counter-revolutionary violence, there is bound to be revolutionary violence to oppose it. It would be impossible to wipe out counter-revolutionary violence without revolutionary violence. The state in which the exploiting classes are in power is counter-revolutionary violence, a special force for suppressing the exploited classes in the interest of the exploiting classes. Both before the imperialists had atomic bombs and rocket weapons, and since they have had these new weapons, the imperialist state has always been a special force for suppressing the proletariat at home and the people of its colonies and semi-colonies abroad, has always been such an institution of violence; even if it is compelled not to use these new weapons, the imperialist state will of course still remain an imperialist institution of violence until it is overthrown and replaced by the people's state, the state of the dictatorship of the proletariat of that country.

Never since the dawn of history have there been such large-scale, such utterly vicious forces of violence as those of present-day capitalist imperialists. For the past ten years and more, the U.S. imperialists have, without any scruples, adopted means of persecution a hundred times more savage than before, trampling upon the outstanding sons of the country's working class, trampling upon the Negro people, trampling upon all progressives, and moreover, recklessly declaring that they intend to put the whole world under their rule of violence. They are continuously expanding their forces of violence, and at the same time the other imperialists also take part in the race to increase their forces of violence.

The bloated military build-up of the imperialist countries headed by the United States has appeared during the unprecedentedly grave general crisis of capitalism. The more frantically the imperialists carry the expansion of their military forces to a peak, the nearer they draw to their own doom. Now even some representatives of the U.S. imperialists have premonitions of the inevitable extinction of the capitalist system. But will the imperialists themselves put an end to their violence? Will those in power in the imperialist countries abandon of their own accord the violence they have set up just because imperialism is drawing near to its doom?

Can it be said that, compared with the past, the imperialists are no longer addicted to violence, or that there has been a lessening in the degree of their addiction?

Lenin answered such questions on several occasions long ago. He pointed out in his book *Imperialism, the Highest Stage of Capitalism*:

> . . . for politically imperialism is in general a striving towards violence and reaction. (*Selected Works*, International Publishers, New York, Vol. V, p. 83.)

After the October Revolution, in his book *The Proletarian Revolution and the Renegade Kautsky* he made a special point of recounting history, comparing the differences between pre-monopoly capitalism and monopoly capitalism, *i.e.*, imperialism. He said:

> Pre-monopoly capitalism, which reached its zenith in the seventies of the nineteenth century, was, by virtue of its fundamental *economic* traits (which were most typical in England and America) distinguished by its relative attachment to peace and freedom. Imperialism, *i.e.*, monopoly capitalism, which finally matured only in the twentieth century, is, by virtue of its fundamental *economic* traits, distinguished by the least attachment to peace and freedom, and by the greatest and universal development of militarism everywhere. (*Selected Works*, International Publishers, Vol. VII, pp. 125–126.)

Of course, these words of Lenin were uttered in the early period of the October Revolution, when the proletarian state was newly born, and its economic forces still young and weak, while with the lapse of forty years and more the face of the Soviet state itself, and of the whole world has undergone a tremendous change, as we have already described. Then, are the foregoing pronouncements of Lenin obsolete, because the nature of imperialism has changed owing to the might of the Soviet Union, the might of the forces of socialism and the might of the forces of peace? Or, is it that imperialism, although its nature has not changed, will no longer resort to violence? Do these ideas conform to the real situation?

The socialist world system has obviously gained the upper hand in its struggle with the capitalist world system. This great historic fact has weakened the position of imperialist violence in the world. But will this fact cause the imperialists never again to oppress the people of their own country, never again engage in outward expansion and aggressive activities? Can it make the warlike circles of the imperialists " lay down the butcher knife " and " sell their knives and buy oxen "? Can it make the groups of munitions merchants in the imperialist countries change over to peaceful pursuits?

All these questions confront every serious Marxist-Leninist, and require deep consideration. It is obvious that whether these questions are viewed and handled correctly or incorrectly has a close bearing on the success or failure of the proletarian cause and the destiny of humanity.

War is the most acute form of expression of violence. One type is civil war, another is foreign war. Violence is not always expressed by war, its most acute form. In capitalist countries, bourgeois war is the continuation of the bourgeois policies of ordinary times, while bourgeois peace is the continuation of bourgeois wartime policy. The bourgeoisie are always switching back and forth between the two forms, war and peace, to carry on their rule over the people and their external struggle. In what they call peace time, the imperialists rely on armed force to deal with the oppressed classes and nations by such forms of violence as arrest, imprisonment, sentencing to hard labour, massacre and so forth, while at the same time they also carry on preparations for using the most acute form of violence—war—to suppress the revolution of the people at home, to carry out plunder abroad, to overwhelm foreign competitors and to stamp out revolutions in other countries. Or, peace at home may exist side by side with war abroad.

In the initial period of the October Revolution, all the imperialist powers resorted to violence in the form of war against the Soviet Union, which was a continuation of their imperialist policies; in the Second World War, the German imperialists used violence in the form of large scale war to attack the Soviet Union, which was a continuation of their imperialist policy. But on the other hand, the imperialists also established diplomatic relations of peaceful coexistence with the Soviet Union in different periods, which is also, of course, a continuation of imperialist policy in another form under certain conditions.

True, some new questions have now arisen concerning peaceful co-existence. Confronted with the powerful Soviet Union and the powerful socialist camp, the imperialists must at any rate carefully consider whether they wouldn't hasten their own extinction, as Hitler did, or bring about the most serious consequences for the capitalist system itself, if they should attack the Soviet Union, attack the socialist countries.

" Peaceful Co-existence "—this is a new concept which arose only after socialist countries appeared in the world following the October Revolution. It is a new concept formed under circumstances Lenin had predicted before the October Revolution, when he said:

> Socialism cannot achieve victory simultaneously in all countries. It will achieve victory first in one or several countries, while the others will remain bourgeois or pre-bourgeois for some time. (" The War Program of the Proletarian Revolution," *Selected Works*, F.L.P.H., Moscow, 1952, Vol. I, part 2, p. 571.)

This new concept is one advanced by Lenin after the great Soviet people overcame the armed imperialist intervention. As was pointed out above, at the outset the imperialists were not willing to co-exist peacefully with the Soviet Union. The imperialists were compelled to " co-exist " with the Soviet Union only after the war of intervention against the Soviet Union had failed, after there had been several years of actual trial of strength, after the Soviet state had planted its feet firmly on the ground, and after a certain balance of power had taken shape between the Soviet state and the imperialist countries. Lenin said in 1920:

> We have won conditions for ourselves under which we can exist alongside the capitalist powers, which are now forced to enter into trade relations with us. (" Our Internal and External Situation and the Party's Tasks," *Collected Works*, 4th Rus. ed., Vol. XXXI, p. 384.)

It can be seen that the realization of peaceful co-existence for a certain period between the world's first socialist state and imperialism was won entirely through struggle. Before the Second World War, the 1920–40 period prior to Germany's attack on the Soviet Union was a period of peaceful co-existence between imperialism and the Soviet Union. During all those twenty years, the Soviet Union kept faith with peaceful co-existence. However, in 1941, Hitler was no longer willing to co-exist peacefully with the Soviet Union, the German imperialists perfidiously launched a savage attack on the Soviet Union. Owing to victory in the anti-fascist war, with the great Soviet Union as the main force, the world saw once again a situation of peaceful co-existence between the socialist and capitalist countries. Nevertheless, the imperialists have not given up their designs. The U.S. imperialists have set up networks of military bases and guided missile bases everywhere around the Soviet Union and the entire socialist camp. They are still occupying our territory Taiwan and continually carrying out military provocations against us in the Taiwan Straits. They carried out armed intervention in Korea, conducting a large-scale war against the Korean and Chinese peoples on Korean soil, which resulted in an armistice agreement only after their defeat—and up to now they are still interfering with the unification of the Korean people. They gave aid in weapons to the French imperialist occupation forces in their war against the Vietnamese people, and up to now they are still interfering with the unification of the Vietnamese people. They engineered the counter-revolutionary rebellion in Hungary, and up to now they are continually making all sorts of attempts at subversion in the East European and other socialist countries. The facts are still just as Lenin represented them to a U.S. correspondent in February 1920: on the question of peace, " there is no obstacle on our side. The obstacle is the imperialism of American (and all other) capitalists." (*Collected Works*, 4th Russ. ed., Vol. XXX, p. 340.)

The foreign policy of socialist countries can only be a policy of peace. The socialist system determines that we do not need war, absolutely would not start a war, and absolutely must not, should not and could not encroach one inch on the territory of a neighbouring country. Ever since its founding, the People's Republic of China has adhered to a foreign policy of peace. Our country together with two neighbouring countries, India and Burma, jointly initiated the well-known Five Principles of Peaceful Co-existence ; and at the Bandung Conference of 1955, our country together with various countries of Asia and Africa adopted the ten principles of peaceful co-existence. The Communist Party and Government of our country have in the past few years consistently supported the activities for peace carried out by the Central Committee of the Communist Party and the Government of the Soviet Union headed by Comrade N. S. Khrushchev, considering that these activities on the part of the Communist Party and the Government of the Soviet Union have further demonstrated before the people of the world the firmness of the socialist countries' peaceful foreign policy as well as the need for the peoples to stop the imperialists from launching another world war and to strive for a lasting world peace.

The Declaration of the Moscow Conference of 1957 states:

> The cause of peace is upheld by the powerful forces of our era: the invincible camp of socialist countries headed by the Soviet Union; the peace-loving countries of Asia and Africa taking an anti-imperialist stand and forming, together with the socialist countries, a broad peace zone; the international working class and above all its vanguard—the Communist Parties; the liberation movement of the peoples of the colonies and semi-colonies; the mass peace movement of the peoples; the peoples of the European countries who have proclaimed neutrality, the peoples of Latin America and the masses in the imperialist countries who themselves are firmly resisting plans for a new war. An alliance of these mighty forces could prevent war.

So long as there is a continuous development of these mighty forces, it is possible to maintain the situation of peaceful co-existence, or even to obtain some sort of official agreement on peaceful co-existence or to conclude an agreement on prohibition of atomic and nuclear weapons. That would be a fine thing in full accord with the aspirations of the peoples of the world. However, even under those circumstances, as long as the imperialist system still exists, the most acute form of violence, namely war, has by no means ended in the world. The fact is not as described by the Yugoslav revisionists, who declare obsolete Lenin's definition that " war is the continuation of politics " (" Active Co-existence and Socialism," *Narodna Armija*, November 28, 1958), a definition which he repeatedly explained and upheld in combating opportunism.

We believe in the absolute correctness of Lenin's thinking: War is an inevitable outcome of systems of exploitation and the source of modern wars is the imperialist system. Until the imperialist system and the exploiting classes come to an end, wars of one kind or another will always occur. They may be wars among the imperialists for redivision of the world, or wars of aggression and anti-aggression between the imperialists and the oppressed nations, or civil wars of revolution and counter-revolution between the exploited and exploiting classes in the imperialist countries, or, of course, wars in which the imperialists attack the socialist countries and the socialist countries are forced to defend themselves. All these kinds of wars represent the continuation of the policies of definite classes. Marxists-Leninists absolutely must not sink into the mire of bourgeois pacifism, and can only appraise all these kinds of wars and thus draw conclusions for proletarian policy by adopting the method of concrete class analysis. As Lenin put it: " Theoretically, it would be quite wrong to forget that every war is but the continuation of politics by other means." (" The War Program of the Proletarian Revolution," *Selected Works*, F.L.P.H., Moscow, 1952, Vol. I, part 2, p. 572.)

To attain their aim of plunder and oppression, the imperialists always have two tactics: the tactics of war and the tactics of " peace "; therefore, the proletariat and the people of all countries must also use two tactics to counter the imperialists: the tactics of thoroughly exposing the imperialists' peace fraud and striving energetically for a genuine world peace, and the tactics of preparing for a just war to end the imperialist unjust war when and if the imperialists should unleash it.

In a word, in the interests of the people of the world, we must thoroughly shatter the falsehoods of the modern revisionists and uphold the Marxist-Leninist viewpoints on the questions of violence, war and peaceful co-existence.

The Yugoslav revisionists deny the inherent class character of violence and thereby obliterate the fundamental difference between revolutionary violence and counter-revolutionary violence; they deny the inherent class character of war and thereby obliterate the fundamental difference between just war and unjust war; they deny that imperialist war is a continuation of imperialist policy, deny the danger of the imperialists unleashing another big war, deny that it will be possible to do away with war only after doing away with the exploiting classes, and even shamelessly call the U.S. imperialist chieftain Eisenhower "the man who laid the cornerstone for eliminating the cold war and establishing lasting peace with peaceful competition between different political systems" ("Eisenhower Arrives in Rome," *Borba*, December 4, 1959); they deny that under the conditions of peaceful co-existence there are still complicated, acute struggles in the political, economic and ideological fields, and so on. All these arguments of the Yugoslav revisionists are aimed at poisoning the minds of the proletariat and the people of all countries, and are helpful to the imperialist policy of war.

IV

Modern revisionists seek to confuse the peaceful foreign policy of the socialist countries with the domestic policies of the proletariat in the capitalist countries. They thus hold that peaceful co-existence of countries with differing social systems means that capitalism can peacefully grow into socialism, that the proletariat in countries ruled by the bourgeoisie can renounce class struggle and enter into "peaceful co-operation" with the bourgeoisie and the imperialists, and that the proletariat and all the exploited classes should forget about the fact that they are living in a class society, and so on. All these views are also diametrically opposed to Marxism-Leninism. They are put forward in an attempt to protect imperialist rule and hold the proletariat and all the rest of the working people perpetually in capitalist enslavement.

Peaceful co-existence of nations and people's revolutions in various countries are in themselves two different things, not one and the same thing; two different concepts, not one; two different kinds of question, and not one and the same kind of question.

Peaceful co-existence refers to relations between nations; revolution means the overthrow of the oppressors as a class by the oppressed people within each country, while in the case of the colonial and semi-colonial countries, it is first and foremost a question of overthrowing alien oppressors, namely, the imperialists. Before the October Revolution the question of peaceful co-existence between socialist and capitalist countries simply did not exist in the world, as there were as yet no socialist countries; but there did exist at that time the questions of the proletarian revolution and the national revolution, as the peoples in various countries, in accordance with their own specific conditions, had long ago put revolutions of one kind or the other on the agenda of the day to determine the destinies of their countries.

We are Marxist-Leninists. We have always held that revolution is each nation's own affair. We have always maintained that the working class can only depend on itself for its emancipation, and that the emancipation of the people of any given country depends on their own awakening, and on the ripening of revolution in that country. Revolution can neither be exported nor imported. No one can prevent the people of a foreign country from carrying out a revolution, nor can one produce a revolution in a foreign country by using the method of " helping the rice shoots to grow by pulling them up."

Lenin put it well when he said in June 1918:

> There are people who believe that the revolution can break out in a foreign country to order, by agreement. These people are either mad or they are provocateurs. We have experienced two revolutions during the past twelve years. We know that revolutions cannot be made to order, or by agreement; they break out when tens of millions of people come to the conclusion that it is impossible to live in the old way any longer. (" The Fourth Conference of Trade Unions and Factory Committees of Moscow," *Selected Works*, International Publishers, New York, Vol. VII, p. 414.)

In addition to the experience of the Russian revolution, is not the experience of the Chinese revolution also one of the best proofs of this? The Chinese people, under the leadership of the Chinese Communist Party, have experienced several revolutions. The imperialists and all the reactionaries, like lunatics, have always asserted that our revolutions were made to order from abroad, or in accordance with foreign agreements. But people all over the world know that our revolutions were not imported from abroad, but were brought about because our people found it impossible to continue to live in the old China and because they wanted to create a new life of their own.

When a socialist country, in the face of imperialist aggression is compelled to launch counter-attacks in a defensive war, and goes beyond its own border to pursue and eliminate its enemies from abroad, as the Soviet Union did in the war against Hitler, is this justified? Certainly it is completely justified, absolutely necessary and entirely just. In accordance with the strict principles of Communists, such operations by the socialist countries must be strictly limited to the time when the imperialists launch a war of aggression against them. Socialist countries never permit themselves to send, never should and never will send their troops across their borders unless they are subjected to aggression from a foreign enemy. Since the armed forces of the socialist countries fight for justice, when these forces have to go beyond their borders to counter-attack a foreign enemy, it is only natural that they should exert an influence and have an effect wherever they go; but even then, the emergence of people's revolutions and the establishment of the socialist system in those places and countries where they go will still depend on the will of the masses of the people there.

The spread of revolutionary ideas knows no national boundaries. But these ideas will only yield revolutionary fruit in the hands of the masses of people themselves, under specific circumstances in a given country. This is so not only in the epoch of proletarian revolution, but also in the epoch of bourgeois revolution. The bourgeoisie of various countries at the time of their revolution took Rousseau's *Social Contract* as their gospel, while the revolutionary proletariat in various countries take as their gospels Marx's *Communist Manifesto* and *Capital* and Lenin's *Imperialism, the Highest Stage of Capitalism* and *The State and Revolution*. Times vary, the classes vary, the ideologies vary and the character of the revolutions varies. But no one can hold back a revolution in any country if there is a desire for that revolution and when the revolutionary crisis there has matured. In the end the socialist system will replace the capitalist system. This is an objective law independent of human will. No matter how hard the reactionaries may try to prevent the advance of the wheel of history, revolution will take place sooner or later and will surely triumph. The same applies to the replacement of one society by another throughout human history. The slave system was replaced by the feudal system which, in its turn, gave way to the capitalist system. These, too, follow laws independent of human will. These replacements were carried out through revolution.

That notorious old revisionist Bernstein once said, " Remember ancient Rome, there was a ruling class that did no work, but lived well, and as a result, this class weakened. Such a class must gradually hand over its power." That the slave-owners as a class weakened was a historical fact that Bernstein could not conceal, any more than the present U.S. imperialists can conceal the fact of their own steady decline. Yet Bernstein, shameless, self-styled " historian " that he was, chose to cover up the following basic facts of ancient Roman history: the slave-owners never " handed over power " of their own accord; their rule was overthrown by protracted, repeated, continuous slave revolutions.

Revolution means the use of revolutionary violence by the oppressed class, it means revolutionary war. This is also true of the bourgeois revolution. Lenin has put it well:

> History teaches us that no oppressed class ever achieved power, nor could achieve power, without going through a period of dictatorship, *i.e.*, the conquest of political power and suppression by force of the most desperate, frenzied resistance always offered by the exploiters. . . . The bourgeoisie . . . came to power in the advanced countries through a series of insurrections, civil wars, the suppression by force of kings, feudalists, slave-owners and their attempts at restoration. (" Theses on Bourgeois Democracy and Proletarian Dictatorship Presented to the First Congress of the Communist International," *Lenin Against Revisionism*, F.L.P.H., Moscow, 1959, p. 488.)

Why do things happen this way?

In answering this question, again we have to quote Lenin.

In the first place, as Lenin said: " No ruling class in the world ever gave way without a struggle." (" Speech at Workers' Conference of Presnia District," *Collected Works*, 4th Russ. ed., Vol. XXVIII, p. 338.)

Secondly, as Lenin explained: " The reactionary classes themselves are usually the first to resort to violence, to civil war; they are the first to ' place the bayonet on the agenda.' " (" Two Tactics of Social-Democracy in the Democratic Revolution," *Selected Works*, F.L.P.H., Moscow, Vol. I, part 2, p. 142.)

In the light of this how shall we conceive of the proletarian socialist revolution?

In order to answer this question we must quote Lenin again.

Let us read the following passage by him.

> Not a single great revolution in history has ever been carried out without a civil war and no serious Marxist will believe it possible to make the transition from capitalism to socialism without a civil war. (" Prediction," *Collected Works*, 4th Russ. ed., Vol. XXVII, p. 457.)

These words of Lenin here explain the question very clearly.

And here is another quotation from Lenin:

> *If* socialism had been born peacefully—but the capitalist gentlemen did not wish to let it be born thus. . . . Even if there had been no war, the capitalist gentlemen would still have done all they could to prevent such a peaceful development. Great revolutions, even when they began peacefully, like the great French Revolution, have ended in desperate wars which have been started by the counter-revolutionary bourgeoisie. ("First All-Russian Conference of Social Education," *Collected Works*, 4th Russ. ed., Vol. XXIX, p. 334.)

This is also very clearly put.

The Great October Revolution is the best material witness to the truth of these propositions of Lenin.

So is the Chinese revolution. No one will ever forget that it was only after twenty-two years of bitter civil war under the leadership of the Chinese Communist Party that the Chinese people and the Chinese proletariat won nationwide victory and captured state power.

The history of the proletarian revolution in the West after the First World War tells us: even when the capitalist gentlemen do not exercise direct, open control of state power, but rule through their lackeys—the treacherous social-democrats, these despicable renegades will surely be ready at any time, in accordance with the dictates of the bourgeoisie, to cover up the violence of the bourgeois White Guards and plunge the proletarian revolutionary fighters into a blood bath. This is just the way it was in Germany at that time. Vanquished, the big German bourgeoisie handed over state power to the social-democrats. The social-democrat government, on coming to power, immediately set about a bloody suppression of the German working class in January 1919. Let us recall how Karl Liebknecht and Rosa Luxembourg, whom Lenin called "the best representatives of the world proletarian International" and "the immortal leaders of the international socialist revolution," shed their blood as a result of the violence of the social-democrats of the day. Let us also recall, in Lenin's words, "the vileness and shamefulness of these murders" (*A Letter to the Workers of Europe and America*, F.L.P.H., Moscow, 1954, p. 16) perpetrated by these renegades—these so-called "socialists" for the purpose of preserving the capitalist system and the interest of the bourgeoisie! Let us, in the light of bloody facts both of the historical part and of the modern capitalist world, examine all this nonsense about the "peaceful growth of capitalism into socialism" put out by the old revisionists and their modern counterparts.

Does it follow, then, that we Marxist-Leninists will refuse to adopt the policy of peaceful transition even when there exists the possibility of such peaceful development? No, decidedly not!

As we all know, Engels, one of the great founders of scientific communism, in the famous work *Principles of Communism* answered the question: "Can private property be eliminated by peaceful means?" He wrote:

> One would wish that it could be thus, and Communists, of course, would be the last to object to this. Communists know well that all plots are not only futile, but even pernicious. They know very well that revolutions cannot be thought up and made as one wishes and that revolutions have always and everywhere been the necessary result of existing conditions, which have absolutely not depended on the will and leadership of separate parties and whole classes. But at the same time, they see that the development of

the proletariat in nearly all civilized countries is being violently suppressed and that in this way the opponents of the Communists are working as hard as they can for the revolution. . . . ("Principles of Communism," *Collected Works of Marx and Engels*, 2nd Russ. ed., Vol. IV, p. 331.)

This was written over a hundred years ago, yet how fresh it is as we read it again!

We also know that for a time following the Russian February Revolution, in view of the specific conditions of the time, Lenin did adopt the policy of peaceful development of the revolution. He considered it "an extraordinarily rare opportunity in the history of revolutions " ("The Tasks of the Revolution," *Collected Works*, 4th Russ. ed., Vol. XXVI, p. 45) and grasped tight hold of it. The bourgeois Provisional Government and the White Guards, however, destroyed this possibility of peaceful development of the revolution and so drenched the streets of Petrograd in the blood of the workers and soldiers marching in a peaceful mass demonstration in July. Lenin, therefore, pointed out:

The peaceful course of development has been rendered impossible. A non-peaceful and most painful course has begun. ("On Slogans," *Selected Works*, F.L.P.H., Moscow, Vol. II, part 1, p. 89.)

We know too that as the Chinese War of Resistance to Japanese Aggression came to an end, there was a widespread and ardent desire for peace in the country. Our Party then conducted peace negotiations with the Kuomintang, seeking to institute social and political reforms by peaceful means, and in 1946 an agreement on achieving peace throughout the country was reached with the Kuomintang. The reactionary Kuomintang clique, however, defying the will of the whole people, tore up this agreement and, with the support of the U.S. imperialists, launched a civil war on a nationwide scale, leaving the people with no option but to counter it with a revolutionary war. As we never relaxed our vigilance or gave up the people's armed forces even in our struggle for peaceful reform but were fully prepared, the people were not cowed by the war, but those who launched the war were made to eat their own bitter fruit.

It would be in the best interests of the people if the proletariat could attain power and carry out the transition to socialism by peaceful means. It would be wrong not to make use of such a possibility when it occurs. Whenever an opportunity for "peaceful development of the revolution " presents itself Communists must seize it, as Lenin did, so as to realize the aim of the socialist revolution. However, this sort of opportunity is always, in Lenin's words, "an extraordinarily rare opportunity in the history of revolutions." When in a given country a certain local political power is already surrounded by revolutionary forces or when in the world a certain capitalist country is already surrounded by socialism—in such cases, there might be a greater possibility of opportunities for the peaceful development of the revolution. But even then, the peaceful development of the revolution should never be regarded as the only possibility and it is therefore necessary to be prepared at the same time for the other possibility, *i.e.*, non-peaceful development of the revolution. For instance, after the liberation of the Chinese mainland, although certain areas ruled by slave-owners and serf-owners were already surrounded by the absolutely predominant people's revolutionary forces, yet, as an old Chinese saying goes, "Cornered beasts will still fight," a handful of the most reactionary slave-owners and serf-owners still gave a last kick, rejecting peaceful reforms and launching armed rebellions. Only after these rebellions were quelled was it possible to carry out the reform of the social systems.

At a time when the imperialist countries and the imperialists are armed to the teeth as never before in order to protect their savage man-eating system, can it be said that the imperialists have become very " peaceable " towards the proletariat and the people at home and the oppressed nations abroad, as the modern revisionists claim, and that therefore, the " extraordinarily rare opportunity in the history of revolutions " that Lenin spoke about after the February Revolution, will become a normal state of affairs for the world proletariat and all the oppressed people, so that what Lenin referred to as a " rare opportunity " is easily available to the proletariat in the capitalist countries? We hold that these views are completely groundless.

Marxist-Leninists should never forget this truth: the armed forces of all ruling classes are used in the first place to oppress their people at home. Only on the basis of oppression of the people at home can the imperialists oppress other countries, launch aggression and wage unjust wars. In order to oppress their own people they need to maintain and strengthen their reactionary armed forces. Lenin once wrote in the course of the Russian revolution of 1905:

> A standing army is used not so much against the external enemy as against the internal enemy. (" The Army and the Revolution," *Collected Works*, 4th Russ. ed., Vol. X, p. 38.)

Is this conclusion valid for all countries where the exploiting classes dominate, for capitalist countries? Can it be said that it was valid then but has become incorrect now? In our opinion, this truth remains irrefutable and the facts are confirming its correctness more and more. Strictly speaking, if the proletariat of any country fails to see this clearly it will not be able to find the way to liberation.

In *The State and Revolution* Lenin centred the problem of revolution on the smashing of the bourgeois state machine. Quoting the most important passages from Marx's *Civil War in France*, he wrote:

> After the revolution of 1848–49, the state power became " the national war engine of capital against labour." (*Selected Works of Lenin*, F.L.P.H., Moscow, 1952, Vol. II, part 1, p. 240.)

The main machine of the bourgeois state power to wage an anti-labour war is its standing army. Therefore, " . . . the first decree of the commune . . . was the suppression of the standing army, and the substitution for it of the armed people. . . ." (*ibid.*, Vol. II, part 1, p. 241.)

So this question, in the last analysis, must be treated in the light of the principles of the Paris Commune which, as Marx puts it, are perpetual and indestructible.

In the seventies of the nineteenth century Marx took Britain and the United States to be exceptions, holding that as far as these two countries were concerned there did exist the possibility of " peaceful " transition to socialism, because militarism and bureaucracy were at an early stage of development in these two countries. But in the era of imperialism, as Lenin put it, " this qualification made by Marx is no longer valid " for these two countries " have today completely sunk into the all-European filthy, bloody morass of bureaucratic-military institutions which subordinate everything to themselves and trample everything underfoot." (" The State and Revolution," *Selected Works*, F.L.P.H., Moscow, 1952, Vol. II, part 1, pp. 237–238.) This was one of the focal points of the debate Lenin had with the opportunists of the day. The opportunists represented by Kautsky distorted this " no longer valid " conclusion of Marx, in an attempt to oppose the proletarian revolution and proletarian dictatorship, that is, to oppose the revolutionary armed forces and armed revolution which are indispensable to the liberation of the proletariat. The reply Lenin gave to Kautsky was as follows:

> The revolutionary dictatorship of the proletariat is violence against the bourgeoisie; and the necessity for such violence is *particularly* created, as Marx and Engels have repeatedly explained in detail, by the existence of *militarism and bureaucracy*. But it is precisely these institutions that were non-existent in England and America in the seventies of the nineteenth century, when Marx made his observations (they *do* exist in England and in America *now*). ("Proletarian Revolution and the Renegade Kautsky," *Selected Works, International Publishers*, New York, Vol. VII, p. 125.)

It can thus be seen that the proletariat is compelled to resort to the means of armed revolution. Marxists have always wanted to follow the peaceful way in the transition to socialism. As long as the peaceful way is there to adopt, Marxist-Leninists will never give it up. But it is precisely this way that the bourgeosie seeks to block when it possesses a powerful, militaristic and bureaucratic machine of oppression.

The above quotation was written by Lenin in November 1918. How do things stand now? Is it that Lenin's words were historically valid, but are no longer so under present conditions, as the modern revisionists allege? Everybody can see that with hardly any exception the capitalist countries, particularly the few imperialist powers headed by the United States, are trying hard to strengthen their militaristic and bureaucratic machine of oppression, and especially their military machine.

The Declaration of the Moscow Meeting of the Representatives of the Communist and Workers' Parties of the Socialist Countries of November 1957, states:

> Leninism teaches, and experience confirms, that the ruling classes never relinquish power voluntarily. In this case the bitterness and forms of the class struggle will depend not so much on the proletariat as on the resistance put up by the reactionary circles to the will of the overwhelming majority of the people, on these circles using force at one or another stage of the struggle for socialism.

This is a new summing up of the experience of the struggle of the international proletariat in the few decades since Lenin's death.

The question is not whether the proletariat is willing to carry out a peaceful transformation; it is rather whether the bourgeoisie will accept such a peaceful transformation. This is the only possible way in which followers of Lenin can approach this question.

So contrary to the modern revisionists who seek to paralyse the revolutionary will of the people by empty talk about peaceful transition, Marxist-Leninists hold that the question of possible peaceful transition to socialism can be raised only in the light of the specific conditions in each country at a particular time. The proletariat must never allow itself to one-sidedly and groundlessly base its thinking, policy and its whole work on the calculation that the bourgeoisie is willing to accept peaceful transformation. It must, at the same time, prepare for alternatives: one for the peaceful development of the revolution and the other for the non-peaceful development of the revolution. Whether the transition will be carried out through armed uprising or by peaceful means is a question that is fundamentally separate from that of peaceful co-existence between the socialist and capitalist countries; it is an internal affair of each country, one to be determined only by the relation of classes in that country in a given period, a matter to be decided only by the Communists of that country themselves.

V

After the October Revolution in 1919, Lenin discussed the historical lessons to be drawn from the Second International. He said that the growth of the proletarian movement during the period of the Second International " was in breadth, at the cost of a temporary fall in the revolutionary level, a temporary increase in the strength of opportunism, which in the end led to the disgraceful collapse of this International." (" Third International and Its Place in History," *Selected Works*, F.L.P.H., Moscow, 1952, Vol. II, part 2, p. 199.)

What is opportunism? According to Lenin, " Opportunism consists in sacrificing fundamental interests in order to gain temporary, partial benefits." (" Speech at Conference of Activists of the Moscow Party Organization," *Collected Works*, 4th Russ. ed., Vol. XXXI, p. 412.)

And what does the fall in the revolutionary level mean? It means that the opportunists seek to lead the masses to focus their attention on their day-to-day, temporary and partial interests only, and forget their long-term, fundamental and overall interests.

Marxist-Leninists hold that the question of parliamentary struggle should be considered in the light of long-term, fundamental and overall interests.

Lenin told us about the limitations of parliamentary struggle, but he also warned communists against narrow-minded, sectarian errors. In his well-known work *Left-wing Communism, an Infantile Disorder*, Lenin elucidated the experience of the Russian revolution, showing under what conditions a boycott of parliament is correct and under what other conditions it is incorrect. Lenin held that every proletarian party should make use of every possible opportunity to participate in necessary parliamentary struggles. It was fundamentally wrong and would only harm the cause of the revolutionary proletariat for a Communist Party member to engage only in empty talk about the revolution, while being unwilling to work perseveringly and painstakingly, and shunning necessary parliamentary struggles.

Lenin then criticized the mistakes of the communists in some European countries in refusing to participate in parliament. He said:

> The childishness of those who " repudiate " participation in parliament consists precisely in the fact that they think it possible to " solve " the difficult problem of combating bourgeois-democratic influences *within* the working-class movement by such " simple," " easy," supposedly revolutionary methods, when in reality they are only running away from their own shadow, only closing their eyes to difficulties and only trying to brush them aside with mere words. (*Selected Works*, F.L.P.H., Moscow, 1952, Vol. II, part 2, p. 443.)

Why is it necessary to engage in parliamentary struggle? According to Lenin, it is for the purpose of combating bourgeois influences within the ranks of the working-class movement, or, as he pointed out elsewhere:

> Precisely for the purpose of educating the backward strata of its own

class, precisely for the purpose of awakening and enlightening the under-developed, downtrodden, ignorant, rural *masses*. (*Selected Works*, F.L.P.H., Moscow, 1952, Vol. II, part 2, p. 383.)

In other words, it is to enhance the political and ideological level of the masses, to co-ordinate parliamentary struggle with revolutionary struggle, and not to lower our political and ideological standards and divorce parliamentary struggle from the revolutionary struggle.

Identify with the masses but no lowering of revolutionary standards—this is a fundamental principle which Lenin taught us to firmly adhere to in our proletarian struggle.

We should take part in parliamentary struggles, but have no illusions about the bourgeois parliamentary system. Why? Because so long as the militarist-bureaucrat state machine of the bourgeoisie remains intact, parliament is nothing but an adornment for the bourgeois dictatorship even if the working-class party commands a majority in parliament or becomes the biggest party in it. Moreover, so long as such a state machine remains intact, the bourgeoisie is fully able at any time, in accordance with the needs of its own interests, either to dissolve parliament when necessary, or to use various open and underhanded tricks to turn a working-class party which is the biggest party in parliament into a minority, or to reduce its seats in parliament, even when it has polled more votes in an election. It is, therefore, difficult to imagine that changes will take place in a bourgeois dictatorship itself as the result of votes in parliament and it is just as difficult to imagine that the proletariat can adopt measures in parliament for a peaceful transition to socialism just because it has won a certain number of votes in parliament. A series of experiences in the capitalist countries long ago proved this point fully and the experiences in various European and Asian countries after the Second World War provide additional proof of it.

Lenin said: "The proletariat cannot be victorious unless it wins over to its side the majority of the population. But to limit or condition this to the gathering of a majority of votes at elections while the bourgeoisie remains dominant is the most utter stupidity or simply swindling the workers." ("Elections to the Constituent Assembly and the Dictatorship of the Proletariat," *Collected Works*, 4th Russ. ed., Vol. XXX, p. 243.) Modern revisionists hold that these words of Lenin are out of date. But living realities bear witness to the fact that these words of Lenin are still the best medicine, though bitter tasting, for proletarian revolutionaries in any country.

Lowering revolutionary standards means lowering the theoretical standards of Marxism-Leninism. It means lowering political struggles to the level of economic ones and restricting revolutionary struggles to within the limits of parliamentary struggles. It means bartering away principles for temporary benefits.

At the beginning of the 20th century Lenin in *What Is to Be Done?* drew attention to the question that "the spread of Marxism was accompanied by a certain lowering of theoretical standards." Lenin cited Marx's opinion contained in a letter on "The Gotha Programme" that we may enter into agreements to attain the practical aims of the movement, but we must never trade in principles and make "concessions" in theory. Afterwards, Lenin wrote the following words which by now are well known to almost all Communists:

Without a revolutionary theory there can be no revolutionary movement. This cannot be insisted upon too strongly at a time when the fashionable preaching of opportunism is combined with absorption in the narrowest forms of practical activity." (" What Is to Be Done? " *Selected Works*, International Publishers, New York, Vol. II, p. 47.)

What an important revelation this is to revolutionary Marxists! It was precisely under the guidance of this thought—that the Bolshevik Party headed by the great Lenin must firmly uphold revolutionary Marxist theory —that the entire revolutionary movement in Russia gained victory in October 1917.

The Chinese Communist Party also gained experience in regard to the above-mentioned question on two occasions. The first was during the 1927 revolutionary period. At that time Chen Tu-hsiu's opportunism as shown over the policy towards the Communist Party's united front with the Kuomintang was a departure from the principles and stand which a Communist Party should uphold. He advocated that the Communist Party should in principle be reduced to the level of the Kuomintang. The result was defeat for the revolution. The second occasion was during the period of the War of Resistance to Japanese Aggression. The Central Committee of the Chinese Communist Party firmly upheld the Marxist-Leninist stand, exposed the differences in principle between the Communist Party and the Kuomintang in their attitudes towards the conduct of the war against Japan, and held that the Communist Party must never make concessions in principle on such attitudes. But the right opportunists represented by Wang Ming repeated the mistakes made by Chen Tu-hsiu ten years earlier and wanted to reduce the Communist Party in principle to the level of the Kuomintang. Therefore, our entire Party carried out a great debate with the right opportunists throughout the Party. Comrade Mao Tse-tung said:

> . . . If the Communists forget this point of principle, they will not be able to guide the Anti-Japanese War correctly, they will be powerless to overcome the Kuomintang's one-sidedness, and they will lower themselves to a stand which is against their principles and reduce the Communist Party to the level of the Kuomintang. They will then commit a crime against the sacred cause of the national revolutionary war and the defence of the motherland. (" After the Fall of Shanghai and Taiyuan," *Selected Works*, Lawrence & Wishart, London, Vol. II, pp. 105–106.)

It was precisely because the Central Committee of our Party refused to make the slightest concessions on question of principle, and because it adopted a policy of both unity and struggle in our Party's united front with the Kuomintang, that we were able to consolidate and expand the Party's positions in the political and economic fields, consolidate and expand the national revolutionary united front and, consequently, strengthen and expand the forces of the people in the War of Resistance to Japanese Aggression. It also enabled us to smash the large-scale attacks launched by the Chiang Kai-shek reactionaries after the conclusion of the War of Resistance to Japanese Aggression and win nation-wide victory in the great people's revolution.

Judging by the experience of the Chinese revolution, mistakes of right deviation are likely to occur in our Party when the proletariat enters into political co-operation with the bourgeoisie, whereas mistakes of " left " deviation are likely to occur in our Party when these two classes break away from each other politically. In the course of leading the Chinese revolution, our Party has waged struggles against " left " adventurism on many occasions. The " left " adventurists were unable to take a Marxist-Leninist viewpoint on the correct handling of the complex class relations in China ; they failed to understand how to adopt different correct policies towards different classes at different historical periods, but only followed the erroneous policy of struggle without unity. Had this mistake of " left " adventurism not been overcome, it would have been impossible for the Chinese revolution to advance to victory.

In line with Lenin's viewpoint the proletariat in any country, if it wants to gain victory in the revolution, must have a genuinely Marxist-Leninist party which is skilled at integrating the universal truths of Marxism-Leninism with concrete revolutionary practice in its own country, correctly determining whom the revolution should be directed against at different periods, settling the question of organizing the main force and its allies and the question of whom it should rely on and unite with. The revolutionary proletarian party must rely closely on the masses of its own class and on the semi-proletariat in the rural areas, namely, the broad masses of poor peasants and establish the worker-peasant alliance led by the proletariat. Only then is it possible, on the basis of this alliance, to unite with all the social forces that can be united with and so establish the united front of the working people with all the non-working people that can be united with in accordance with specific conditions in the different countries at different periods. If it fails to do so, the proletariat will not be able to achieve its purpose of gaining victory in the revolution at different periods.

The modern revisionists and certain representatives of the bourgeoisie try to make people believe that it is possible to achieve socialism without a revolutionary party of the proletariat and without the series of correct policies of the revolutionary party of the proletariat mentioned above. This is sheer nonsense and pure deception. The *Communist Manifesto* by Marx and Engels pointed out that there were different kinds of " socialism," there was petty-bourgeois " socialism," bourgeois " socialism," feudal " socialism," etc. Now, as a result of the victory of Marxism-Leninism and the decay of the capitalist system, more and more of the mass of the people in various countries are aspiring to socialism and a more motley variety of so-called " socialisms " have emerged from among the exploiting classes in certain countries. Just as Engels said, these so-called " socialists " also " wanted to eliminate social abuses through their various universal panaceas and all kinds of patchwork, without hurting capital and profit in the least," they " stood outside the labour movement and looked for support rather to the ' educated ' classes." (" Preface to the German Edition of the Manifesto of the Communist Party," *Selected Works of Marx and Engels*, F.L.P.H., Moscow, 1958, Vol. I, p. 31.) They only put up the signboard of " socialism " but actually practise capitalism. In these circumstances it is extremely important to adhere firmly to the revolutionary principles of Marxism-Leninism and to wage an irreconcilable struggle against any tendency to lower the revolutionary standards, especially against revisionism and right opportunism.

In regard to the question of safeguarding world peace at the present time there are also certain people who declare that ideological disputes are no longer necessary, or that there is no longer any difference in principle between communists and social democrats. This is tantamount to lowering the ideological and political standards of communists to those of the bourgeoisie and social democrats. Those who make such statements have been influenced by modern revisionism and have departed from the stand of Marxism-Leninism.

The struggle for peace and the struggle for socialism are two different kinds of struggle. It is a mistake not to make a proper distinction between these two kinds of struggle. The social composition of those taking part in the peace movement is, of course, more complex; it also includes bourgeois pacifists. We communists stand right in the forefront in defending world peace, right in the forefront in opposing imperialist wars, in advocating peaceful co-existence and opposing nuclear weapons. In this movement we shall work together with many complex social groups and enter into necessary agreements for the attainment of peace. But at the same time we must uphold the principles of the working-class party and not lower our political and ideological standards and reduce ourselves to the level of the bourgeois pacifists in our struggle for peace. It is here that the question of alliance and criticism arises.

" Peace " in the mouths of modern revisionists is intended to whitewash the war preparations of the imperialists, to play again the tune of " ultra imperialism " of the old opportunists, which was long since refuted by Lenin, and to distort our communist policy concerning peaceful co-existence of countries with two different systems into elimination of the people's revolution in various countries. It was that old revisionist Bernstein who made this shameful and notorious statement: The movement is everything, the final aim is nothing. The modern revisionists have a similar statement: The peace movement is everything, the aim is nothing. Therefore, the " peace " they talk about is in practice limited to the " peace " which may be acceptable to the imperialists under certain historical conditions. It attempts to lower the revolutionary standards of the peoples of various countries and destroy their revolutionary will.

We communists are struggling in defence of world peace, for the realization of the policy of peaceful co-existence. At the same time we support the revolutionary wars of the oppressed nations against imperialism. We support the revolutionary wars of the oppressed people for their own liberation and social progress because all these revolutionary wars are just wars. Naturally, we must continue to explain to the masses Lenin's thesis concerning the capitalist-imperialist system as the source of modern war; we must continue to explain to the masses the Marxist-Leninist thesis on the replacement of capitalist imperialism by socialism and communism as the final goal of our struggle. We must not hide our principles before the masses.

VI

We are living in a great new epoch in which the collapse of the imperialist system is being further accelerated, the victory of the people throughout the world and their awakening are constantly advancing.

The peoples of the various countries are now in a much more fortunate situation than ever before. In the forty-odd years since the October Revolution, one-third of all mankind have freed themselves from oppression by capitalist imperialism and founded a number of socialist states where a life of lasting internal peace has really been established. They are exerting their influence on the future of all mankind and will greatly speed the day when universal, lasting peace will reign throughout the world.

Marching in the forefront of all the socialist countries and of the whole socialist camp is the great Soviet Union, the first socialist state created by the workers and peasants led by Lenin and their Communist Party. Lenin's ideals have been realized in the Soviet Union, socialism has long since been built and now, under the leadership of the Central Committee of the Communist Party of the Soviet Union and the Soviet Government headed by Comrade Khrushchev, a great period of the extensive building of communism is already beginning. The valiant and enormously talented Soviet workers, peasants and intellectuals have brought about a great, new labour upsurge in their struggle for the grand goal of building communism.

We, the Chinese Communists and the Chinese people, cheer every new achievement of the Soviet Union, the native land of Leninism.

The Chinese Communist Party, integrating the universal truths of Marxism-Leninism with the concrete practice of the Chinese revolution, has led the people of the entire country in winning great victories in the people's revolution, marching along the broad common road of socialist revolution and socialist construction charted by Lenin, carrying the socialist revolution to full completion and it has already begun to win great victories on the various fronts of socialist construction. The Central Committee of the Chinese Communist Party creatively set down for the Chinese people, in accordance with Lenin's principles and in the light of conditions in China, the correct principles of the general line for building socialism, the big leap forward and the people's communes, whch have inspired the initiative and revolutionary spirit of the masses throughout the country and are thus day after day bringing about new changes in the face of our country.

Under our common banner of Leninism, the socialist countries in Eastern Europe and the other socialist countries in Asia have also attained progress by leaps and bounds in socialist construction.

Leninism is an ever victorious banner. For the working people throughout the world, holding firm this great banner means taking hold of truth and opening up for themselves a road of continuous victory.

Lenin will always live in our hearts. And when modern revisionists endeavour to smear Leninism, the great banner of the international proletariat, our task is to defend Leninism.

All of us remember what Lenin wrote in his famous work *The State and Revolution* about what happened to the teachings of revolutionary thinkers and leaders in the past struggles of various oppressed classes for liberation. Lenin wrote that after the death of these revolutionary thinkers and leaders distortions ensued, " emasculating the essence of the revolutionary teaching, blunting its revolutionary edge and vulgarizing it." Lenin continued,

> At the present time, the bourgeoisie and the opportunists within the working-class movement concur in this " doctoring " of Marxism. They omit, obliterate and distort the revolutionary side of this teaching, its revolutionary soul. They push to the foreground and extol what is or seems acceptable to the bourgeoisie. (" The State and Revolution," *Selected Works*, F.L.P.H., Moscow, 1952, Vol. II, part 1, p. 202.)

Just so, at the present time we are again confronted by certain representatives of U.S. imperialism who once again assuming the pious mien of preachers, even declare that Marx was " a great thinker of the nineteenth century " and even acknowledge that what Marx predicted in the nineteenth century about the days of capitalism being numbered, " is well-grounded " and " correct "; but, these preachers continue, after the advent of the twentieth century, and especially in recent decades, Marxism has become incorrect, because capitalism has become a thing of the past and has ceased to exist, at least in the United States. After hearing such nonsense from these imperialist preachers, we cannot but feel that the modern revisionists are talking the same language as they do. But the modern revisionists do not stop at distorting the teachings of Marx, they go further to distort the teachings of Lenin, the great continuer of Marxism who carried Marxism forward.

The Declaration of the Moscow Meeting pointed out that "the main danger at present is revisionism, or, in other words, right-wing opportunism." Some say that this judgment of the Moscow Meeting no longer holds good under today's conditions. We hold this to be wrong. It makes the people overlook the importance of the struggle against the main danger—revisionism, and is very harmful to the revolutionary cause of the proletariat. Just as from the beginning of the seventies of the nineteenth century there was a period of "peaceful" development of capitalism during which the old revisionism of Bernstein was born, so under the present circumstances when the imperialists are compelled to accept peaceful co-existence and when there is a kind of "internal peace" in many capitalist countries, revisionist trends find it easy to grow and spread. Therefore, we must always maintain a high degree of vigilance against this main danger in the working-class movement.

As pupils of Lenin and as Leninists, we must utterly smash all attempts of the modern revisionists to distort and carve up the teaching of Lenin.

Leninism is the complete and integrated revolutionary teaching of the proletariat, it is a complete and integrated revolutionary world outlook which, following Marx and Engels, continues to express the thinking of the proletariat. This complete and integrated revolutionary teaching and revolutionary outlook must not be distorted or carved up. We hold the view that the attempts of the modern revisionists to distort and carve up Leninism are nothing but a manifestation of the last ditch struggle of the imperialists facing their doom. In face of continuous victories in building communism in the Soviet Union, in face of continuous victories in building socialism in the socialist countries, in face of constant strengthening of the unity of the socialist camp headed by the Soviet Union and of the steadfast and valiant struggles being waged by the increasingly awakened peoples of the world seeking to free themselves from the shackles of capitalist imperialism, the revisionist endeavours of Tito and his ilk are completely futile.

Long live great Leninism!

[*Red Flag*, No. 8, 1960. (Translated in *Peking Review*, No. 17, 1960.)]

"Forward Along the Path of the Great Lenin"

U.S. imperialism holds nothing but venom for the peace efforts of the socialist camp headed by the Soviet Union. It openly proclaims a policy of hostility to the People's Republic of China, and brazenly attacks the just stand of the Chinese people in safeguarding world peace and opposing imperialist war. The Chinese people have made a timely exposure of the fact that the U.S. Government headed by Eisenhower is, since the Camp David talks between Comrade Khrushchev and Eisenhower last September, still continuing to actively carry out arms expansion and war preparations and enlarging its aggression. U.S. imperialist spokesmen spread the slander that the Chinese people do not seem enthusiastic about relaxing the international situation. But this monstrous lie is really too brazen for words. Since the U.S. Government and Eisenhower himself are in actual fact engaged in arms expansion, war preparations and enlarging aggression, and this runs counter to the demand for easing the international situation, how would it help the international situation if this should be concealed or even whitewashed, prettified and extolled? On the contrary, that would only make the tension-makers all the more reckless and unbridled.

Facts speak louder than eloquence. Just have a look at the following brief summary of the words and deeds of the U.S. Government and Eisenhower against peace since the Camp David talks last September:

On October 16, 1959, U.S. Assistant Secretary of State Andrew H. Berding said in a speech that the United States could not accept peaceful co-existence because it would mean accepting the status quo of the socialist camp.

On October 21, the U.S. railroaded an illegal resolution on the so-called " Tibet question " through the United Nations General Assembly interfering in China's internal affairs and slandering the putting down by the Chinese Government of the rebellion of a reactionary group of serf-owners in the Tibet region.

On October 22, the U.S. State Department issued a statement on the third anniversary of the counter-revolutionary revolt in Hungary, slandering the Hungarian and Soviet Governments and "honouring" the counter-revolutionary elements who launched the revolt. . . .

The facts listed here are, of course, far from exhaustive, and are limited to data issued openly by the U.S. Government and American publications. Nevertheless, we should like to ask: Are these still not facts? Are these still not the principal facts of present U.S. policy? Can it be said that all this has been concocted by the Chinese Communists? Can it be said that these are only insignificant, trifling survivals of former times in U.S. policy? Naturally, the facts do not bear this out. The fact is, even after the Camp David talks and even on the eve of the East-West summit conference, we see no change at all in substance in U.S. imperialist war policy, in the policy carried out by the U.S. Government and by Eisenhower personally. U.S. imperialism is not only doing its utmost to expand its aggressive military strength, but is also impatiently fostering the militarist forces of West Germany and Japan and turning these countries into hotbeds of new war Let it be clearly understood that all this is affecting the fate of all mankind. It is absolutely necessary to oppose militarism in West Germany and Japan, and militarism fostered by the United States in other countries. But now it is, first of all, the war policy of U.S. imperialism that plays the decisive role in all this. Departing from this point is departing from the heart and essence of the matter. If the peace-loving people of the world do not concentrate their strength on continuously and resolutely exposing this war policy of the U.S. authorities and waging a serious struggle against it, the result will inevitably be a grievous calamity.

What right have the Chinese people, standing in the foremost ranks of the struggle for peace together with the peoples of the Soviet Union and the other socialist countries, to maintain silence on all these facts? What right have we to let Americans do, say and know about all these things, and not let the peoples of China and other countries know about them? Can it be bad for peace, can it aggravate tension, if we explain the true state of affairs to the Chinese and world public, or can concealing the truth help peace and help relax tension? Can it be that, according to the logic of the U.S. imperialists, that is how peace is to be " preserved "? Or is this the " peace in freedom " referred to by Eisenhower and his ilk?

The U.S. imperialists who actively plan for new war do indeed hope that we will conceal the true state of affairs; hope that we will abandon the standpoints of Marxism-Leninism; hope that we will believe the nature of imperialism can change or even that it has already changed; hope that in the struggle to safeguard world peace we, just like the bourgeois pacifists, will not mobilize and rely on the broadest masses of people who are against imperialism, against imperialist war, and against imperialist aggression; hope that we will exaggerate as much as possible the peace gestures which the imperialist aggressive forces are compelled to make and put the masses off their guard or exaggerate the might of the imperialist aggressive forces in war, and so throw the masses of the people into a panic. In short, the plotters of new war hope that we, like them, will not really want peace and will not want real peace, so that they can suddenly force war on the peoples, just as they did in the First and Second World Wars. . . .

[*People's Daily*, editorial, April 22. From text in *Peking Review*, No. 17, 1960.]

THE SOVIET REPLY

The Soviet reply to " Long Live Leninism! " and, presumably, to Chinese representations to Moscow during the preceding months was given by Otto Kuusinen, a member of the CPSU Presidium who had been prominent in the international Communist movement during Comintern days. In his speech at the Lenin anniversary meeting at Moscow's Sports Palace on April 22, Kuusinen made the first public allegation that those who opposed the CPSU's " creative development " of Leninism with respect to peace, war and peaceful co-existence were adopting a " dogmatic position." He reasserted the conclusions of the CPSU's Twentieth and Twenty-first Congresses, reaffirming the import- ance of the " powerful factors " making for peace.

These factors still did not include the national liberation movement; the statement that " imperialism *has* been weakened by the collapse of the colonial system " (emphasis added) would seem to refer to countries like India which had already achieved independence rather than to rebel movements like the Algerian FLN. The importance of Kuusinen's failure to include the national liberation movement here is underlined by the way in which he refers to it later in his speech. He states that even though the imperialists may achieve temporary successes, they can never defeat the anti-colonialist struggle. His attitude seems to be that the Communist *bloc* does not need to concern itself too much with the national liberation movement because it will take care of itself.

At this point it may be convenient to discuss the importance of the national liberation movement in the Sino-Soviet dispute. The opposing positions of Moscow and Peking first came to the surface during the Middle Eastern crisis after the Iraqi revolution in the summer of 1958. Chinese propaganda indicated that if Mao had been in Khrushchev's shoes he would have moved troops into Iraq to guard against the danger of a counter-coup that the American move into the Lebanon must have made the Communists think possible. Khrushchev, however, was fully aware that any such action on his part might well lead to a Russo-American clash on the ground with a high probability of a nuclear war ensuing. This risk he could not take and instead he called for a summit conference. However, Chinese representations at this time were clearly very strong for Khrushchev felt compelled to fly secretly to Peking and attempt to co-ordinate Sino-Soviet views. As the prospect of American intervention in Iraq soon faded, he was able, in effect, to abandon his demands for a summit conference.[10]

From the development of that crisis, Khrushchev probably drew two conclusions: (1) that any Soviet involvement with the national liberation movement would certainly worsen East-West relations and carry with it the risk of a Russo-American clash; and (2) that involvement was unnecessary since the national liberation movement would succeed anyway.

It was doubtless such conclusions that caused Khrushchev to handle the FLN very gingerly whereas the Chinese soon officially recognised the movement as the Algerian Government. The Chinese position was that by encouraging such movements the West was weakened more considerably and more quickly. They were prepared, it seemed, to risk world war if that was what the policy involved. Khrushchev was not—hence the consistent Soviet underplaying of the importance of the national liberation movement in the " fight for peace."

In his speech, Kuusinen again made the distinction between " thick-skulled opponents of peace " and " sober-minded statesmen " among whom he presumably included Eisenhower. Even more important, he rejected the Chinese attempt to minimise the significance of the invention of nuclear weapons with the theoretical argument that man, not technique, determined the fate of mankind. Kuusinen, referring to Lenin, suggested that weapons could indeed have a decisive influence on the likelihood of war.

Finally, we must note that Khrushchev took this opportunity also to

10 Khrushchev had originally called for a " summit " within the framework of the Security Council; after his visit to China he called instead for a " summit " outside the UN, ostensibly so that he would not have to deal with Nationalist China. While the Chinese might well have resented Khrushchev's readiness to sit down with the Nationalists, the point to note is that the Soviet change of attitude made a " summit " far less likely, as Khrushchev must have known it would. The diminishing fervour of Soviet demands for a " summit " can also be taken as a sign of Soviet intentions.

justify Soviet aid to neutralist countries. His argument seems to be that this policy increases confidence in the Soviet Union on the part of the neutralists—and that this confidence will bring the neutralists' diplomacy more into line with Soviet diplomacy as well as increase the pro-Communist forces within the neutralist countries. (" The confidence . . . will have its bearing on the further strengthening of peace and social progress.")

Kuusinen's Speech at the Lenin Anniversary Meeting

The great teaching of Lenin—Leninism—is the Marxism of our epoch. As a loyal Marxist, Lenin further developed the teaching of Marx in conformity with changing historical conditions. Allegiance to the teaching of Lenin demands of our party that it, too, taking present-day conditions into consideration, should further develop Marxism-Leninism, always applying its fundamental provisions in a creative way.

Such allegiance to Leninism is demanded of our party by its responsibility to the working class, to the entire Soviet people, and also to the international communist movement. For our party, thanks to its wealth of experience, has set an example of struggle for socialism, an example of the successful accomplishment of the most complicated tasks of building socialism and communism.

Our party proves its allegiance to Marxism-Leninism by its deeds and by its policy. Lenin wrote that politics is a science and an art. Emphasising the unbreakable ties between the theory and practice of Marxism, he pointed out: " Marxism lies in the ability to determine what policy should be pursued in the given conditions."

What is the specific policy our party is pursuing in the present conditions? How does it fulfil Lenin's behests? What is the aim of the policy of the party and the Soviet government?

It seems to me appropriate at this meeting, devoted to the memory of our unforgettable teacher, to try to throw light on these questions. . . .

Policy of Friendship with the Peoples Who Have Cast Off the Yoke of Colonialism

Comrades, true to the behests of Lenin, our party has always backed the liberation struggle of the oppressed peoples and their right of self-determination. When, after the Second World War, Lenin's forecasts concerning the liberation of the peoples of the East came true on a gigantic scale and when dozens of new independent states were founded on the wreckage of colonial empires, our Soviet state was confronted with new and important tasks.

The peoples who for centuries had borne on their shoulders the yoke of colonial exploitation now needed, not only moral and political support, but also economic assistance in developing their national economy.

As for our relations with countries of the socialist camp—the Chinese People's Republic, the Korean Democratic People's Republic and the Democratic Republic of Viet Nam, the Mongolian People's Republic—those relations have been determined from the very outset by the principles of socialist internationalism. Close alliance and fraternal friendship, mutual assistance and co-operation in building socialism and communism—that is the foundation of these relations.

But we have a broader understanding of the international duty of our socialist country—we understand it as rendering assistance to those liberated peoples, too, who are not included in the world system of socialism. All-round, disinterested assistance in strengthening their political and economic independence is the foundation of our relations with the newly-created states. Of course, we do not impose assistance on anyone, but we help when we are asked to do so.

The road to the consolidation of the independence of the liberated countries is the road of developing their national economy, promoting the advance of their culture and improving the living standards of the people. Industrialisation is of tremedous importance for such countries. It is precisely here that the young states need support most of all. Understanding this, the Soviet Union is accordingly developing its economic co-operation with them.

The supplying of up-to-date industrial equipment, assistance in building large enterprises, in prospecting for and exploiting natural resources, in training national cadres of specialists—these are the principal aspects of Soviet assistance. The Soviet Union's participation in building the gigantic steel works at Bhilai, in the construction of the Aswan High Dam, a steel works in Indonesia and dozens of other industrial projects accords with the vital interests of the peoples of the East.

One often hears the claim that the western countries also have a strong desire to help the peoples who have cast off the yoke of imperialism. Generally speaking, it would only be fair if the colonial powers were to return to the owners even a part of the wealth they have appropriated. However, this is not the case here.

The western powers, as in the past, still continue to hinder the independent development and industrialisation of underdeveloped countries. The nature of their " assistance " is determined, as we know, by their military plans, which are obviously a danger to the independence of the recipient countries.

It is said in the West that a struggle for the countries of the East has now developed and it is alleged that the Soviet Union is seeking to tie them to its chariot. But does the Soviet Union seek to draw the eastern countries into war *blocs* like S.E.A.T.O., Cento, etc.? Does the Soviet Union attach political strings to its assistance? Does it demand the right to intervene in domestic affairs? No, that is precisely how the western powers act.

Thus, the liberated peoples have two aspects of assistance, two policies before their eyes. Is it surprising that those peoples increasingly dissociate themselves from the policy of the West? They understand that assistance is a good thing if it is disinterested, and friendship is firm if it is sincere.

The consolidation of independence and the successful development of the liberated countries brings closer the time when they will achieve their legitimate right, on an equal footing with other states, to take part in the solution of all major international problems. This was rightly pointed out by Nikita Khruschev when he addressed the Indonesian Parliament.

The confidence which Soviet policy enjoys in the countries of the East is a matter of great importance. It will have its bearing on the further strengthening of peace and social progress. We owe this confidence to the fact that underlying Soviet policy are the principles worked out by the great Lenin.

Struggle for Peace and Peaceful Co-existence

Lenin's behest to our party and all communists was: Fight tirelessly for peace and work to end wars. He said: "The ending of wars, peace between the nations, the stopping of plunder and violence—it is precisely this that is our ideal." (*Works, vol. 21, p. 264, Russian edition.*)

In the West at the present time there are glib propagandists who allege that Lenin was against the peaceful co-existence of the two systems. These falsifiers pick out individual quotations from Lenin's works, or even fragments of quotations dating back to the time of the Civil War and military intervention. But it was the world bourgeoisie itself which, by its intervention, added to the struggle of the Russian proletariat the character of an international clash. It is clear that at the time of the intervention the question of the peaceful co-existence of socialism and capitalism was relegated to the background.

But then, these gentlemen carefully pass over in silence Lenin's entire policy during the first years of Soviet power, his line towards establishing businesslike co-operation with capitalist states, the line which was clearly expressed in Lenin's directives to the Soviet delegates to the first international conferences, for instance in Genoa in 1922.

In that period Lenin developed his idea of the peaceful economic competition of the two systems. To use Lenin's expression, this is the " rivalry of two methods, two formations, two kinds of economy—communist and capitalist."

"We shall prove," Lenin continues, "that we are the stronger."

" Of course, the task is a difficult one, but we have said and continue to say that socialism has the power of example. Force is of avail in relation to those who want to restore their power. But that exhausts the value of force, and after that only influence and example are of avail. We must demonstrate the importance of communism practically, by example." (*Works, vol. 31, p. 426, Russian edition.*)

The principles of peaceful co-existence, both then and now, form the basis of the whole of Soviet foreign policy. During recent years our party has been creatively developing this idea of Lenin's. Of decisive importance in this connection was the conclusion drawn by the 20th and 21st Party Congresses about there being no fatal inevitability of wars in our epoch, about the possibility of preventing wars. By drawing this conclusion, the party has made a new contribution to Marxism.

Of course, aggressiveness is inherent in the nature of imperialism. But one should not dogmatically consider only this aspect of the matter. The fact that powerful forces counteracting war have appeared should not be ignored. One should not overlook the fact that the time has gone, never to return, when imperialism had the whole world under its sway. Capitalism can no longer make the whole world follow its laws. A powerful world system of socialism is already in existence; imperialism has been weakened by the collapse of the colonial system; a vast " zone of peace " has come into being; the forces of peace and democracy are now more closely united and better organised even in the imperialist countries themselves. Don't these powerful factors have practical significance in settling the question of peace and war?

Therefore, in order to be loyal to Marxism-Leninism today it is not sufficient to repeat the old truth that imperialism is aggressive. The task is to make full use of the new factors operating for peace in order to save humanity from the catastrophe of another war. A dogmatic position is a backward position. The correctness of our foreign policy of creative Leninism, making use of all the factors for peace, is proved best of all by the success of this policy. The persistent struggle of the Soviet government, abounding in initiative, has yielded fruit. A tangible easing of international tension has been achieved. The cold war is gradually receding. Business-like relations, including cultural contacts, are being established between states with different social systems. The most burning questions of the international situation have, at long last, become the subject of serious East-West negotiations.

The active struggle of the Soviet government for peace and peaceful co-existence gives our foreign policy an innovative and creative character. This is demonstrated in the frankness with which the most burning issues of world politics are approached, in the combination of firmness, based on principle, with readiness to agree to sensible compromises. This is a truly democratic foreign policy which is being carried out openly before the eyes of the peoples.

In its practical activity the Soviet government is widely cultivating personal contacts with both statesmen and public leaders of bourgeois countries.

The numerous state visits to foreign countries by the head of the Soviet government, Nikita Krushchev, have, as we know, acquired tremendous importance. They have been of historic significance in improving the Soviet Union's relations with other states and in improving the international situation as a whole. These visits have confirmed once again that the Leninist policy of the peaceful co-existence of states with different social systems, pursued by our party and the Soviet government headed by Comrade Nikita Khrushchev, is the only correct and viable policy. All of us remember full well the moving demonstrations of friendship by masses of people during Nikita Krushchev's stay in the United States of America, India, Indonesia, Burma, Afghanistan and France on his great mission of goodwill.

The change in the balance of forces on the international scene, the growing might of the socialist camp and the obviously disastrous con-sequences of another war—all this leads to a split in the ruling circles of the imperialist states. There appear, alongside the thick-skulled opponents of peace, sober-minded statesmen who realise that a war with the use of weapons of mass destruction would be madness.

Such are the dialectics of military-engineering progress: A new weapon created for war begins to exert an influence in favour of peace. For Marxists there is nothing mysterious in this. The classics of Marxism have never denied the fact that new types of weapons can not only bring about a radical change in the art of war but can also influence politics.

For instance, Engels wrote about this in *Anti-Dühring*. And Nadezhda Krupskaya tells us that Lenin foresaw that " the time will come when war will become so destructive as to be impossible."

Lenin told Krupskaya about his talk with an engineer who had said that an invention was then in the making which would render it possible to destroy a large army from a distance. It would make a war impossible.

119

" Ilyich," Krupskaya writes, " talked about it with great enthusiasm. It was obvious that he passionately wanted war to become impossible."

The division among influential circles of the bourgeoisie is undoubtedly of importance for a successful struggle for peace. Already Lenin pointed out that it is by no means a matter of indifference to us, of course, whether we are dealing with those representatives of the bourgeois camp who are inclining towards a military solution of a problem, or with representatives of the bourgeois camp who are inclining towards pacifism, even of the most feeble kind and one which, from the communist viewpoint, will not stand up to the slightest criticism (*Works, vol. 33, p. 236, Russian edition*).

The achievements in the struggle for peace provide a favourable basis for further advancement. The main task now is to achieve disarmament. It is very significant that it was precisely our socialist state, which possesses a generally recognised superiority in the military sphere, which put forward the proposal for general and complete disarmament and made this task the pivotal point of world politics.

Just imagine, comrades, a situation in which all these famous sputniks, luniks and our other celestial envoys had been made in the United States, and our country had been sending up rockets which persisted in coming down. Who would believe, then, that the American authorities would make a proposal for total disarmament? I don't believe it, nor do you. Obviously, no one would believe it! The diehard imperialists, naturally, are doing everything in their power to prevent the Soviet proposals from being accepted.

They represent the interests of those groups of monopoly capital which by no means want to give up the fat profits they get from the policy of militarisation and of the arms race. They are the leaders of the Pentagon— the American Defence Department, which continues to call recklessly for new military gambles. They are the " big shots " of N.A.T.O., who see the only meaning of their activity in turning the peaceful fields of Europe into the theatre of another destructive war. They are the militarist revenge-seeking forces who are rearing their heads in Western Germany and Japan. Yes, the cause of peace has many enemies. The danger they represent should not be underestimated. They are real vultures. Therefore the vigilance of the peoples must not be weakened.

A vigorous struggle against the bellicose imperialists is necessary in order to frustrate their aggressive plans. There is only one way to bring the aggressors to their senses; they must be convinced beyond a shadow of doubt that if they dare to unleash another war, then a formidable force will rise against them everywhere, at the front and in the rear, and will not let them escape just retribution. This force must constantly re-remind the enemies of peace: *Memento mori*!—Remember that you must die! If you start a war, you will be hanged as the Nazi ringleaders were hanged in Nuremberg! Crimes against humanity will not go unpunished. Thus, the foreign policy line of our party, inspired by the ideas of the great Lenin, has stood the test of life and has earned wide international recognition. Being fully in keeping with the interests of the Soviet people, this line, at the same time, is imbued with consistent internationalism. It expresses the vital interests of the international working-class movement and of all progressive mankind.

The Century of the Implementation of Lenin's Great Ideas

Comrades, our century—the 20th century—is a most important stage in the history of mankind. This is the century which is witnessing the implementation of Lenin's great ideas. . . .

Naturally, Marxism-Leninism does not indulge in the futile forecasting of events. But that does not mean that it is altogether impossible to foresee the historical prospects of the second half of our century. We see clearly the basic tendencies of historical progress.

Firstly, it is perfectly clear that the Soviet people will carry out ever more successfully the great programme of communist construction. The majestic goals of the Seven-Year Plan will be achieved ahead of schedule. . . .

Secondly, the other countries of the socialist camp will go forward side by side with the Soviet Union. . . .

Thirdly, judging by everything, the second half of our century will bring complete liberation to the oppressed and dependent nations.

Following its major victories in the middle of the century, the Asian national liberation movement is continuing to achieve ever new successes in the struggle for the complete political and economic independence of the nations. Most of the Arab nations have already thrown off the imperialist yoke in Africa. The Negro nations of Africa have also awakened and set up their first independent states. All the African colonies have proclaimed the militant slogan of their peoples' movements: "Independence during the lifetime of our generation!" Africa has now voiced an even stronger demand: "Immediate independence!" A national movement is also surging in the formally free, but actually dependent, countries of Latin America.

Of course, we must not ignore the fact that the imperialists will do everything possible to smother the national liberation movement of the oppressed nations. But haven't they done everything possible in that direction before? Nevertheless, the movement has continued to grow and has become an invincible force.

The imperialists have achieved temporary successes only in countries where they have obtained the support of corrupt local reactionaries. But can the freedom-loving peoples be expected to tolerate for long the rule of traitors to the nation—accomplices of foreign imperialists? Of course not. The days of colonialism are numbered.

Fourthly, the great struggle of the peoples to safeguard lasting peace throughout the world will grow year by year.

Already today, the correlation of forces is such that the peoples and states advocating the cause of universal peace are the stronger. However, the most rabid imperialists threaten to unleash a terrible nuclear war, which would subject the peoples to brutal mass annihilation. That is why the peoples cannot give up the struggle for reliable guarantees of peace. This is a question of life and death for them.

All the factors which have made for the successes recently achieved in the effort to safeguard peace and lessen international tension, will continue to assume ever greater scope. Lenin's idea of struggling to deliver mankind from the terrible nightmare of war has gripped the minds of vast bodies of people in all continents and has therefore become a major force which will continue to grow and will, finally, make any military aggression impossible.

It is from this that the tempestuous streams of historical progress are now flowing, in spite of all kinds of obstacles.

As for the prospects of the countries of modern capitalism, it will be best if we leave the concrete evaluation of those prospects within the competence of the Marxist-Leninists of each particular capitalist country. After all, they know the situation in their countries better than anyone else. Here we can only state the general directions in which the basic laws of social development, laid down by the science of historical materialism, are operating and will continue to operate in those countries. . . .

[From text published in *Soviet News* (London: Soviet Embassy) No. 4255.]

4. Battle Joined

The U-2 incident and the resultant disruption of the summit conference at the beginning of May gave a great fillip to the Chinese campaign against Khrushchev's policies. On the one hand, the Chinese now had the kind of evidence they needed to clinch their case that nothing had altered since Camp David; furthermore Eisenhower's assumption of responsibility for the incident meant that the Soviet distinction between advocates of the cold war and sober-minded Western statesmen, and Khrushchev's personal guarantee of Eisenhower's sincerity had been completely undermined.[11] From the practical point of view, the worsening of East-West relations meant that the Chinese need not fear any Soviet deal with America in the near future.

However, Khrushchev's speech in East Berlin immediately after the summit fiasco made it clear that he was not abandoning his policies. One of the consequences was that the Chinese chose to try and thrash out the dispute at an international forum, the general council session of the Communist-dominated World Federation of Trade Unions (WFTU) which met in Peking from June 5 to 9. The reason for raising the issue at this particular meeting must have been that the Chinese hoped to convert workers' leaders to their advocacy of revolutionary struggle.

A principal Chinese delegate, Liu Chang-sheng, Vice-Chairman of the WFTU and Vice-Chairman of the All-China Federation of Trade Unions, emphasised the distinction between *world* war and other wars which Mao had possibly failed to make in 1957,[12] accepting the possibility of preventing world war, but asserting that wars of national liberation were inevitable and just and should be supported. He rejected as an " unrealistic illusion " the idea that America would agree to general disarmament, though he admitted the possibility of a nuclear test ban. He suggested that the kind of " peace diplomacy " favoured by Khrushchev was less important for the Communist cause than revolutionary struggle.

Behind the scenes at the council session, however, the Chinese were not allowed to have things their way as the reports of Italian delegates showed.

The Chinese Attack at the WFTU Meeting

Liu Chang-sheng said that the question of war and peace is one with which everyone is concerned and he wished to express some views on this question. With regard to the question of war and peace, he said, we have

---

[11] See above p. 61.   [12] See above p. 80.

always stood for safeguarding world peace, for peaceful co-existence between countries with different social systems, for the relaxation of international tension and for disarmament. But on this question there still exist some problems involving basic principles that must be clarified, otherwise people would go astray in regard to the question of safeguarding peace.

As to what attitude we should adopt towards war, Liu Chang-sheng said, we must first of all make a distinction as to its nature. A war between imperialist countries in a scramble for colonies is an unjust war. An imperialist war to suppress the colonial people and the people at home and to commit aggression against other countries is also an unjust war. On the other hand, a revolutionary war waged by the colonial peoples and by the oppressed peoples of the imperialist countries for their own liberation is a just war. Since the imperialists use armed force to suppress the oppressed peoples and nations, the oppressed peoples and nations cannot but take up arms themselves. We must stand for and uphold just revolutionary wars, and oppose and stop unjust wars. It is wrong to talk indiscriminately about whether or not war should be supported or whether or not it should be opposed, without making a specific analysis of its nature.

Liu Chang-sheng continued: The question of whether or not war can be averted, in our opinion, refers mainly to a world war. As to whether a world war can be averted, it should be pointed out that, on the one hand, under the conditions of the steady growth of the forces of the socialist countries, the forces of the liberation movements in the colonies and semi-colonies and the forces of the revolutionary movements and peace movements of the peoples of the countries the world over, and the united struggle of these forces, there exists the possibility of stopping the imperialists from unleashing a new world war. But, on the other hand, so long as there is imperialism, the root cause of war remains, the breeding ground of war remains, and the war maniacs remain, and that is why there still exists the danger of imperialism launching a new world war. If we only talk about the possibility of stopping the imperialists from launching a world war, but not about the danger of imperialism launching a world war, and are not on the alert against the military adventures of the war maniacs, we will only lull ourselves and the people. This will only help imperialism in its arms expansion and war preparations and, once it launches a war, the peoples of various countries, taken off guard, may be thrown into a state of alarm and confusion and even suffer unduly heavy losses. It is entirely wrong to believe that war can be eliminated for ever while imperialism still exists. The spreading of such illusions about imperialism among the peoples of all lands will lead to evil consequences of a serious nature and, in fact, we can already see such consequences at present.

Liu Chang-sheng said that as to imperialist wars of suppression against colonies and semi-colonies, national liberation wars of the colonial and semi-colonial peoples against imperialism, wars of suppression against the people by the exploiting classes and people's revolutionary wars in the capitalist countries, wars of such nature have always existed in history, and have never stopped in the capitalist world since the Second World War. The wars in Indo-China, in Algeria, over the issue of the Suez Canal and in Cuba are all such wars. In the future, as long as imperialism and the exploiting system are still in existence, such wars of different nature will still be unavoidable. The belief that wars of the above-mentioned types can be avoided is entirely wrong and contrary to fact. Such views will deprive the oppressed peoples of their fighting spirit and in the face of armed suppression by the enemy, prevent them from arming themselves to actively fight the enemy, who is armed to the teeth, and to liberate themselves. This will, in effect, keep the oppressed peoples for ever in the state of enslavement.

Liu Chang-sheng went on: We stand for peaceful co-existence between socialist and capitalist countries. Since World War II, we socialist countries have spared no effort in striving for peaceful co-existence and have unswervingly pursued various policies of peace, but the imperialist countries headed by the United States have all along clung to their cold war policy, persisted in arms expansion and war preparations and created tension. We should make it clear to the people that they should not be intimidated by the cold war waged by imperialism, that they should resolutely oppose its cold war policy, expose its ugly face and wage a head-on struggle against it. Only thus can the cold war be prevented from developing into a hot one.

Liu Chang-sheng further stated: We must take into full account the fact that because internal crises are worsening day by day in the imperialist countries and because they want to intensify their oppression and rule over the people at home and in the colonial countries, the imperialists will, for a long time to come, keep up their cold war policy, impose cold war on the people of the world and continue to maintain their massive military forces and the entire state machine. To safeguard world peace and oppose imperialism will, therefore, be a long-drawn-out struggle for the peoples of various countries.

Liu Chang-sheng said: We support the disarmament proposals put forward by the Soviet Union. It is of course inconceivable that imperialism will accept proposals for general and complete disarmament. The purpose of putting forward such proposals is to arouse the people throughout the world to unite and oppose the imperialist scheme for arms drive and war preparations, to unmask the aggressive and bellicose nature of imperialism before the peoples of the world in order to isolate the imperialist bloc headed by the United States to the greatest extent, so that they will not dare unleash a war lightly. But there are people who believe that such proposals can be realised when imperialism still exists and that the " danger of war can be eliminated " by relying on such proposals. This is an unrealistic illusion. As to the view that after disarmament, imperialism would use the funds earmarked for war purposes for " the welfare of the labouring masses " and for " assisting underdeveloped countries " and that this would " bring general progress to people as a whole without exception " —this is downright whitewashing and embellishing imperialism, and indeed this is helping imperialism headed by the United States to dupe the people throughout the world.

Liu Chang-sheng pointed out that only when socialist revolution is victorious throughout the world can there be a world free from war, a world without arms. Such a world is inconceivable while imperialism still exists. This is not a question of whether we want it or not; the question is that the imperialists will never lay down their arms of their own accord. They will not lay down their arms because they want to suppress the people of their own countries; they will not lay down their arms because they want to suppress the colonies; they will not lay down their arms because they want to carry on expansion and aggression against other countries. History has confirmed and will continue to confirm this.

We hold that the utmost efforts must be made to reach agreement on the banning of nuclear weapons and to prevent the outbreak of a nuclear war in the world, Liu Chang-sheng said. The mastery of nuclear weapons by the Soviet Union has now deprived U.S. imperialism of its atomic monopoly. The Soviet Union and the other socialist countries should continue to develop their lead in the sphere of atomic energy and at the same time the people throughout the world should wage a more extensive struggle against imperialism and against nuclear weapons. Only in these circumstances can such agreement be reached. But even if agreement is reached, imperialism can still tear it to pieces. And even if in their own interests the imperialists dare not unleash a large-scale nuclear war, they still can wage war with the so-called conventional weapons. Therefore, in all circumstances people throughout the world should maintain sharp vigilance against imperialism and should not adopt a naïve attitude towards U.S. and other imperialism.

Liu Chang-sheng pointed out: To win world peace, the struggle of the world's peoples and diplomatic negotiations carried out by the socialist countries should go hand in hand. It should not be supposed that since diplomatic negotiations are needed, the struggle of the peoples can thus be dispensed with. On the contrary, diplomatic negotiations must be backed up by the united struggle of the world's peoples. To win world peace, we should mainly rely on the struggles waged by the peoples of various countries. We should increase the might of the socialist countries, continuously develop the strength of the liberation movements in colonial and dependent countries, continuously expand the revolutionary forces of the people within the imperialist countries, and continuously expose the imperialist bloc headed by the United States and the modern revisionists who are in the service of imperialism. At the same time, we should make full use of our tactics and exploit the contradictions between the imperialist countries and the various monopoly capital groups within the imperialist countries. We hold that as long as we make the above-mentioned efforts and rally all the forces that can be united around the anti-imperialist struggle to form a broad united front, we can certainly defeat the bellicose forces of imperialism and win the great victory in the defence of world peace.

[Liu Chang-sheng at the WFTU Council session, June 8, 1960. *Peking Review* No. 24, 1960.]

INFANTILE LEFTISM

Meanwhile the Russians had evidently been preparing to take action against the propagation of the " dogmatist " views of the Chinese in the international Communist movement. On June 10, an article appeared in *Sovyetskaya Rossiya* to mark the fortieth anniversary of Lenin's *Left-wing Communism—An Infantile Disorder* by D. Shevlyagin. It warned against two leftist mistakes—contempt for making compromises with the bourgeoisie in working towards Communism and condemnation of the policy of peaceful co-existence. In fact the Chinese had never taken up such positions publicly, for obvious reasons; but certainly the views

126

they had officially committed themselves to indicated that that might well be how they felt. Another commemorative article, this time in *Pravda*, seemed designed to reactivate the commune controversy of 1958. The author asserted that the desire to build socialism " on the basis of imperialist handouts " (Tito) or " attempts to skip entire historic stages " (Mao) served only " the enemies of the working class. . . ." This article also hinted at Peking's indignation at Khrushchev's American visit.

" Fighting Weapon of Communist Parties "

The Communist movement develops and strengthens together with the growth of the working-class movement, and it is constantly its task in the first instance to solve more and more new, general and specific problems of the class struggle of the proletariat and its allies. It happens that not only groups of Communists but also the leadership of individual parties are not up to the task of solving such problems, lose their Marxist-Leninist orientation and fall into leftism or right-wing opportunism. An example of this are the revisionist standpoints of the present leadership of the Union of Communists of Yugoslavia.

In the years of the Second World War the Communist Party organisations of Spain, which had correctly begun an armed partisan movement, in their leftish manner continued this struggle for a long time even after the end of the war, although the international situation and internal conditions had already changed substantially. This error was exposed by the Party and corrected in 1948-49, and the activities of Communists were directed towards work in the masses, including the various fascist organisations, which has already yielded many positive results. . . .

The book *Left-wing Communism—An Infantile Disorder* takes on particularly great significance in connection with the fact that in recent years a number of Communist Parties have appeared in countries which have recently achieved or are still striving for national independence. The Communist movement in these countries is living through its " childhood days," and for it this Leninist work will be of very great help.

By the end of the Second World War and in the post-war years, as a result of the rapid upsurge of the working-class and national-liberation movement, many Communist Parties, which thanks to their war-time service had grown into large parties, emerged from prolonged underground activities. Certain parties, however, revealed inability to orientate themselves in the new conditions. The methods and means of long years of underground struggle against the class enemy were no longer suitable. In the new conditions it was necessary to establish relations with the broader masses of the working people, to seek allies in the middle strata of town and village and also, according to circumstances and the latest tasks of the struggle, temporary agreements with specific strata of the national bourgeoisie, particularly in countries where the main task was liberation from imperialist and colonial oppression. In this connection it is useful to recall Lenin's instruction to the effect that " history in general, and the history of revolutions in particular, is always richer in content, more diverse, more multiform, more vital, more ' cunning,' than is imagined by the best Parties, the most conscious vanguards of the most advanced classes."

Lenin understood the good intentions of those comrades who were in a hurry to race ahead, to accelerate the oncoming of socialist revolution, but he most resolutely warned against the danger of degenerating into Blanquists, who, not wishing to remain "at intermediary stations and not wanting to compromise," as Engels expressed it, could not be considered Communists.

Lenin's doctrine about the conditions of compromise, which are worked out in great detail in *Left-wing Communism—An Infantile Disorder*, are the basis of the struggle of Communists for the achievement of unity of action of the working class with all strata of the petty and middle bourgeoisie in the joint struggle against the arbitrary rule of the monopolies and their alliance with the imperialist forces of other countries. This struggle does not do away with or replace the tasks of carrying out socialist revolution, but, on the contrary, is directly bound up with this task, since it unleashes the initiative of the masses, brings them into political, general democratic and gradually also into revolutionary struggle for the victory of a socialist revolution.

Lenin's doctrine about "compromises" acquires great importance in modern conditions, when Communists, especially in countries where many tasks of bourgeois-democratic revolution and the achievement of national independence still have to be solved, must be able to conclude alliances not only with the peasantry but also with certain strata of the national bourgeoisie in the interests of struggle against foreign oppression. Here, as Lenin pointed out, "one has only to take a small step beyond this—apparently a step in the same direction—and the truth becomes error." The point is not to be at the tail-end of events, but also not to rush ahead, not to put forward precocious slogans of socialist transformations where conditions are not ripe for this. . . .

For the purpose of drawing into active political life the broadest masses of the working people and the middle strata of town and village and bringing up among them allies of the working class in the struggle for transition to socialism, Communist Parties have worked out programmes of struggle for democratic reforms (the agrarian question, nationalisation of monopolies, the establishment of a democratic government, proclamation of the policy of not joining aggressive *blocs* and the policy of peaceful co-existence). However, on the path of the implementation of these programmes, even Communist Parties which are powerful and hardened in class struggle are running up against survivals of leftism, the erroneous views of comrades whom V. I. Lenin ironically described as "terrible revolutionaries." Essentially the standpoint of these comrades is nothing more than the passive awaiting of that certain "hour" when, in their view, the general collapse of capitalism must automatically occur. . . .

Present-day leftism in the Communist movement is also manifested in both concealed and overt resistance to the Communist parties' policy of establishing collaboration with working people in the ranks of the social-democratic, Catholic and various other bourgeois-radical parties and organisations. The policy of achieving peaceful co-existence, of cessation of the arms race and establishment of peace and friendship between peoples of capitalist and socialist countries is interpreted by present-day leftists as a "deviation" from Marxism-Leninism, and they take the slightest aggravation of the international situation as proof of their sectarian views. Although from the outside they seem "terribly revolutionary," they do harm to the cause of rallying the working class to the struggle against the aggressive designs of the imperialists, for the cessation of the "cold war" and the strengthening of peace throughout the world. . . .

[D. Shevlyagin in *Sovyetskaya Rossiya,* June 10, 1960.]

"The Ideological Weapon of Communism"

The search for a separate path to socialism for each country individually, the desire to build socialism on the basis of imperialist handouts or attempts to skip entire historic stages serve only the enemies of the working class interested in weakening socialism. Unmasking the false, anti-marxist views of the advocates of "separate paths," Comrade N. S. Khrushchev said: "If such a point of view is adopted, it may well result in so many ' paths ' that people will get lost, as in a forest, and will not know how to reach their goal. In life there is only a single, Leninist path toward the construction of socialism and Communism, a path tested by historical experience, the path of the great October socialist revolution. . . ."

V. I. Lenin demonstrated the unsoundness and harm of the slogans of the leftists who rejected the idea of Communist compromises with other parties and groups. He said that the leftists, though considering themselves Marxists, had forgotten the fundamental truths of Marxism. Vladimir Ilyich (Lenin) recalled a statement by F. Engels who once criticised the Blanquists (followers of Blanqui, an early French Communist) for wanting to skip through all intermediate stages directly to Communism without taking account of the new historical development, and remarked that if power will be in their hands, "Communism will be introduced" the day after tomorrow. Engels described as childish naivety the Blanquists' attempts to put forward their own impatience as a theoretically convincing argument.

"Naive and utterly inexperienced people," Lenin wrote, "imagine that it is sufficient to admit the permissibility of compromises in general in order to obliterate the dividing line between opportunism, against which we wage and must wage an uncompromising struggle, and revolutionary Marxism or Communism.

"But if such people do not yet know that all dividing lines in nature and in society are mutable and, to a certain extent, conditional, they cannot be assisted in any way other than by a long process of training, education, enlightenment, political and everyday experience."

Creatively developing Marxist-Leninist theory under the new conditions and generalising the great experience of socialist construction in our country in full accordance with the principles of social development, the Twenty-first Party Congress laid out a well-grounded, full-fledged programme for the transition from socialism to Communism. That programme is the concrete embodiment of the general line of the Communist Party in the present stage.

Characterising the process of transition from socialism to Communism, Comrade N. S. Khrushchev told the Twenty-first Party Congress:

"We must not hurry and hastily introduce what has not yet ripened. That would lead to distortions and compromise our cause. But neither must we rest on our laurels because such a course would lead to stagnancy."

The course of social development is objective. We consider erroneous and incorrect the statements of leftists in the international Communist movement to the effect that since we have taken power into our hands we can at once introduce Communism, by-passing certain historical stages in its development.

Such statements contradict Leninism. Lenin taught us that to try to anticipate the result of a fully developed, fully consolidated and established, fully unfolded and matured Communism amounts to the same thing as to try to teach higher mathematics to a four-year-old child.

The left-sectarian sentiments and tendencies against which Lenin's book was directed find their expression in some places even in our time. Some persons mistakenly consider the course of the achievement of peaceful co-existence of our countries with different political systems, the struggle to halt the arms race and to strengthen peace and friendship among peoples and the talks between leaders of socialist and capitalist countries as some kind of deviation from the positions of Marxism-Leninism.

Lenin taught that the very complex struggle for Communism and the struggle against the international bourgeoisie could not be waged while renouncing in advance agreements and compromises on specific questions with possible, even if temporary, unstable allies for the exploitation, even though temporarily, of contradictory interests among the enemies.

While pursuing in some cases compromises in the name of the interests of development of the revolutionary movement, Communists never depart from positions of principle. "In questions of ideology," said Comrade N. S. Khrushchev, "we have firmly stood and will continue to stand firmly, like a rock, on the principles of Marxism-Leninism." . . .

V. I. Lenin's book teaches us a truly creative approach to the solution of practical problems arising in life and serves as a mighty ideological weapon of the Communist and workers' parties in the struggle for peace and socialism.

Forty years have passed since the publication of the first edition of *Left-Wing Communism—An Infantile Disorder*. During that time the conditions of the class struggle have changed repeatedly both in the international and in the national arenas. A world-wide socialist system has been formed and the balance of power has changed radically in favour of socialism.

There has been a great increase in the number of Communist and workers' parties. While there were a total of forty Communist parties and groups when V. I. Lenin wrote his book, there are now Communist and workers' parties in eighty-six countries, with a total membership of more than 36,000,000 people.

In recent years the Communist parties have demonstrated great creative enthusiasm. True to Lenin's behests, the fraternal parties are creatively developing Marxist-Leninist theory and applying it to present-day conditions. A great contribution to the cause of the further development of Marxism-Leninism was made by our Party at its Twentieth and Twenty-first Congresses.

Of major importance for international affairs have been the decisions of the congresses on such questions of principle as the peaceful co-existence and competition of the two systems, the possibility of preventing war in this era, the form of transition of various countries of socialism, and the ways of strengthening the world socialist system. The congress decisions were approved unanimously by all Communist and workers' parties.

All the basic statements in Lenin's book are still vital at the present time. They are directed against rightist opportunists, present-day revisionists and leftist doctrinaires. The Communist parties, while regarding revisionism as their greater danger, draw attention at the same time to sectarianism and dogmatism, which can also represent great danger at certain stages of development of a given party. . . .

The great force and vitality of Leninism lie in the successful and multi-faceted activity of the Communist and workers' parties. They are reflected in the fiery speeches of Communists for peace, against war, for general disarmament, and for peaceful co-existence of countries with different social-political systems. The vitality and force of Leninism are also evident in the upsurge of the workers' movement in the capitalist countries and in the successes of the national liberation movement of peoples against colonialism. The vitality and force of Leninism are also found in the great achievements of the Soviet people in successfully building Communism and in the victories of all socialist countries that unswervingly pursue Lenin's course.

[N. Matkovsky in *Pravda*, June 12, 1960.]

5. The Bucharest Conference

According to Indian Communist sources,[13] the Chinese did not expect the onslaught upon their views made by Khrushchev before all the leaders of the East European Communist parties, except Albania's Enver Hoxha, at the Rumanian party congress in Bucharest in June. Khrushchev dealt scornfully with those who " mechanically " repeated the words of Lenin decades after they had been formulated under very different historical conditions. As to the specific problem of accounting for the break-up of the summit conference and the disappearance of the Camp David spirit, Khrushchev still clung to the distinction between sober-minded Western statesmen (among whom he included de Gaulle and Macmillan) and the advocates of the cold war. Since he could no longer count Eisenhower among the former, he put his faith in the election of a more amenable American president at the end of the year.

Khrushchev laid great stress on the destructiveness of a nuclear war, omitting any claim that only imperialism would be wiped out in the event of such a catastrophe. He also cautioned that a local war could lead to a world nuclear conflict. He did not list the national liberation movement as a factor making war less likely.

The chief Chinese delegate to the Rumanian Congress, P'eng Chen, would not appear to be the kind of man to be cowed by Khrushchev's attack.[14] He took his stand firmly on the 1957 Declaration and called for Communist unity. According to Indian Communist sources, he said that the Chinese central committee would discuss and reply to the criticisms later on.[15] In any event, the communiqué issued after the discussions of the international situation merely reaffirmed support for the 1957 Declaration.

Khrushchev's Bucharest Speech

Comrades, questions of international relations, questions of war and peace, have always deeply concerned the mass of the people. That is natural. More than once in history the anti-national policy of the imperialists, their desire for a redivision of the world, for the seizure of new colonies, have subjected mankind to the horrors of devastating wars. But no matter how terrible wars have been in the past, if the imperialist circles should succeed in unleashing another world war, its calamities would be incomparably more terrible. For millions of people might burn in the

---

[13] Quoted in the *Hindustan Times* of New Delhi, November 14, 1960.
[14] A burly, self-confident looking man, P'eng is a senior member of the Chinese Politburo and ranks second to Teng Hsiao-p'ing in the Party secretariat.
[15] *Hindustan Times, loc. cit.*

conflagration of hydrogen explosions, and for some states a nuclear war would be literally a catastrophe. That is why the Marxist-Leninist parties, in all their activity, have always been consistent champions of a reasonable peace-loving policy, of the prevention of another world war. . . .

The Communists are realists; they are aware that in present conditions, when there are two world systems, it is imperative to build mutual relations between them in such a way as will preclude the possibility of war breaking out between states. Only madmen and maniacs can now call for another world war. As for people of sound mind—and they are in the majority even among the most deadly enemies of Communism—they cannot but be aware of the fatal consequences of another war.

It is common knowledge that the Soviet government and the governments of the other socialist countries have by their deeds, by their realistic policy, proved to all the peoples of the world their loyalty to the idea of peaceful co-existence between states. The proposals on general and complete disarmament and on the ending of nuclear weapon tests and the complete prohibition of those tests, the reduction in the armed forces of the socialist countries—I do not think there is any need to list here all the peaceable actions taken by our side—all this is concrete evidence of our desire to prevent war and really strengthen the cause of peace.

We made serious preparations for the Paris conference of the heads of government of the four powers. It will be recalled that the United States Administration, by its cynical provocations, torpedoed the conference before it had even begun. The name of the spy pilot Powers, though he is only a small poisonous bug in the service of the Pentagon brass, will go down covered with ignominy in the history of the United States, together with the names of those who sent him on that piratical flight.

The events in Paris were not accidental. These are the tactics of imperialism. The imperialists, headed by the aggressive circles of the United States of America, have been opposed and are now opposed to the policy of peaceful co-existence between states.

I remember a conversation with Mr. Dillon, the U.S. Under-Secretary of State, at Camp David.

Since it happened on a Sunday, the United States President flew off in a helicopter to pray to God and he told me that Mr. Dillon would like to have a talk with me on economic matters and questions of trade.

That worshipper there probably prayed to God for a safe flight for Powers. This, by the way, seems to indicate that the Lord does not serve the imperialists now. The President of the United States prayed to God for a safe flight for the spy plane, and we shot that plane down. Whom did God help? He sided, so to speak, with socialism. When I told Mr. Dillon during the conversation that it was necessary to create conditions for peaceful co-existence, he asked me the cynical question: " What does co-existence mean? I don't understand it."

You see what a cynical person Mr. Dillon is. Of course, he and his like would prefer to exist alone, without the socialist countries. However, that is no longer within their power.

The question might be asked: If the imperialists oppose peaceful co-existence, how did they come to agree to the meeting of the heads of government which was to have been held in Paris?

One must bear in mind that the attitude to the question of peaceful co-existence is not everywhere the same in the imperialist countries. During the conversations I had in Paris with President de Gaulle and Prime Minister Macmillan, it seemed to me that they showed a certain understanding of the necessity for peaceful co-existence and were even persuading me themselves that the policy of co-existence must be the guiding principle in the future relations between states with different social systems.

Not all representatives of the ruling circles of the United States of America have as yet learned to pronounce the words "peaceful co-existence," and some of them, like Dillon, claim that they don't understand the meaning of these words and refuse to carry through their policy in a spirit of peaceful co-existence.

Time, however, is the best teacher and it will also teach those diehards. Sooner or later they will realise that the alternative to peaceful co-existence is a bloody war. Let them make their choice. And victory will be on our side!

As for the American people, it must be expected that they will draw the appropriate conclusions and will produce leaders who understand the necessity for peaceful co-existence between states with different social systems.

It must also be borne in mind that the imperialist countries are not monolithic; they have their internal contradictions. On the one hand, there is the working class, the working peasantry and the working intelligentsia, and on the other, there are the monopolists, the capitalists who wax fat on the exploitation of the working class, of all the working people.

The peoples of those countries, especially the working class, the peasantry, the working intelligentsia, and even part of the bourgeoisie, do not want a war or are afraid of war. Some do not want it and others are afraid of it. The slogans of the struggle for peace, against war, are close to the hearts of the peoples. And under the pressure of these popular forces the governments of the imperialist states were driven to consent to a meeting between the heads of government. But they planned in advance to wreck that meeting and to blame it on the Soviet Union. The persons who wrecked the conference are now shedding crocodile tears. They are grieving as Judas did after he had betrayed Christ.

They crucified that conference and now they allege that the Soviet Union is to blame because it did not of its own free will get caught in the snares which were laid by the imperialist powers.

We are not living in the days when the legend of Christ was created; we are living in the twentieth century. Sober-minded representatives of the capitalist world now admit that it is impossible to halt the progress of socialism. And this robs some gentlemen of their common sense; they resort to steps which can be bluntly called provocative. They are getting nervous, they are raving. In such conditions even persons who don't want to unleash war might get unduly frightened, press the wrong button, and the consequences would be irrevocable.

That is why it is necessary to arouse the conscience of the peoples, enhance their vigilance, organise and strengthen the struggle against the aggressive policy of imperialism, against colonialism, and to support and help the peoples who are fighting to liberate themselves from imperialist, colonial oppression. It is necessary to assist those peoples who have already gained their political independence but are economically dependent and to enable them to grow stronger and firmly pursue a policy that is in keeping with the interests of peace. All this means that we must still more actively expose the evils of imperialism, its vices. In order to prevent war—including a local war, because a local war might grow into a world war—each people in their own country must bring pressure to bear on their government and force it to adhere to the principles of peaceful co-existence between states with different social sytems. . . .

Though the Paris conference was wrecked by the aggressive circles of the United States, this did not remove the urgent problems still awaiting solution. In order to establish normal relations between states and to preclude the possibility of another world war, we must solve the problem of general disarmament, destroy the means of waging war and disband the national armed forces, it goes without saying, under appropriate international control. We must eliminate the remnants of the Second World War, conclude a peace treaty with the two German states and solve the problem of West Berlin on this basis. . . .

What conclusion can be drawn from the collapse of the conference? If the United States government continues the policy proclaimed by Herter, if it continues overflights—this will, of course, have the most serious consequences for the cause of peace.

The statesmen now directing United States policy have shown their aggressiveness and irreconcilability. They are so much blinded by hatred for Communism that this does not let them understand correctly the prevailing conditions in the world. The present leaders of the United States are evidently unable to cultivate in the proper way relations between states with differing social systems.

It is not for us, it is for the American people to decide who will be the next President of the United States. But our state, our people, who want to live in peace and friendship with the American people, are naturally interested in the election of such a President and the formation of such a government that would understand and correct the mistakes made by the present government of the United States.

The Soviet Union and the United States are great world powers. History itself has assigned them such a place. Much depends on our two powers how the international situation will develop in the future—along the road of strengthening peace or along the road of straining relations.

The Soviet government has done everything for the further development of the relations which had slightly improved between our two countries. But the American leaders are doing everything so that the world reverts to the worst times of the cold war. And this is not being done accidentally; it is being done according to plan, as Secretary of State Herter and the President of the United States have virtually admitted. For they have confirmed that the spy plane was deliberately sent into the Soviet Union. Naturally, every government and every thoughtful statesman understands that the dispatch of a spy plane and intrusion into the air-space of another country cannot be conducive to the improvement of relations between states, cannot facilitate a solution of the problems which should have been discussed at a summit meeting.

What line must we pursue in these conditions? Should we accept this "challenge" and give up the efforts exerted by the peoples of our countries to secure a relaxation of international tension, the ending of the cold war and the normalisation of international relations? No, such a policy would be incorrect. Had we embarked upon this road, it would have meant that we had taken the cue from the imperialists, who wax rich on the cold war and arms race. This would have met their wishes. Consequently, they would have been, so to say, rewarded for their provocative actions. We cannot allow this to happen. By bringing down the U-2 we have not only brought down a spy and *agent provocateur*, but also the self-conceit of the American imperialists, of the Pentagon military.

All the peoples want peace, including the American nation. I did not doubt this before my visit to the United States and became even more convinced of this after I had been there. And if today some people are intoxicated by the torpedoing of the meeting, the lies, slander and the all-out efforts to stir up the cold war, this is a temporary circumstance which sooner or later will have to give way to a more healthy atmosphere.

What has happened is another convulsion of imperialism. Aggressive circles will continue their attempts to provoke us. This is why we, the representatives of the socialist world, the representatives of the working class, the representatives of the working peasantry, must bravely and resolutely rebuff the militarists and foil their aggressive designs. . . .

We do not intend to yield to provocations and to deviate from the general line of our foreign policy, which was laid down by the 20th C.P.S.U. Congress and approved in the Declaration of the Communist and Workers' Parties, adopted in 1957, during the celebrations of the 40th anniversary of the Great October Socialist Revolution.

This is a policy of co-existence, a policy of consolidating peace, easing international tension and doing away with the cold war.

The thesis that in our time war is not inevitable has a direct bearing on the policy of peaceful co-existence proclaimed at the 20th and 21st Congresses of our party. Lenin's propositions about imperialism remain in force and are still a lodestar for us in our theory and practice. But it should not be forgotten that Lenin's propositions on imperialism were advanced and developed tens of years ago, when the world did not know many things that are now decisive for historical development, for the entire international situation.

Some of Lenin's propositions on imperialism date back to the period when there was no Soviet Union, when the other socialist countries did not exist.

The powerful Soviet Union, with its enormous economic and military potential, is now growing and gaining in strength; the great socialist camp, which now numbers over 1,000 million people, is growing and gaining in strength; the organisation and political consciousness of the working class have grown, and even in the capitalist countries it is actively fighting for peace. Such factors are in operation now as, for instance, the broad movement of peace champions; the number of countries coming out for peace among nations is increasing. It should also be pointed out that imperialism no longer has such a rear to fall back upon as the colonial system which it had formerly.

Besides, comrades, one cannot mechanically repeat now on this question what Vladimir Ilyich Lenin said many decades ago on imperialism, and go on asserting that imperialist wars are inevitable until socialism triumphs throughout the world. We are now living in such a period when the forces of socialism are increasingly growing and becoming stronger, where ever-broader masses of the working people are rallying behind the banner of Marxism-Leninism.

History will possibly witness such a time when capitalism is preserved only in a small number of states, maybe states for instance, as small as a button on a coat. Well? And even in such conditions would one have to look up in a book what Vladimir Ilyich Lenin quite correctly said for his time, would one just have to repeat that wars are inevitable since capitalist countries exist?

Of course, the essence of capitalism, of imperialism, does not change even if it is represented by small countries. It is common knowledge that a wolf is just as bloodthirsty a beast of prey as a lion or a tiger, although he is much weaker. That is why man fears less to meet a wolf than a tiger or a lion. Of course, small beasts of prey can also bite, essentially they are the same but they have different possibilities, they are not so strong and it is easier to render them harmless.

Therefore one cannot ignore the specific situation, the changes in the correlation of forces in the world and repeat what the great Lenin said in quite different historical conditions. If Lenin could rise from his grave he would take such people, as one says, to task and would teach them how one must understand the essence of the matter.

We live in a time when we have neither Marx, nor Engels, nor Lenin with us. If we act like children who, studying the alphabet, compile words from letters, we shall not go very far. Marx, Engels and Lenin created their immortal works which will not fade away in centuries. They indicated to mankind the road to Communism. And we confidently follow this road. On the basis of the teaching of Marxism-Leninism we must think ourselves, profoundly study life, analyse the present situation and draw the conclusions which benefit the common cause of Communism.

One must not only be able to read but also correctly understand what one has read and apply it in the specific conditions of the time in which we live, taking into consideration the existing situation, and the real balance of forces. A political leader acting in this manner shows that he not only can read but can also creatively apply the revolutionary teaching. If he does not do this, he resembles a man about whom people say: " He looks into a book, but sees nothing!"

All this gives grounds for saying with confidence that under present conditions war is not inevitable.

He who fails to understand this does not believe in the strength and creative abilities of the working class, underestimates the power of the socialist camp, does not believe in the great force of attraction of socialism, which has demonstrated its superiority over capitalism with the utmost clarity.

Is the possibility of the imperialists unleashing war under present conditions ruled out? We have said several times and we repeat once again: No, it is not. But the imperialist countries cannot fail to take into account the power of the Soviet Union, the power of the socialist camp as a whole. Naturally, the imperialists do not want to trigger off war in order to perish in it. They would like to destroy the socialist countries. Therefore today even the stupid, frenzied representatives of the imperialist circles will think twice about our power before they start a military gamble.

Even the crazy Hitler, if he had believed that the war which he launched against the Soviet Union would end in the routing of his fascist hordes and in his hiding in a Berlin shelter in the fifth year of the war and shooting a bullet into his head, he would not have taken such a mad decision on war against our country. This is quite clear!

And if the imperialists do unleash a war, will our socialist camp be in a position to cut it short? Yes, it will. Let me cite an instance. When France, Britain and Israel attacked Egypt in 1956, our intervention put an end to this imperialist war which had been started by the aggressive forces to deprive Egypt of her independence. We helped the people of Egypt who were heroically fighting for the freedom of their country. . . .

The Soviet government addressed messages to Anthony Eden, Guy Mollet, and Ben-Gurion, warning them that there was a country which could deal a devastating blow unless aggression was stopped. And the war ended literally 22 hours later. Eden and Mollet—that so-called socialist leader, but actually a rabid imperialist colonialist—and Ben-Gurion, their errand boy, immediately had their tails between their legs.

Thus the Soviet Union and all the countries of the socialist camp fulfilled their duty and the war was ended. Was it not a demonstration of the strength of socialism? And this happened soon after the 20th Congress of our party proclaimed the thesis that under the present conditions war is not inevitable and that, in the event of it being unleashed, we have the possibility of thwarting the adventurist plans of the aggressors, to make the developments take the desired turn.

It is to be remembered that this happened in 1956. Now, the Soviet Union has created such powerful military facilities of which the imperialists have no full idea, in spite of all their espionage flights.

Or let us take another example. In 1957 we prevented Syria from being attacked by Turkey, which was incited to this adventure by the United States imperialists. And in 1958, after the revolution in Iraq, the Americans and British concentrated their forces and were preparing to attack Iraq. The American imperialists egged on Turkey, Iran and Pakistan to attack Iraq. The Americans were in such a hurry preparing for this attack that they even violated Austria's sovereignty by flying their troops stationed in Germany right over the territory of neutral Austria to Lebanon and Jordan. But in that case as well they had to stop short and did not dare to start aggression against Iraq in view of the resolute warning served by the Soviet Union and other socialist countries. They flew there, stayed for a while and flew away with nothing to show for their efforts. And the Iraq Republic continues to exist and grow in strength.

It should be emphasised that in the case of Syria, as in the case of Iraq, the point in question was to beat off the aggression which the United States —the strongest imperialist state—was preparing against those countries.

The American imperialists and their adventurist policy have discredited themselves to such an extent that they have come to be hated, not only by the peoples of the socialist countries, but also by the population of their allied states.

The bloody puppet Syngman Rhee has been thrown out of South Korea with ignominy. The former Turkish Premier, Menderes, the obedient executor of the will of the Americans, is now in prison.

Even on Taiwan, that American-occupied island, the United States Embassy was smashed up in spite of the brutal terror of Chiang Kai-shek, that American lackey. You know very well that millions of Japanese are coming out against the American invaders with contempt and hatred. To put the matter in a nutshell, in the countries from which the American imperialists are not as yet being kicked out the peoples' anger is welling up and the forces of protest are maturing. And it is common knowledge that if lightning strikes, a thunderbolt is bound to come too. . . .

The U.S.S.R. pursued a policy of peace even when it stood alone, facing the powerful camp of imperialist states. We are also pursuing this policy now when the forces of peace are undoubtedly superior to the forces of war and aggression.

This position of ours stems from our firm belief in the stability of the socialist system, in our system, and therefore don't worry about the future of socialism.

No world war is needed for the triumph of socialist ideas throughout the world. These ideas will get the upper hand in the peaceful competition between the countries of socialism and capitalism. . . .

[Speech to Rumanian Communist Party Congress in Bucharest on June 21. From text in *Soviet News* (London: Soviet Embassy), June 22, No. 4292, 1960.]

P'eng Chen's Reply

U.S. imperialism, the most vicious enemy of the people of the world, is now more isolated than ever. In trying to extricate itself from its plight, it has, in the past few years, taken great pains to play the trick of faking peace while actually preparing for war. It has worked in every way to use peace as a camouflage for its aggression and preparations for a new war. However, it only serves as a good teacher by negative example. Recently the crimes of the United States in intruding into the Soviet airspace and sabotaging the four-power conference of government heads have stripped U.S. imperialism and its head, Eisenhower, of all their disguises and bared the utterly ferocious features of U.S. imperialism. This has provided an instructive lesson to the people of the world. Imperialism is, after all, imperialism and its fine words can never be trusted. . . .

Comrades! The development of the international situation has fully testified to the correctness of the Declaration of the Moscow Meeting of the Communist and Workers' Parties of the Socialist Countries two and a half years ago. The Declaration pointed out on the one hand that " so long as imperialism exists there will always be soil for aggressive wars," that the aggressive circles of the United States are " the centre of world reaction " and " the sworn enemies of the people," and that " all the nations must display the utmost vigilance in regard to the war danger created by imperialism." On the other hand the Declaration pointed out that " the forces of peace have so grown that there is a real possibility of averting war." So long as there is unity among the socialist camp headed by the Soviet Union, the international working class and its vanguard, the peoples of Asia, Africa and Latin America struggling for their liberation, the peoples of various capitalist countries fighting against monopoly capital and all peace-loving countries and peoples in the world, it is possible to check war and safeguard peace. This is to say that the aggressive and predatory nature of imperialism will never change, that U.S. imperialism is the arch enemy of world peace, and that the peoples of the world must never entertain any unrealistic illusions about imperialism, especially U.S. imperialism. They must maintain a high degree of vigilance, carry on a persistent struggle against U.S. imperialism and its lackeys and maintain solidarity and mutual support in the struggle.

This is also to say that the forces of the masses of the people of various countries and their struggle are the decisive factor in checking war and defending world peace. War can be held at bay and world peace preserved only by continually strengthening the forces of the people in the countries of the socialist camp, the liberation movements of the Asian, African and Latin American peoples and the revolutionary struggle of the people in various capitalist countries and by relying on their alliance in the resolute struggle against U.S. imperialism and its lackeys so as to isolate U.S. imperialism to the greatest extent.

In the face of the powerful growth of the struggle waged by the people in the world against imperialism and its lackeys, our sacred duty as Communists is to strengthen the unity of our socialist camp and the international communist movement on the basis of the Moscow Declaration. At the same time we must unite all the international forces with whom it is possible to unite to form the broadest anti-imperialist united front with this great unity as its core. The unity of the socialist camp and the international communist movement is the most reliable guarantee for the cause of world peace, liberation of the working class and all the oppressed nations. Imperialism fears most this unity of ours and is trying by every means to disrupt it. Modern revisionists, represented by the Tito clique, exactly in keeping with the needs of imperialism, are doing their utmost to disrupt this great unity of ours, thus serving imperialism and especially U.S. imperialism. For the defence of the unity of the socialist camp and the international communist movement, we must carry the struggle against modern revisionism to the end. We must thoroughly expose them for the renegades they are, completely wipe out the ideological poison spread by them and utterly smash all their criminal sabotage activities. . . .

[Speech on June 22, 1960; *Peking Review*, No. 26, 1960.]

The Bucharest Communiqué

Representatives of the Communist and Workers' Parties of the socialist countries, attending the Third Congress of the Rumanian Workers' Party . . . decided to take advantage of their stay in Bucharest to exchange opinions on current problems of the present international situation, and the conclusions for the fraternal parties coming from them.

The participants in the conference noted unanimously that all international events and the developments of the countries of the world socialist system fully reaffirmed the correctness of the Marxist-Leninist theses of the Declaration and the Peace Manifesto adopted by the Communist and Workers' Parties in Moscow in November 1957.

The participants in the conference reaffirmed their allegiance to the principles of the Declaration and Peace Manifesto, which are the charter of the present-day Communist and workers' movement, a programme of its struggle for peace, democracy and socialism.

The representatives of the Communist and Workers' Parties of the socialist countries believe that all the conclusions of the Declaration and the Peace Manifesto—on peaceful co-existence between countries with different social systems, on the possibility of preventing wars in the present period, on the need for vigilance of the peoples with regard to the danger of war, since the existence of imperialism means there is a basis for wars of aggression—can be fully applied in the present situation, too.

"The Communist Parties," the Declaration emphasises, "regard the struggle for peace as their paramount task. Shoulder to shoulder with all peace-loving forces they will do their utmost to prevent war."

The Declaration also draws an important conclusion about the forms of the transition of countries from capitalism to socialism. "In the present conditions in a number of capitalist countries, the working class, headed by its vanguard, has the possibility . . . of breaking the resistance of reactionary forces and creating the necessary conditions for the peaceful accomplishment of the socialist revolution." All the same, it is also necessary to take into account the possibility of the working class gaining victory for the socialist revolution by non-peaceful means. . . .

Bucharest, June 24, 1960.

[From text in *Soviet News* (London: Soviet Embassy) No. 4296, June 28, 1960.]

6. Renewed Soviet Attacks

THERE were a number of indications during the new few months that the dispute continued.[16] The absence of Mikoyan from Moscow and of Teng Hsiao-p'ing and P'eng Chen from Peking in late summer was accompanied by reports that they were attempting to hammer out a compromise in south Russia. The Chinese, however, refrained from any further major assaults on the Soviet position, perhaps feeling that the U-2 incident, the collapse of the summit conference and the cancellation of Eisenhower's visit to Japan were sufficient vindication of their cause until the whole dispute could be thrashed out at some form of conference. But the Soviet press renewed its attacks on the Chinese, presumably after the matter had been discussed at the CPSU central committee session in mid-July.

Writing in *Pravda* on August 7, Yu Frantsev, a leading Soviet theoretician, conceded that the national liberation movement was an important force making for the preservation of peace, though he did not list it second in the Chinese manner. As if to extract a *quid pro quo* for this concession, Frantsev asserted that the Bucharest conference confirmed that all ruling Communist Parties supported the conclusions of the CPSU's *Twenty-first* Congress, a claim for which there was certainly no visible proof.

Frantsev also attempted to prove that Lenin had foreseen the kind of international situation now existing and would have analysed it in much the same way as Khrushchev himself. To earlier Chinese charges that over-optimistic talk about peace would dull the vigilance of the proletariat, Frantsev retorted that leftist views on peace and war sapped the morale of the proletariat and enabled the imperialists to accuse Communists of aggressiveness.

An article by S. Titarenko reproduced in a number of Soviet provincial papers on August 16 contained an implied threat that Soviet aid might be withheld if China did not fall into line. An article published in *Pravda Ukrainy* on August 30 compared the dogmatists to Trotskyists. A. Belyakov and F. Burlatsky, writing in *Kommunist* (No. 13, 1960) emphasised, as Khrushchev had done at Bucharest, that nuclear war would be a disaster for the " whole of humanity," clearly rejecting the comforting Maoist thesis that it would result only in the destruction of imperialism and " certainly not . . . the annihilation of mankind." [17] They asserted, too, that Soviet advocacy of peaceful co-existence did not imply advocacy of peace between classes within states—but at the same

---

[16] See above p. 25.
[17] See " Long Live Leninism!", p. 93.

142

time reaffirmed the possibility of " peaceful transition to socialism " under conditions of peaceful co-existence. This argument reinforced the earlier attack in a *Pravda* article by Academician E. Zhukov on dogmatists who allowed themselves to sneer at bourgeois nationalist revolutions in Africa and Asia.

" Problems of War and Peace in Present-day Conditions "

The Great October Revolution marked the beginning of a new historical epoch whose content is the transition from capitalism to socialism. Socialism has triumphed fully and definitively in our country: the Soviet people are successfully building a communist society. A world system of socialism has arisen and is growing stronger. No single phenomenon in the world can now be correctly understood unless one regards the world system of socialism as of paramount importance.

A third of mankind has cast off the yoke of capitalism, is creating a new type of society and has achieved gigantic successes in subduing the forces of nature and developing technology to an astounding extent. Millions of people have been freed from the yoke of colonialism. The question arises: In these conditions can the imperialists, as in the old days, arbitrarily drive the peoples into bloody slaughter? Will the bloody element of war rage over the globe as in the past?

An answer to this most important question was given by the Twentieth Congress of the CPSU, which on the basis of profound Marxist-Leninist analysis of the present day reached the conclusion that in our time there is no fatal inevitability of war. The transformation of socialism into a world system, the growth of the might of the Soviet Union, of all the countries of socialism, the growth of the consciousness and organisation of all the forces standing for peace in capitalist countries, the unprecedented development of the peace movement, the appearance of " peace zones " on the map of the world, the growth of the national-liberation movement—all this has radically altered the world situation. There are now no forces in the world that could halt the dynamic development of the world system on socialism.

The implementation of the economic plans of the USSR and of all the other socialist countries will introduce still greater changes into the international situation. When the USSR becomes the world's first industrial power, when the Chinese People's Republic becomes a mighty industrial power and all the socialist countries together turn out more than half the world's industrial production, then the influence of the socialist countries on the strengthening of the peace-loving forces will grow still further. The present-day Peace Partisan Movement, which has embraced all countries and all peoples, represents a great social force, whose activity in the struggle against war will grow more and more. The idea of the impermissibility of war will take still deeper root in the minds of the peoples. Relying on the might of the camp of socialism, the peace-loving peoples will then be able to compel the militant circles of imperialism to abandon their plans for a new world war. These ideas form the basis of the conclusions of the Twenty-first Congress of the CPSU to the effect that even before the complete victory of socialism on the earth and while capitalism continues to exist in part of the world, a real possibility will arise of excluding world war from the life of society.

The proposition that it is possible in our time to prevent war and preserve peace was developed in the Declaration and Peace Manifesto adopted at the Conference of Fraternal Parties in Moscow in the autumn of 1957. The principles of the Declaration and Peace Manifesto, which constitute the charter of the present day communist and working-class movement, have triumphed in the struggle against revisionism, dogmatism and sectarianism, which are contrary to the creative character of Marxism-Leninism and impede the mobilisation of all the forces of the socialist camp, of the revolutionary working-class and liberation movement, to the struggle for peace and socialism against imperialism.

The Conference of Representatives of the Communist and Workers' Parties of the Socialist Countries held in Bucharest in June 1960 confirmed with fresh force that the Communist and Workers' Parties unanimously support the conclusions of the Twentieth and Twenty-first Congresses of the CPSU, which have exerted a tremendous influence on the international situation in the interests of peace and socialism, and support the principles of the Declaration and Peace Manifesto. The Conference in Bucharest demonstrated the fidelity of the international communist movement to Marxism-Leninism, the readiness of all the fraternal parties to continue to strengthen the solidarity of the world socialist camp and to preserve like the apple of their eye the unity of the international communist movement. The July Plenum of the Central Committee of the CPSU adopted unanimously a resolution on the results of the Conference of Representatives of Communist and Workers' Parties in Bucharest. The Plenum fully and entirely approved the political line and activity of the CPSU Delegation headed by Comrade N. S. Khrushchev at this Conference and the communiqué of the Conference. The Central Committee of the CPSU confirmed its fidelity to the principles of the Declaration and Peace Manifesto and expressed complete solidarity with the statement by the Communist and Workers' Parties which participated in the Bucharest Conference to the effect that the struggle for peace remains the cardinal task of the communist movement.

Has the Nature of Imperialism Changed?

Imperialism no longer dominates the whole globe, as in the past. Barring the way to the implementation of its plans there now stands not one socialist country in capitalist encirclement, but a world system of socialism. Imperialism does not have its former hinterland in the form of the colonial system. The peoples of countries which have liberated themselves from colonial oppression and also of countries which are struggling for their national independence are resolutely opposed to imperialism, to its rapacious colonial policy and predatory aggressive wars. On the international arena the number of states coming out for peace is increasing. Within the capitalist countries the organisation and consciousness of the working class is growing. Is the aggressive nature of imperialism changing in the course of these processes? No, it is not. By its social nature imperialism remains rapacious. But do the imperialists still have their former opportunities to manifest their rapacious nature unimpeded on the world arena? No, these opportunities are diminishing. . . .

The aggressive nature of imperialism remains, but its opportunities are diminishing—this is the peculiarity of the present-day international situation. Whoever notices only one side of a question and closes his eyes to the other

144

is not a Marxist and cannot correctly understand the present-day international situation.

Contemporary revisionists and reformists close their eyes to the aggressive nature of imperialism and proclaim that imperialism has allegedly changed since the time when the classics of Marxism-Leninism wrote about it, and that the wolves have allegedly been " transformed " into sheep. The point, the revisionists and reformists preach, is not that it is getting more and more difficult for the wolves to use their teeth but that the wolves do not have any teeth and no longer have any desire to live at the expense of others. In that case there would be no need to wage the struggle for peace.

On the other hand, the dogmatists and sectarians claim that while imperialism exists it retains its rapacious nature and even now the question of whether there will be a war or not allegedly depends on its whim. In this case, the struggle for peace loses its perspective.

The position of creative, consistent Marxism-Leninism on these questions is different. . . .

At the present time there is no fatal inevitability of wars. But it would be mistaken to suppose that it is possible to ensure lasting peace without a struggle. The issue is decided by the struggle of the masses, in the first place by the assiduous and consistent struggle for peace of the camp of socialism and the world communist movement. Communists are not fatalists and are not Utopian dreamers. In the struggle for peace they rely on actual possibilities contained in the historical situation and convert these possibilities into reality. The characteristic feature of the present-day international situation consists precisely in the fact that imperialism, without changing its aggressive nature, is forfeiting its former opportunities of lording it on the world arena, while the opportunities of the world socialist system to curb the aggressive aspirations of the imperialists are growing.

War is the continuation of politics by other means. In order to continue imperialist policy on the world arena by force of arms, with the help of war, it is necessary to dispose of the appropriate means and opportunities. The desire alone of the imperialists is not enough. It is well-known that the imperialists have undertaken wars, proceeding from the balance of forces, at a time when they have been able to count on success. Beasts of prey undertake wars in the hope of booty and not in order to break their teeth. This is the ABC of Marxism. Even a wild beast chooses the moment for the most successful attack and also chooses its victim, in accordance with its own strength. The issue of war is decided by the correlation of forces on the world arena. And at present the balance of these forces is not in favour of the imperialists. . . .

The conclusions of the Twentieth and Twenty-first Congresses of the CPSU and of the Declaration and Peace Manifesto on the possibility of averting war are based on a scientific analysis of the contemporary international situation; they are confirmed by the whole course of world events and retain their full validity. These conclusions are an expression of the creative character of Marxist-Leninism.

Lenin on War and Peace in the Epoch of Imperialism

V. I. Lenin taught us to approach the question of wars from the point of view of dialectical materialism. But such an approach requires that one take account of the concrete situation, of the changed balance of strength in the world. In combating the right- and "left"-wing opportunists, Lenin stressed that the question of wars could be decided only in the light of the new historical situation. . . .

V. I. Lenin showed that predatory wars stemmed from the fact that the imperialists enjoyed undivided sway in the world, from the fact that they had divided the world up amongst themselves and were waging a struggle for its redivision. He wrote about the first world war: "The objective conditions of socialism have fully ripened, and the present war is a war of capitalists for the privileges and monopolies which might defer the collapse of capitalism." The imperialists would like, with the help of war, to prolong the existence of capitalism, to slow down the historical process which is inevitably leading to the replacement of capitalism by a new, socialist system of society. The working class, the working people, on whom fall all the burdens of imperialist wars, are the opponents of these wars: predatory wars are at variance with the socialist system, based on the international solidarity of the peoples, which is being created by the working people.

While fighting against the deception of the people by pacifist phrases, Lenin indicated to mankind the correct road to peace. He taught the working people that "the blessings which they expect from peace are impossible without a series of revolutions." He spoke out against the illusion that "present governments, present ruling classes, are *capable*, without being 'trained' (or removed) by a series of revolutions, of [achieving] a peace in some way satisfactory to democracy and the working class."

Why did Lenin write about a *series of revolutions* which alone can radically change the world situation and create conditions for the appearance of those blessings of peace awaited by the masses? Lenin did not entertain any illusions as to how the capitalist world would greet the socialist revolution after it had triumphed initially in one country: a country in which the socialist revolution triumphed might be subjected to intervention by capitalist states. The people, having taken the fate of their country into their own hands, would reply to this intervention with a just, defensive war. Lenin wrote that "socialism having triumphed in one country does not in any way immediately exclude all wars in general." He pointed out that this was a matter for the future, the result of a series of revolutions.

Now there has occurred a series of revolutions which have removed capitalism from tremendous expanses of the globe. There exists a world system of socialism. The time has irrevocably passed when international relations were an arena for the arbitrary will of imperialists, aggressors and invaders.

During Lenin's life there was no world system of socialism, but the brilliant strategist of the proletarian revolution foresaw that mankind would inevitably be faced with the historic "task of transforming a dictatorship of the proletariat from a national one (*i.e.*, existing in one country and incapable of determining world politics) into an international one (*i.e.*, a dictatorship of the proletariat in at least several of the advanced countries, capable of exerting a decisive influence on the whole of world politics)." At the present stage, as Lenin foresaw, the mighty world system of socialism is already capable of exerting and is exerting a decisive influence on world politics.

The General Line of our Foreign Policy

Leninism proceeds from the fact that in the final analysis the question of the victory of the new social system over the old is decided in the most important sphere of man's activity, in production. " Labour productivity," wrote Lenin, " is in the last analysis the most important and chief thing for the triumph of the new social system." This is one of the basic ideas of Leninism which determine the process of the transition from capitalism to communism. Socialism is developing its gigantic potentialities in the sphere of creative productive labour. Through the smoke of the battles of the civil war Lenin clearly saw this most important task of the new society. At the height of the fierce battles against Denikin's followers he pondered the question of relations with the technically and economically advanced capitalist countries " during the period when socialist and capitalist states will exist side by side." Lenin put forward and substantiated the principle of the peaceful co-existence of countries with different social systems.

For the contemporary historical period the principle of peaceful co-existence put forward by Lenin is the only correct and necessary one in the relations between the countries of socialism and capitalism. The policy of peaceful co-existence conforms to the interests of the working class, of all working people, to the interests of communism. Today, while struggling against the " cold war " policy, we are winning over to our side wide sections of the public in the capitalist countries and we are isolating the most aggressive representatives of monopoly capital both in the world arena and inside capitalist countries. This is promoting the triumph of the cause of peace, democracy and socialism.

The struggle for peace, for the peaceful co-existence of countries with different social systems, is the general line of the foreign policy of the socialist camp. The peace-loving foreign policy of the Soviet Union and of the other socialist states is meeting with the support and approval of all peoples. The Soviet proposals for universal and total disarmament, whose implementation could save mankind from the fear of a new war, are a graphic manifestation of this policy.

A new and immeasurably more favourable situation has now come about in the struggle for communism compared with the time when the working class in our country had only just taken power into its hands. " Even at that time," N. S. Khrushchev has noted, " we spoke of the broad opportunities which communism opens up before people, while we ourselves in fact were going around in torn breeches, barefoot and hungry. Certain bourgeois leaders hoped then that our people would be tempted by the ' charms of bourgeois civilization.' But now the Soviet Union—a country where a communist society is being built—has the opportunity of demonstrating communism before the whole world not only as the most advanced doctrine but also of demonstrating the material and spiritual riches which the Soviet man is receiving as a result of building a socialist system."

The nearer our country advances towards communism the less will the " charms of bourgeois civilization " tempt the working people of the capitalist countries. The policy of the " carrot and the stick," on which the bourgeoisie places its main reliance, will suffer one failure after another. The new world situation is bringing into prominence the struggle for the utilisation of all the gigantic advantages which the socialist system possesses. The imperialists have long feared this historical prospect. They have openly attempted to frustrate with the help of wars the peaceful competition of socialism with capitalism. Then, going over to the "cold war" methods, they tried, as N. S. Khrushchev has said, "to compel the socialist countries to expend their material means on non-productive purposes." By imposing on us the arms race, they evidently counted not only on halting the development of the science and culture of socialist countries but in bringing them to ruin and in this way discrediting the socialist system. All these plans of the imperialists have failed.

The time is not far distant when the socialist camp will overtake the advanced capitalist countries in per capita production. The Soviet Union will be the country with the highest standard of living for the working people and with the shortest working day, and its population will be exempted entirely from taxes.

In peaceful competition with capitalism, socialism is winning great victories. Over the past six years our industrial production has increased by 90 per cent., while that of the U.S.A. has gone up by 15 per cent. Over the last six years per capita output of industrial products in the USSR has grown by 71 per cent., and in the U.S.A. by 0·3 per cent. Industrial production as a whole in the countries of the socialist system has grown almost six-fold compared with the pre-war level, while in the capitalist countries industrial production has increased approximately two-fold over the same period.

The successes of the Soviet Union and of the socialist camp are now acknowledged by all. Recently the *New York Times* wrote: "The times have long passed when Americans could permit themselves to scoff at communist plans for economic growth, and both our main parties have tacitly admitted this fact during the past few weeks."

Socialist society proposes to capitalism, instead of producing means of destroying people, to organise competition in the production of means of production and of means of consumption. The fact that the imperialists have waged the "cold war" without risking going over to open direct war against the socialist countries shows the growing might of the camp of socialism, in the first place of the Soviet Union. At the present time the Soviet Union, the world camp of socialism, has real possibilities of successfully fighting for the liquidation of the "cold war." The imperialists have repeatedly based their calculations on the hope that our party and the Soviet government would depart from the Leninist general line of their foreign policy and that people who are alien to Leninism would deflect communists from the Leninist path in the sphere of world politics. Then it would be easier for the imperialists to spread their absurd fables about the "aggressiveness of communism." The imperialists have for a long time frightened countries with these fables. But as a result of the consistent peace-loving policy of the Soviet Union, of our Party, the imperialists have now been revealed in their true aspects as aggressors, and the mask of "peaceableness" has been torn off them. All people of common sense can see that the communists, the Soviet Union, all the countries of the socialist camp, are fighting undeviatingly for peace, and that communism is an ideology and policy of construction, of peaceful creation by the masses.

Do not Slacken Vigilance

In 1918 the "left" phrase-mongers asserted that for the Soviet country to maintain peaceful relations with the capitalist countries would mean the

" legalisation " of imperialism. In criticising the writings of the " left " communists, Lenin asked them: " Perhaps the authors think that the interests of the international revolution required that it be given a *push*, and that such a push would be a war, and not peace, which might produce on the masses an impression that imperialism was being ' legalised '? " And Lenin answered this question most decisively: " Such a ' theory ' would signify a complete break with Marxism, which has always rejected the idea of giving a ' push ' to revolutions, which develop in accordance with the acuteness of the class contradictions which give rise to revolutions."

In present-day conditions a revival of views like those of the " left " communists would merely play into the hands of the imperialists by helping them to spread false stories about the " aggressiveness of communism." A revival of such left sectarian views would merely have a demoralizing influence on the builders of the new society: why construct, build, create, if one knows in advance that all the fruits of one's labour will be destroyed by the tornado of war? Such views have nothing in common with communism. Nor can one fail to see that as a result of modern warfare the productive forces, including the main productive force—the working people —would suffer considerably and mankind would experience tremendous difficulties in erecting the new social system on the ruins remaining after a military catastrophe. A destructive war would only make difficult the process of constructing a new society.

The socialist system not only does not create military conflicts between peoples, it destroys the soil from which such conflicts can arise. It removes this soil in economics, politics and ideology. The socialist states are fighting for the elimination of the distrust between peoples which has been nurtured by capitalism.

Imperialism, in kindling enmity between peoples, is attempting to drown in the blood of the peoples everything of value that there is in modern civilization.

By extending and intensifying its influence in world politics socialism is striving to set limits to the activity of the imperialists in the sphere of international relations so that the aggressors shall not be able at their own whim to unleash wars and doom the millions of working people to torment and destruction.

While the imperialists refuse to disarm, the greatest vigilance is necessary against all their intrigues, and readiness to deal a crushing rebuff to any provocation by them. Through the efforts of the Party the Government and the whole people, we have created tremendous possibilities for once and for all discouraging the aggressors from undertaking military provocations.

Our Party, the Soviet Government, are waging an indefatigable struggle for peace, for peaceful co-existence. With pride in our Party, in our Government, we repeat today Lenin's words: " Our peaceful policy is approved by an overwhelming majority of the world's population." In the struggle for peace the whole Soviet people is taking part, enhancing by its selfless labour the influence of our State, of the whole socialist camp on the development of the world, bringing nearer the triumph of communism.

[Yu. Frantsev in *Pravda*, August 7, 1960.]

A Threat to Cut Off Aid?

Now, when there is a great commonwealth of socialist countries forming a mighty bulwark of peace and social progress, it is necessary to approach in a new way the question of the conditions and the possibilities of victorious socialist construction in various countries. In the period when the USSR was the only country of proletarian dictatorship in the world, it did not have the possibility of relying on anybody's direct economic or military aid. The working class and the working peasantry of the USSR could count only on their own strength and resources both in the construction of a socialist economy and in ensuring the country's military security.

The situation is now completely different. The working class of any country knows well that, in the struggle for socialism, it will always receive fraternal support from the Soviet Union and the whole camp of socialism. Lenin's teaching about the victory of socialism in particular countries should now be considered in direct connection with the successes of the socialist camp.

Could one imagine the successful construction of socialism going on in present day conditions even in so great a country as, let us say, China, if that country were in a state of isolation and could not rely on the collaboration and aid of all other socialist countries? While being subjected to an economic blockade by the capitalist countries such a country would be subjected simultaneously to military blows from outside. It would experience the greatest difficulties even if it succeeded in withstanding the furious attacks of the enemy. . . .

[S. Titarenko in *Sovyetskaya Latvia*, August 16, 1960.]

"Outstanding Factor of Our Times"

Under the onslaught of the peoples rising to freedom, the last mainstays of present-day imperialist slaveowners in colonial countries are crumbling. Academician E. Zhukov writes in *Pravda* today in an article headlined "Outstanding Factor of our Times," in which he analyses the most essential problems of the contemporary national liberation movement.

The emergence of new national states and the progressive development of certain states which have existed relatively for a long time as a result of the disintegration of the colonial system of imperialism, the author stresses, is a significant phenomenon of our days. Dogmatists and sectarians, Academician Zhukov goes on, who fail to understand the laws of social development, contend that the realisation of the Leninist principle of peaceful co-existence retards the development of the national liberation movement and dooms it to stagnation. Describing this point of view as deeply erroneous, Zhukov goes on: The experience of development of the USSR and other socialist nations, their active policy of peace and the unselfish aid they are rendering to underdeveloped countries inspire the peoples of these countries and strengthen their confidence in the success of their just cause.

Further, Academician Zhukov writes: Only petty-bourgeois leftists and hopeless dogmatists can deny the great historic significance of the fact of the formation of national states in Asia and Africa, even though many of these states have not yet attained economic independence and have not solved a number of pressing social problems advanced by life.

After noting that most of the new national states of Asia and Africa are headed by bourgeois politicians appearing under the flag of nationalism, the author notes that this, however, does not detract from the progressive historic significance of the present breakthrough of the front of imperialism. Doctrinaires and "leftists," the article goes on, who allow themselves to sneer at such forms of national liberation movement as do not fit into the customary sociological schemes forget that there exists no such thing in nature as " pure " revolutionary processes. It is quite natural that in the national liberation anti-imperialist movement, the front of participants is much wider than in a social revolution. Failure to understand the multiplicity of forms of national liberation movement, Zhukov goes on, and a haughty attitude towards anti-imperialist actions when, in definite historic conditions, non-proletarian elements come to the forefront, represent sectarianism of a most dangerous kind leading to self-isolation. Citing then Lenin's words about the unequal development of capitalism in various countries, the author writes: Hence it follows that it is impossible to skip over a definite historic stage and consequently the task of socialist transformation cannot be mechanically placed on the order of the day in all countries [at the same time, Tass Russian version added]. What is needed is a concrete historic approach to the solution of the question of the paths of development of any given country.

Speaking about the relations between socialist countries and states fighting for independence, the author goes on: The main and most essential thing which unites socialist states and non-socialist national states is their common anti-imperialist position, their common interest in the earliest liquidation of the colonial system and in the all-round economic and cultural progress of peoples who temporarily fell back in their development, in establishing genuine equality of nations and consolidating lasting peace on earth.

Only imperialist provocateurs, the author stresses, who have made anti-communism their banner in the policy of aggression and fresh colonial adventures, raise the cry of " Communist conspiracy " about any just national liberation struggle of the peoples, no matter who stands at its head. Marxism-Leninism, Academician Zhukov writes in this connection, resolutely condemns as a reactionary Utopia the very idea of " exporting " revolution to other countries and rejects any imposition upon other countries of social systems and institutions which are not the product of internal development. The Soviet Union, the article says, is rendering and will continue to render unselfish support to national states defending their sovereignty from imperialist encroachments and in doing so it has no other aims except seeing these states free and prosperous as quickly as possible.

The continuing disintegration of the colonial system, Academician Zhukov writes in conclusion, strikes the imperialist colonialists with fear. This is eloquently attested by the events in the Congo, where the colonialists are attempting to confront a young sovereign state which expresses the indomitable will of the Congolese people to independence and freedom with their own united front, using for this purpose " NATO solidarity," the venality of certain tribal chiefs and the obsequiousness of highly-placed manipulators from the United Nations machine. Colonialists spare no efforts to retard the historic process of regeneration of formerly enslaved peoples. Vain efforts! The lesson of life is: Wherever the people rise to freedom the entire process of social life is accelerated, along with an intense upsurge of national economy and culture.

[Text of Tass summary in English, August 26, 1960. Reproduced in *Summary of World Broadcasts* (London: B.B.C.), Part 1, SU/421/B/1.]

151

"The Struggle for Peace is the Primary Task"

The international "weather" is changeable. Do you remember how clearly the barometer turned to "clear" when N. S. Khrushchev's visit to America took place? But recently, as a result of a number of provocations by American rulers the wind of the "cold war" has again blown up. This changeability reflects to a certain extent the effect on the world scene of two conflicting forces—the progressive forces of socialism and the reactionary forces of capitalism. And although with every year we can see more clearly the tendency towards a steady improvement of the international situation, which is an undoubted achievement of the progressive forces, the forces of reaction sometimes manage to halt the approach of warm weather and even to induce some fog.

There are, however, people who do not see and do not wish to see which is the predominant tendency. Their whole attention is absorbed by current changes in the international situation. They can't, as we say, see the wood for the trees.

Some of them exploit every bright period on the international horizon to shout repeatedly at the top of their voices: "We have long been asserting that imperialism is now nothing like what it was when Marx and Lenin described it, it has become good—'humane,' 'popular,' 'peace-loving.' . . ."

The others—they usually raise their voices imperiously when the international situation has deteriorated—declare gloomily: "Our epoch is the epoch of imperialism, wars and proletarian revolutions; so long as imperialism exists, wars are inevitable, and so said Lenin." Yes, they base themselves on Marxism-Leninism but not on its essential features, not on its living soul but on the letter, the formality, forgetting that Lenin himself more than once ridiculed those who treat Marx's teaching as a dogma. Lenin himself more than once stressed the creative character of Marxism and its continuous development in accordance with changes in the life of society. Failing to take these changes into account, the prophets of gloom draw obviously incorrect conclusions from Lenin's formulae: If, they say, wars are inevitable under imperialism, then what sort of peaceful co-existence can you talk about? And the struggle for peace, they say, has no future, it only distracts revolutionary parties from their main tasks in the development of the class struggle. People who make such assertions are dogmatists and sectarians. . . .

Even now, such weapons are being produced that their use in the event of war would have catastrophic consequences for the whole of humanity. The Soviet Union's great service lies in the fact that it has not permitted the imperialists to acquire a monopoly over the new weapons and has equipped its army with powerful weapons which are superior to the weapons of foreign military adventurers. Today even the most rabid maniacs from the Pentagon must realise that with modern weapons war will be suicide for the person who launches it.

And even with such superiority we are against war. The first secretary of the C.C. of the Communist Party of Czechoslovakia, Antonin Novotny, has stated: "We are fighting with all our strength for the final defeat of imperialism. But we are convinced that our strength gives us the possibility of achieving complete victory by peaceful means. The devastation which would be brought about by another war would be too great a price to pay for our victory, it would throw humanity back hundreds of years and would inflict great harm on the cause of proletarian revolution. . . . We are fighting for the victory of life over death and therefore our banner is peace. . . ."

The adventurist policy of the Trotskyists and the Bukharinists of playing at revolution in 1918 almost spelled the end of the young Soviet Republic. In our time the emergence of views, similar to the views of the " left communists," can only play into the hands of the communists who spread false stories about the aggressive nature of world communism. . . .

Any kind of attempt to assess the policy of peaceful co-existence, of averting wars and the struggle for disarmament as a retreat from Marxist-Leninist positions on the class struggle of the proletariat, attempts to spread doubt about the correctness of the theoretical principles laid down by the Twentieth and Twenty-first Congresses of the CPSU, is a retreat from Marxism-Leninism, a demonstration of dogmatism and sectarianism which is capable of causing serious harm to the development of the international communist movement. . . .

[G. Nikolnikov in *Pravda Ukrainy*, August 30, 1960.]

" Lenin's Theory of the Socialist Revolution and Present-day Conditions "

There are two erroneous approaches to Lenin's theory of the socialist revolution—the revisionist and the dogmatic.

The revisionists try to impose the idea, openly or covertly, that this theory has allegedly become outdated. . . .

The supporters of the other erroneous theory, the dogmatic one, shut their eyes to the new factors which the present era introduces into the theory of scientific socialism. Admitting in words that big shifts have occurred in the world in the last couple of dozen years, the supporters of this point of view nevertheless fail to draw the necessary conclusions from them. They question the new principles of theory and tactics of a socialist revolution worked out by the communist movement in recent years, and try to dispute them, referring to quotations from the works of V. I. Lenin taken out of context. In these cases Lenin's ideas are either misinterpreted or else are mechanically extended to new historical conditions.

It must be emphasised that in general such a bookish approach is unacceptable in Marxism-Leninism as a creative teaching and is absolutely inapplicable to the theory of a socialist revolution. It must be rejected in principle as being contrary to the spirit of Leninism. . . .

An appreciation of the internal situation of the world capitalist system as a whole and of each country in particular remains the starting point, as before. However, it is impossible to limit ourselves to this under present-day conditions. Today it is necessary to take into account not only the tendencies in the development of imperialism, but also the new position which capitalism occupies in the world, the balance of forces of the two systems, the influence of the successes in the building of socialism and communism on the world liberation movement, and the part played by the national liberation fight of the peoples. . . .

Today, when the U.S.A. no longer holds a monopoly in atomic weapons, when the might of the world system of socialism has grown out of all knowledge, the possibility of paralysing imperialist interference in a revolution, in the internal affairs of this or that country, has tremendously increased. Is not that proved by the stopping of the Anglo-Franco-Israeli aggression against Egypt on the demand of the USSR and other peace-loving forces? Is not that proved by the successful development along the revolutionary road by the heroic people of Cuba, despite the burning hatred of the American imperialists and all their attempts to strangle the revolution? . . .

Generally speaking, the relationship between war and revolution is much more complicated than some people imagine. It must be considered from every angle, and that is a concretely historical way. The influence of wars on the social processes, on the liberation movement of the masses and the conditions of its development have always been of a contradictory character. Wars have always been tremendous disasters for the popular masses, causing the worker starvation and destruction in the rear and death and disablement at the front. They led to the destruction of the productive forces of the community and thereby obstructed its progress. Besides that, the preparations for a predatory war and the war itself led to a strengthening of reaction, to an active attack by the ruling classes against the rights and liberties of the masses and against their militant organisations. . . .

It is notable that the October revolution was carried out under the banner of peace, whilst the civil war was started, not by the communists, but by the forces of internal and foreign counter-revolution. . . .

A world war with the employment of thermo-nuclear weapons would make no distinctions between front and rear. It would lead to the complete destruction of the main centres of civilisation and the wiping out of whole nations, and would bring immeasurable disaster to the whole of humanity. It is only madmen who could wish for such a catastrophe. . . .

It is obvious, therefore, that modern nuclear war of itself could in no way be a factor which would hasten revolution or bring nearer the victory of socialism. On the contrary, it would throw back humanity, the world revolutionary workers' movement and the cause of building socialism and communism for many dozens of years. . . .

The policy of peaceful co-existence assists in taking advantage of the struggle between two tendencies among the ruling circles of the capitalist countries—the militant aggressive one and the moderate sober one—in the interests of peace. People are to be found, however, who assert that the thesis of peaceful co-existence almost amounts to preaching " class peace." Such people misinterpret Lenin's conception of peaceful co-existence which, as is well known, applies to the sphere of inter-state (and by no means inter-class) relations and in no way implies a cessation of the fight between the two systems or some kind of armistice in the contradictions between socialism and capitalism. The contradictions continue and the class war in the international arena continues, but the forms of that war are different—economic competition and an ideological fight in place of war. . . .

Thus there can be no doubt that the strengthening of peace and peaceful co-existence is a factor which favours the expansion of the liberation movement and the activisation of the class war in the capitalist countries. Lasting peace creates more favourable conditions for accelerating the development of the socialist system, improves the prospects of the liberation movement and increases the possibilities for a revolutionary snapping of more links in the capitalist system. . . .

Anti-fascist unity was achieved on a wide scale during the second world war. Peoples-Democratic revolutions which developed in the countries of Europe and Asia served as an obvious example of the importance which universal democratic aims and movements have assumed in our days. These revolutions developed under anti-fascist democratic slogans (and in places where survivals of feudalism had been preserved, under anti-feudalist slogans as well). Experience has also shown that under proper direction by the working class and its Marxist-Leninist parties, democratic revolutions have a tendency to develop into socialist revolutions relatively swiftly. . . .

In the post-war period, the communist parties in the capitalist countries have enriched the tactics of the democratic, anti-monopolistic fight with new ideas and forms. The new features which have been introduced by the communist parties into this question can be found in a summarised form in the decisions of the Rome conference of representatives of the communist parties of the capitalist countries held in November 1959. The programme for the anti-monopoly war proposed by this conference is a model of a creative approach to the assessment of the modern conditions of the fight of the working class and the working out of the tactical slogans and forms of this fight. . . .

Communists are by no means opposed in principle to regulation of the economy by the state. The working class accepts battle on the field which has been created by the process of the objective development of capitalism itself. If the ruling groups of monopolistic capitalism resort on a wide scale to measures of government interference in economic life, the working class does not of necessity have to reject state interference as such. We are talking about something different. Would it not be possible by means of an organised fight by the working class and all the popular masses to achieve the introduction of such regulating measures as would be directed against the ruling sections of the bourgeoisie, the monopolies, and would be in the interests of the people? In other words, government regulation becomes one of the new objectives around which the fight of the main social forces of the modern capitalist society develops. . . .

Dogmatically minded people spring up to ask: "But is any fight for democratic transformation really necessary? Would it not be better to immediately carry out a socialist revolution which would once and for all settle the problems of peace and the problems of democracy? Does not the fight for democratic transformations distract the working class from the prospects of revolution?" Some people even maintain that the decisions of the Rome conference are contrary to the Marxist theory of the class war, since they do not contain any call for the direct revolutionary overthrow of capitalism and the establishment of a dictatorship of the proletariat. It would be a good thing to remind such people of the following statement by Lenin on combining the fight for the immediate and final objectives of the working class, for reform and revolution: "For a genuine revolutionary the greatest danger, and even perhaps the only danger, is to exaggerate revolutionary feelings, to disregard the limits and conditions for an able and successful application of the revolutionary method. It was this that led real revolutionaries, more than anything else, to break their necks, when they began to write 'Revolution' in capital letters, to exalt 'Revolution' into something almost divine, to lose their heads, to lose the capacity to realise, weigh up and make sure, in the most cool-headed and sober way, at what moment and in what circumstances, in what sphere of action it was necessary to be able to act in a revolutionary way, and at what moment and in what circumstances, in what sphere of action it was necessary to change to a reformist type of action " (*Works*, Vol. 33, pp. 86–87). . . .

In the process of the fight for peace and democracy the masses are able to recognise the true features of the monopolies as being the chief enemies of peace, independence and national liberty, the people responsible for the deterioration of the position of various sections of the population. It is only in the course of a fight of this kind that there can be forged a coalition of the anti-monopolist forces, where the working class will assume its leading position, whilst its allies will acquire confidence in its leadership and its programme of radical social transformations. . . .

Lenin constantly stressed that the proletariat must become proficient in all forms of fighting, both non-peaceful and peaceful. He wrote that the revolutionary class, in order to secure its ends, " must master *all*, without the smallest exception, forms and sides of social activity " and must be prepared to make " the most sudden and unexpected switch from one form to another " (*Works*, Vol. 31, p. 76). This principle rests today, as formerly, at the foundation of the approach of the Marxist-Leninist parties to the problem of the means by which the working class is to capture power. Any attempt to ignore the diversity of methods for the seizure of power by the working class, to identify revolution with an armed rising and civil war, throws the workers' movement back. . . .

When Marx and Engels were prepared to admit a peaceful transition to socialism in Britain and the U.S.A., they indicated the main internal factor which distinguished these countries from the countries of the European continent, the comparative weakness of the military and bureaucratic castes. At the same time the working class already predominated in the population of Britain. Under such conditions a socialist overthrow would not of necessity cause the bourgeoisie to use the most extreme forms of violence and therefore would not call for corresponding counter-measures by the proletariat. In the era of monopoly capitalism, when these countries did not differ from the countries of the European continent in the increase of militarism and bureaucracy, the question of a peaceful proletarian revolution in the U.S.A. and Britain ceased to apply, as Lenin pointed out. . . .

The case may be different in a transition to socialism under conditions of peace and peaceful co-existence. Here, for a number of countries, it is more probable than it was formerly that there may be peaceful roads to revolution, a conquest of power without a civil war or an armed rising. But for this it would be necessary that the ruling classes should be deprived of the possibility of taking up arms, of using the police, army and government machinery to crush the revolutionary movement of the masses. A situation of this kind might develop from a number of causes—the weakening of militarism as the result of a successful disarmament policy; a considerable part of the army and the government machine coming over onto the side of the people; the recognition by the ruling circles of the hopelessness of an open fight against the masses. It is obvious that if such favourable conditions are absent, the revolutionary struggle will inevitably assume non-peaceful forms.

[A. Belyakov and F. Burlatsky in *Kommunist*, No. 13, 1960.]

7. The Moscow Conference

WITH the announcement on November 4 of the composition of the Chinese delegation to the celebration of the forty-second anniversary of the Bolshevik revolution in Moscow, it became immediately apparent that the Chinese were determined to fight to the bitter end for their views. Mao was not going, presumably because he did not want to suffer the loss of " face " that a defeat would mean. But Mao's number two in the party, Liu Shao-ch'i, the head of state, was to lead the delegation with Teng Hsiao-p'ing, the party's general secretary, as his deputy. All the previous principal characters on the Chinese side were included—P'eng Chen, Lu Ting-yi, K'ang Sheng. The presence of Liao Ch'eng-chih, Chairman of the Chinese Afro-Asian Solidarity Committee, and Liu Ning-yi, Chairman of the All-China Trade Union Federation, men who had done a good deal of travelling in pursuit of their international " front organisation " activities, meant that the Chinese were well aware they would need to use all possible influence with Communist Parties from outside the *bloc* and, in particular, from Asia, Africa and Latin America. The delegation, made up of six Politburo members and five other members of the central committee, contained every senior Chinese theoretician or propagandist apart from Mao and the editor of *Red Flag,* Ch'en Po-ta, who presumably stayed at home to be ready to loose thunderbolts from Peking if necessary.

The stage was set for the conference by three articles in the Chinese press and the speech by Frol Kozlov, the member of the Soviet Presidium who currently appears destined to succeed Khrushchev, at the traditional meeting in the Moscow Sports Palace on November 6, the eve of the anniversary of the Bolshevik revolution.

The Chinese articles consisted of two on the Bolshevik revolution and one on the experience of the Chinese revolution to mark the publication of the fourth volume of Mao's selected works.

The major theme common to all these articles was on the need for revolutionary violence to smash bourgeois state power; this, it was affirmed, was the lesson taught by both the Soviet and Chinese revolutions. The *Red Flag* article on Mao's works affirmed that the Chinese revolution proved the validity of the lessons of the Paris Commune (also alluded to at the beginning of " Long Live Leninism! ") and the Bolshevik revolution in a " big eastern country." This appears to be a counter-attack against the views outlined in the article by Belyakov and Burlatsky (see above p. 156), a rejection of the idea that " peaceful transition " may be possible in other " big, eastern " countries such as India or Indonesia. In particular, this article emphasised the importance of disorganising the bourgeois army, whereas the Soviet article just mentioned talked somewhat loosely of the army " coming over " to the side of the proletariat. At the same time, the article goes to some lengths to prove that Mao has always been against " leftism," presumably to refute Soviet charges against his current policies; it also affirmed that Mao had never been against the use of parliamentary struggle.[19] It would seem that the Russians when criticising the Chinese for advocating revolutionary violence as opposed to " peaceful transition " argued that the Chinese themselves had co-operated with the bourgeoisie —to which the Chinese replied in this article that this was a " muddle-headed " confusion of the seizure of power by violence and the carrying out of socialist transformation by peaceful means. The Chinese also lambasted " certain muddle-headed people " for thinking that national revolutions would endanger world peace, citing their own revolution as evidence that they would in fact increase the power of the peace forces.

The *People's Daily* editorial of November 7 reaffirmed the importance of the national independence movements for the Communist cause.

Kozlov repeated the Soviet acceptance of the national liberation movement as a force for peace. He indicated that the resolution on colonialism which Khrushchev had proposed to the U.N. on September 23, 1960, had been in part designed to counter Chinese allegations that peaceful co-existence implied " softness " on colonialism. Kozlov withdrew the Soviet claim that the signing of the Bucharest communiqué implied the acceptance by all ruling Communist Parties of the conclusions of the CPSU's Twenty-first Congress on peace and war. He could not report much success in Khrushchev's dealings with the West; he even scratched Macmillan off the list of " soberminded " Western statesmen. But he did not abandon hope of negotiations producing results.

One of the few " inside " accounts of the course of the Moscow conference confirms Western speculation that it must have been extremely bitter, lasting as it did most of November.[20] According to this version, the conference began with a preparatory meeting at which the

[19] Any Communist familiar with Chinese Communist history would have been aware that the leftists cited by the article had been acting under Soviet orders.

[20] Edward Crankshaw in the London *Observer*, February 12 (" The Moscow-Peking Clash Exposed ") and February 19 (" Moscow-Peking Clash: More Disclosures "). The fact that no admission that a conference was being held was made until it was over and a final document could be published, indicates that it was feared agreement might be impossible.

Chinese disputed every point of a draft declaration drafted by Mr. Suslov. Later, in full session, Teng Hsiao-p'ing led the Chinese attack, condemning the CPSU as opportunist, revisionist, and lacking deep knowledge of Marxism-Leninism. He described its ideas about disarmament as absurd, criticised aid to Nehru and Nasser as a mistake which could only help imperialism, and asserted that peaceful co-existence should be regarded as nothing more than a tactical weapon with which to deceive the enemy.[21]

Towards the end of the conference, the *People's Daily*, breaking the Communist press silence on the points in dispute, maintained since the conference had begun, anticipated the anniversary of the 1957 Declaration to emphasise the importance of the national liberation struggle. *Pravda* replied by reaffirming the CPSU's positions on peaceful co-existence.

"The Path of the Great October Revolution is the Common Path of the Liberation of Mankind"

Forty-three years ago, the proletariat and all other working people of Russia, led by V. I. Lenin, the great teacher of revolution, continuing the cause of the Paris commune, carried out an armed uprising, overthrew the counter-revolutionary rule of the landlord-capitalist class and won a great victory in the world-shaking proletarian revolution. Subsequently, after three years of heroic struggle, they smashed the armed intervention by fourteen capitalist countries, crushed the domestic counter-revolutionary rebellions and safeguarded the great victory of the October Revolution. As Lenin pointed out, "Revolutionary violence won a magnificent victory in the October Revolution.". . .

Fundamentally speaking, the path of the October Revolution is the common bright path of advance of entire humanity. Historical facts have times on end proved to us that without smashing the state machine of the capitalist class by revolutionary means, without establishing the dictatorship of the proletariat, there can be no socialism, no genuine liberation of the proletariat and the other labouring people. Lenin had more than once pointed out that the theory of the dictatorship of the proletariat is the most important component of Marxism and "only he is a Marxist who extends the recognition of the class struggle to the recognition of the dictatorship of the proletariat. This is what constitutes the most profound difference between the Marxist and the ordinary petty (as well as big) bourgeois." Lenin had also constantly pointed out that to recognise the dictatorship of the proletariat required that the Party go deep among the tens of millions of the labouring masses, devote its main efforts to leading the masses to carry out struggle, constantly raise their revolutionary level, make long, painstaking and persistent preparations for realising the dictatorship of the proletariat, combine the struggle for the immediate interests of the proletariat with the struggle for its long-term interests and oppose the erroneous tendency of sacrificing the fundamental interests of the proletariat in favour of the immediate interests. To put into effect the programme of the dictatorship of the proletariat, Lenin, in leading the revolution, waged persistently a firm

21 Crankshaw, *Observer*, February 12.

struggle against the opportunists and revisionists of the second international and their Russian counterparts, the Mensheviks. On the eve of the October Revolution, these opportunists and revisionists did everything to oppose the launching of an armed uprising by the Russian proletariat. After the October Revolution, they again tried their utmost to oppose the conversion of the Soviets into a state organisation of the dictatorship of the proletariat, the dissolution of the reactionary constituent assembly of the capitalist class, the defeat and rout of the reactionary troops etc. Lenin stressed: "The point is whether the old state machine (bound by thousands of threads to the bourgeoisie and permeated through and through with routine and inertia) shall remain, or be destroyed and replaced by a new one. Revolution consists not in the new class commanding, governing with the aid of the old state machine, but in this class smashing this machine and commanding, governing with the aid of a new machine. Kautsky slurs over this basic idea of Marxism, or he has utterly failed to understand it." . . .

Lenin wrote the great work *The State and Revolution* on the eve of the outbreak of the October Revolution, theoretically defending and developing the fundamental idea of Marxism on smashing the state machine of the capitalist class and realising the dictatorship of the proletariat, further elucidating in detail the path of the Paris Commune and laying a solid theoretical foundation for the victory of the Russian proletariat in the October socialist revolution and the realisation of the dictatorship of the proletariat. This was of extremely great significance for the revolutionary cause of the proletariat of the whole world and the cause of mankind's liberation. . . .

The experiences of the Soviet Union and other socialist countries prove that only under the conditions of the dictatorship of the proletariat is it possible to realise the socialist transformation of the national economy and carry out socialist and Communist construction. . . .

The declaration of the Moscow meeting of Communist and Workers' Parties of the Socialist Countries which is of great historic significance sums up the experience of the international Communist movement in the past hundred years, especially the past forty years. The declaration points out that the " guidance of the working masses by the working class, the core of which is the Marxist-Leninist party, in effecting a proletarian revolution in one form or another and establishing one form or another of the dictatorship of the proletariat is a major universal law." The modern revisionists represented by the Yugoslav Tito clique deny the historical necessity of carrying out the proletarian revolution and the dictatorship of the proletariat in the period of transition from capitalism to socialism and do all they can to oppose the proletarian revolution and the dictatorship of the proletariat. Their " revision " of Marxism-Leninism is precisely an attempt to depart from the highroad of the liberation of the proletariat. Therefore, the task of all Communists is to resolutely oppose revisionism and defend this Marxist-Leninist path blazed by the October Revolution.

Compared with forty-odd years ago, the situation of the world has changed considerably. Socialism has triumphed in areas inhabited by more than one-third of the population of the globe and comprising one-fourth of its territory. The socialist countries headed by the Soviet Union, aiding each other and working closely together, are successfully building socialism, and enjoying an economic upsurge in common. With the support of the socialist and other progressive forces of the world, the national liberation movement has made tremendous progress in the colonies and semi-colonies of Asia, Africa and Latin America. The workers' movement in the capitalist countries and the world-wide peoples' movement for peace, have also grown remarkably. As a result of these changes, the domain of imperialism has become daily smaller, the contradictions within the imperialist system are steadily sharpening, and the imperialist countries are having a very hard time. The situation in the world today shows that we are living in a new epoch in which the forces of peace prevail over the forces of war, the forces of the people over the forces of reaction and the forces of socialism over the forces of imperialism, a new epoch which is unprecedentedly favourable to the proletarian revolution in different countries of the world, a new epoch which is unprecedentedly favourable to the national revolution in the colonies and semi-colonies, a new epoch in which the collapse of the imperialist system is being further accelerated and the victory of the people throughout the world and their awakening are constantly mounting. At present, the primary task of the peoples of the world is to form the broadest united front against imperialism headed by the United States, resolutely oppose U.S. imperialism's policies of aggression and war, stand firm against colonialism, promote the growth of the national liberation movement and facilitate the progress of the revolutionary struggle of the working people in the imperialist countries against the bellicose groups and monopoly capital, so as to achieve the aim of preventing imperialism from starting a world war and safeguarding world peace.

Imperialism will never reconcile itself to its doom. Imperialism, U.S. imperialism in particular, is making frantic efforts to expand armaments and prepare for war, to uphold everywhere the system of national oppression and enslavement and foster reactionary governments and forces in all parts of the world, and sparing no effort to plot for the subversion of the socialist countries. The socialist camp headed by the great Soviet Union is the strong bulwark for the defence of world peace and the struggle for the liberation of mankind. To continue to develop and increase the might of the socialist camp and consolidate its unity is the sacred duty of the peoples of the socialist countries. The Chinese people have done, are doing and will continue to do their utmost to fulfil this sacred duty. Imperialism and its running dogs, the modern revisionists, have used all despicable tactics to undermine the unity of the countries of the socialist camp. However, their acts of sabotage have invariably ended in ignominious failure, and will inevitably suffer one defeat after another in the future as well. . . .

[*Red Flag*, No. 20–21, 1960. From text released by NCNA, October 31, 1960.]

" Hold High the Red Banner of the October Revolution. March from Victory to Victory "

Since the great October Revolution, the national liberation movements in colonies and semi-colonies have entered a new stage. Today, the nationalist, democratic movements in Asia, Africa and Latin America are in a new upsurge. The Soviet Union and the other socialist countries have given warm support and tremendous encouragement to the national independence movements in various countries; the people in all the countries which are struggling for national independence look upon the Soviet Union and the other socialist countries as their most faithful friends. The successful development of national independence movements has greatly weakened the strength of the imperialist system and at the same time rendered tremendous support to the building of socialism in the socialist countries and to the struggle of the world's people for peace. The October Revolution has closely linked together the cause of socialist revolution of the proletariat in all countries and the struggle of all oppressed nations for liberation. The linking together of the socialist revolution and the national liberation movement has accelerated the collapse of the imperialist system and speeded up the victorious progress in the struggle of all oppressed nations for national independence, democracy and freedom. . . .

[*People's Daily*, November 7, 1960. From text released by NCNA on same day.]

" A Basic Summing-up of Experience Gained in the Victory of the Chinese People's Revolution "

In summing up the experience of the Paris Commune, Karl Marx put forward the famous proposition that the working class cannot simply lay hold of the ready-made state machinery and wield it for its own purposes. . . .

Why was the great October Revolution able to succeed? Because the Russian proletariat under the leadership of the great Lenin's Bolshevik Party thoroughly smashed the old Russian militarist, bureaucratic state machine, established the dictatorship of the proletariat and set up a new Soviet state machine, transforming the state from an instrument for suppression of the majority of people by the exploiting few into one of suppression of the exploiting few by the majority.

The establishment of the system of the people's democracies in a series of European and Asian countries towards the end of and after the Second World War was also due to the smashing of the old militarist, bureaucratic state machine in these countries, by their own people, or by their own people with the assistance of the Soviet Army which was pursuing the bandit troops of the German fascists.

The Central Committee of the Chinese Communist Party has stressed repeatedly that the Chinese Revolution was the continuation of the October Revolution. Why was the great revolution of the Chinese people able to succeed? For the same reason. How could victory have been achieved if we did not overthrow the counter-revolutionary dictatorship of the big landlord class and the big bourgeoisie and smash the old state machine of the war-lords, bureacrats and secret agents? The victory of the Chinese revolution substantiated afresh, in a big eastern country, the Marxist-Leninist theory of the state and revolution.

The specific historic conditions underlying the revolution are usually not completely identical in various countries; they often vary from country to country. The concrete process whereby the reactionary state machine was smashed and the revolutionary state machine established during the Chinese revolution had its own characteristics.

The October Revolution started with the armed uprising of the Russian working class in the capital. Its course of development was characterised by the taking over first of the cities and then of the countryside. But the Chinese revolutionary war which began in the autumn of 1927, namely the revolutionary war under the independent leadership of the Chinese Communist

Party, first succeeded in a number of rural areas on the basis of the agrarian revolution, then the success was gradually extended and finally victory was achieved in the cities. In other words, its course was characterised by growth from setting up small revolutionary bases in the rural areas to large revolutionary bases; from the establishment of a few revolutionary bases to the establishment of many and from encirclement of the cities by the rural areas to the ultimate taking over of the cities.

This process means that the seizure of political power by the Chinese people took place at first in one place and then another and area by area, and so did their smashing of the reactionary state machine. Through this process of revolutionary development, which took twenty-two years to accomplish, the Chinese proletariat and the Chinese people won victory throughout the country and achieved their aim.

This course of development of the Chinese revolution was propounded by Comrade Mao Tse-tung....

After the betrayal of the revolution by Chiang Kai-shek, the former capitulationists represented by Ch'en Tu-hsiu joined hands with the counter-revolutionary Trotskyites and became liquidationists. They declared that the Chinese revolution had ended and held that the Chinese people should not touch Chiang Kai-shek's counter-revolutionary state machine but should only engage in legal activities under the reactionary rule of Chiang Kai-shek, with a "National Assembly" as the central slogan. They also shamelessly acclaimed Chiang Kai-shek's counter-revolutionary wars and slandered the revolutionary wars and guerrilla wars of the peasants led by the proletariat as a "Movement of Roving Insurgents" which was doomed to fail. Comrade Mao Tse-tung refuted the counter-revolutionary babble of the Trotskyite–Ch'en Tu-hsiu liquidationists and held firmly to the banner of the Chinese people's revolution. He maintained that "a single spark can start a prairie fire" and that revolutionary armed forces and revolutionary bases, though small and existing only in the rural areas as they did, had great vitality and an unlimited future.

On the other hand, there were in our revolutionary ranks at that time a group of petty-bourgeois "Left" adventurists who controlled the leading organs of the party for several years and beat down a large number of correct leading comrades headed by Comrade Mao Tse-tung so that they could not raise their heads. These "Left" adventurists denied the protracted nature and the tortuous character of China's revolutionary struggle, failed to comprehend that the Chinese revolution had to pass through a process of developing from small to big and from the countryside to the cities and impatiently wanted to take big cities. They were unwilling to carry out among the people the arduous task of building up the forces of the revolution, engaged in wishful thinking that the Chinese revolution could be won overnight and that Chiang Kai-shek's counter-revolutionary state machine could be smashed root and branch in one, single "decisive battle." It was in fact, impossible for "Left" adventurism to achieve the aim of overthrowing the reactionary rule of Chiang Kai-shek and really strengthen and extend the forces of the revolution. On the contrary, such blind actions could only lead to the weakening of the revolutionary forces, and the position of the revolution. During the ten years' civil war in 1927–36, Comrade Mao Tse-tung unceasingly opposed this anti-Marxist-Leninist "Left" opportunist line and forcefully drew attention to the necessity of establishing a solid foundation of revolutionary bases in the countryside "thus placing ourselves in an invincible position."

Comrade Mao Tse-tung maintained that above all the bases in the countryside which at the beginning were small in area and still few in number should be firmly held and continuously expanded and developed; in this way it would be possible "to come ever nearer the goal of attaining nationwide political power." Comrade Mao Tse-tung's victory against "Left" adventurism in 1935 led to the quick resuscitation of the forces of the revolution which had dwindled at that time to only one-tenth of their former strength and guaranteed the Chinese revolution a path of sound development. . . .

Comrade Mao Tse-tung said during the period of the war of resistance to Japanese aggression in his *Problems of War and Strategy,* "According to the Marxist theory of the state, the army is the main component of the political power of the state. Whoever wants to seize state power and to keep it must have a strong army."

Armed revolution against armed counter-revolution, which the Chinese people conducted for a long period, was precisely a process of unceasingly smashing the armed forces of the counter-revolution and building up the armed forces of the revolution, precisely a process of unceasingly shattering the state machine of the counter-revolution and building up the state machine of the revolution, and precisely a process of unceasingly reducing the area under the rule of the counter-revolution and expanding the revolutionary bases and the liberated areas.

In the same article mentioned above, Comrade Mao Tse-tung said: "The task of the proletarian parties in the capitalist countries is to prepare for the final overthrow of capitalism by educating the workers and building up strength through a long period of legal struggle. There we find long legal struggle, the utilisation of the platform of the legislative body, economic and political strikes. . . ." And he further said that in those countries, "War or . . . armed insurrection should not be launched until the bourgeoisie becomes really helpless, until the majority of the proletariat are determined to take up arms and wage war and until the peasant masses are willing to give assistance to the proletariat." But China was in a condition different from this. According to Comrade Mao Tse-tung, in a semi-colonial and semi-feudal country like China, there was no parliament to be utilised, nor did there exist the legal right to organise the workers to conduct strikes. "In China the main form of struggle is war and the main form of organisation is the army." Such a war was mainly a peasants' war and such an army was an army with the peasants as its main component.

We Communists are aware that even in the capitalist countries parliaments are only an ornament of the bourgeois dictatorship. To fail to understand this is utter stupidity. Of course it is also stupidity if, when the circumstances call for it, the political parties of the proletariat do not make use of such an instrument as the parliament to conduct legal struggle. In China, we say, there was no parliament to make use of, and so our main form of struggle was revolutionary war and our main form of organisation was the army; but this by no means signified that all the possible conditions for carrying on legal struggle should not be made use of; such a notion was also stupid. But in the period of the ten years' civil war the "Left" opportunists within our party committed precisely this stupidity.

Either to restrict revolutionary struggle solely to legal struggle or to refuse completely to make use of such legal struggles as are possible and necessary is equally mistaken. Comrade Mao Tse-tung has always sharply criticised such errors.

Comrade Mao Tse-tung has always maintained that a revolutionary party must seize every opportunity to make use as far as possible of the contradictions of the enemy, develop the progressive forces, win over the middle-of-the-road forces and isolate the reactionary forces. He has opposed all kinds of one-sidedness. He said that our policy " is neither unity to the exclusion of struggle nor struggle to the exclusion of unity, but a combination of both. . . ."

Combating Right opportunism, Comrade Mao Tse-tung repeatedly stated the following truth: "Without armed struggle there would be in China no place for the proletariat, the people or the Communist Party and no victory for the revolution." (Introductory remarks to *The Communist*.)

Is not this the fact?

The Chinese Communist Party held a series of talks with Chiang Kai-shek in the period after the Japanese surrender and before Chiang Kai-shek launched a new, all-out counter-revolutionary civil war. Comrade Mao Tse-tung personally went to Chungking for direct talks with Chiang Kai-shek and agreement was reached on peace and national reconstruction. The "summary of conversations between the representatives of the Kuomintang and the Chinese Communist Party," signed on October 10, 1945, laid down in its very first article "The Basic Policy on Peace and National Reconstruction," providing unequivocally for "determined efforts to avert civil war." But, three days after the signing of the agreement, on October 13, Chiang Kai-shek secretly released an order for so-called "Bandit suppression," for attacks on the liberated areas. The political consultative conference closed on January 31, 1946, yet scarcely ten days later, on February 10, an incident occurred at Chiaochangkou, Chungking, in which Kuomintang secret agents wrecked the mass rally held to celebrate the Political Consultative Conference and committed brutal acts of suppression there. From January to June 1946, the Kuomintang and the Communist Party concluded cease-fire agreements on three occasions, yet each was immediately violated by ever bigger military attacks by Chiang Kai-shek. . . .

Chiang Kai-shek often made this proposition to Chinese Communists: You hand over your army, and I will give you democracy and let you join the organs of political power. The Right opportunists lent a willing ear to these words from Chiang Kai-shek and showed much interest in them. Comrade Mao Tse-tung on the contrary always reminded us that we must not fall into this trap laid by Chiang Kai-shek. In circumstances where the Chiang Kai-shek reactionaries continuously strengthened their counter-revolutionary state machine, would it have been possible to win democracy peacefully? Would it have been possible to win political power peacefully? Obviously not.

The Right opportunists did not believe that the masses of the people are the creators of history and did not see the great strength of the people; what they perceived was only the phenomenon of the superficial strength of the Chiang Kai-shek reactionaries, not the weakness which was the essence. The Right opportunists' illusions about Chiang Kai-shek's Kuomintang meant in fact that they were cowed by its superficial strength. Marxist-Leninists scorned this weak-kneed, impotent attitude of the Right opportunists and held that the task was to expose the reactionaries as only outwardly strong but really weak inside, and so to inspire the masses of the people to dare to wage struggle and seize victory. Comrade Mao Tse-tung fulfilled precisely this task. At a time when Chiang Kai-shek with the backing of U.S. imperialism expanded his army to well over four million men, that is to say at the time when the counter-revolutionary state machine of China's big landlords and big bourgeoisie reached its peak, Comrade Mao Tse-tung penetratingly pointed out that the Chiang Kai-shek reactionaries were nothing but paper tigers and that the Chinese people should prepare themselves, and indeed they had the strength, to overthrow the reactionary rule of Chiang Kai-shek's Kuomintang, found a new China of people's democracy and make themselves the masters of their country.

Things turned out exactly as Comrade Mao Tse-tung predicted; the massive counter-revolutionary army under Chiang Kai-shek, hammered and battered by the People's Liberation Army, rapidly fell to pieces in just over three years. . . .

As Lenin once pointed out in contending with the renegade Kautsky: " Not a single great revolution has ever taken place, or ever can take place, without the ' disorganisation ' of the army. For the army is the most ossified instrument for supporting the old régime, the most hardened bulwark of bourgeois discipline, buttressing the rule of capital, and preserving and fostering among the working people the servile spirit of submission and subjection to capital." (Lenin: *The Proletarian Revolution and the Renegade Kautsky*.) By this Lenin meant that it was not possible for the oppressed classes to gain emancipation and put themselves in the ruling position unless they smashed the old, counter-revolutionary army, unless they smashed this principal component of the counter-revolutionary state machine. These words of Lenin, written after the October Revolution, take us back some forty years, but can we say they have become outdated? Of course not. In the forty years and more since the great October Revolution the revolutionary experience of a whole series of countries in Europe and Asia, the experience of the great revolution of the Chinese people, plus the experience gained from the revolutionary struggles which the people of various countries are now waging, have proved, and are still proving with ever greater force, that these words of Lenin have not become outdated at all; they have proved, and are still proving with ever greater force the vitality of the truth revealed in Lenin's words.

For the proletariat and the masses to take political power, smash the old, reactionary state machine and set up a new, revolutionary state machine is one thing. It is quite another thing, having taken political power and relying on it, to proceed to the socialist transformation of the system of ownership of the means of production. The two must not be confused. Only when the former exist can the latter be done. This is how it was in the Soviet Union; this is how it was in the socialist countries in Europe and Asia, and this is how it was in the People's Republic of China, too.

It is muddle-headed to confuse these two things—the seizing of political power by the proletariat and the carrying out by the proletariat of socialist transformation by peaceful means after it seizes political power. Such muddle-headedness conceals the most fundamental question, expounded time and again by Lenin, namely: " The basic question in any revolution is that of state power."

History tells us that people's revolutions in all countries stem from the needs of the people and are the result of the development of class struggle. These revolutions are made within a country by certain oppressed classes to overthrow certain oppressing classes, by certain exploited classes to overthrow certain exploiting classes. Marxist-Leninists have always held that revolution cannot be imported, nor can it be exported. To say that revolution can be imported or exported is entirely wrong. Precisely this is the slander the imperialists and reactionaries in various countries hurl against the people's revolution in any country, but such slanders can in no way check the advance of the revolutionary movement in any country or prevent the rise of revolution in any country.

No Marxist-Leninist party advocates that the socialist countries resort to war between states to spread revolution. The Titoist clique of Yugoslavia slanders the socialist countries with intending to use " war between states " to spread revolution. This is nothing but nonsense in the service of imperialism.

The development of the revolutionary forces of the people in the various countries and their successes in revolution are fundamental factors in preventing imperialism from launching a world war and in preserving world peace. The victory won by the Chinese people in their great revolution and the founding of the Chinese People's Republic have added to the strength of the socialist camp headed by the Soviet Union, expanded the forces standing . guard over world peace and to a great extent frustrated the adventurist policies and plans of the imperialists for starting a new world war. The stronger the socialist camp becomes, the greater the development of the people's revolutionary movements in the various countries and the more countries that win victory in their revolution, the greater will be the safeguards for world peace. The modern revisionists and certain muddle-headed people pit the revolutions in the various countries against world peace, alleging that revolution cannot be carried out if world peace is to be preserved. This is a completely preposterous standpoint which runs fundamentally counter to Marxism-Leninism. . . .

The socialist revolution cannot triumph at a single stroke in all the countries of the world simultaneously. It will come, separately and gradually, as a result of the inherent factors of society in the various countries and the political awakening of the people themselves, their own efforts and their preparations for revolution. . . .

[*Red Flag*, No. 20–21, 1960. From text released by NCNA, November 2, 1960.]

Kozlov's Anniversary Speech

The emergence of socialism beyond the confines of a single country represents one of the greatest victories in the age-old struggle between labour and capital.

It has entailed fundamental changes in the political, economic and ideological life of all mankind. The time of the universal rule of imperialism is gone irrevocably. The world socialist system, the formation of which constitutes the greatest event in history after the victory of the Great October Socialist Revolution, is now becoming the decisive factor in the development of human society.

On the world scene there has also emerged a group of states which refuse to take their cue unconditionally from the imperialist powers. The peoples of Asia, Africa and Latin America, who in hard-fought struggle against the colonialists have won independence or are fighting for it, are taking an increasingly active part in international life and are making their contribution to the weakening of the positions of imperialism.

The positions of the working class have become stronger in the countries of monopoly capital. There has been an increase in the influence of the Marxist-Leninist parties, of which there are now 87 uniting 36 million communists. The working class has greatly increased its ability to rally the vast majority of the people in the struggle to isolate the reactionary aggressive monopoly circles, for new victories in the struggle for peace, democracy and socialism.

In these conditions even more vital becomes the policy of the peaceful co-existence of states with different social systems proclaimed and substantiated by V. I. Lenin. This policy answers the demands of contemporary social development and the real balance of world forces. It is in the interests of all peoples.

Creatively developing Marxism-Leninism, the Communist Party of the Soviet Union drew an important conclusion at its 20th Congress: Today war is not fatally inevitable; war can be averted. This conclusion enlisted the unanimous support of the fraternal Communist and Workers' Parties in a document of programmatic importance—in the Declaration of the Moscow conference of representatives of Communist and Workers' Parties of the socialist countries. The theses of the Moscow Declaration were reaffirmed in the communiqué of the Bucharest conference of the Marxist-Leninist parties.

A further advance of the theory of Marxism-Leninism was the conclusion of the 21st Congress of the Communist Party of the Soviet Union, which said: " Even before the complete victory of socialism on earth, given the preservation of capitalism in a part of the world, there is a real possibility of excluding world war from human society."

In drawing this conclusion our party proceeded from the fact that the fresh successes of the socialist camp would lead to the further growth of the peace forces throughout the world, while the number of countries advocating the consolidation of peace would increase. Our party took into consideration the fact that the idea of the impermissibility of war would strike ever deeper roots in the minds of the peoples, and, backed by the might of the socialist camp, they would be able to compel the bellicose circles of imperialism to abandon their plans for unleashing new wars.

The entire course of developments reaffirms the correctness of the analysis made by the communists. The socialist camp, backed by all the peace forces, has in recent years more than once cut short attempts by imperialist aggressors to engineer local wars through which imperialism threatens mankind with a new world war. This is striking evidence showing that the inception of the world socialist system and the successes of socialism have fundamentally changed the balance of power in the world in favour of socialism and the supporters of peace. Real forces have taken shape in the world in our time able to curb the imperialist aggressors. Imperialism can no longer settle at its discretion the issue of whether there will or will not be war.

Fighting for peace, the Marxist-Leninists, of course, take into consideration that the cause of war remains as long as imperialism exists. The reactionary forces representing the interests of the capitalist monopolies might seek to unleash war. Imperialism has been and remains aggressive: its wolfish nature has not changed and will not change. That is why the socialist countries and all the peace forces must maintain the greatest vigilance and be ready to administer a crushing rebuff if the imperialists should risk starting a war.

Peace is the most cherished desire of all the peoples of the world. Men and women now have no greater desire than to avert the threat of another war of extermination.

But peace cannot be consolidated without fighting for it. That is why the pursuit by the socialist states of an active foreign policy whose general line is the principle of peaceful co-existence, the further mobilisation of all peace forces, making the peoples confident that another world war can now be averted—that is why all this is an urgent necessity of our time. Lenin said: " We must help the peoples to intervene in the issues of war and peace." Our party follows this behest of Lenin with the consistency and persistence inherent in communists.

Striving for peace, our party well remembers Lenin's directive that socialism victorious exerts the main influence on the destinies of mankind by its economic successes. And these successes can be multiplied only in conditions of peace. In peaceful economic competition with capitalism, socialism will undoubtedly gain a decisive economic victory and will ensure the peoples of its countries higher living standards than they now have. This will demonstrate even more clearly than now the superiority of our socialist system and will provide for all the peoples of the world a powerful impetus in their struggle against capitalism and for socialism.

Comrades, all of us have witnessed the resolute actions of the Soviet government in defence of peace.

The Soviet Union has fought persistently for the realisation of the proposals for general and complete disarmament which were supported last year by the United Nations General Assembly. As a result of the persistent actions of the Soviet government in the struggle for general and complete disarmament a 10-power committee was formed. We hoped that this committee would be able to clear away the obstacles which had piled up in the disarmament talks. Last January we adopted a new law on a new unilateral reduction of the Soviet armed forces by 1,200,000 men.

Our economic contacts and cultural relations with many states have been extended. We continue to render selfless aid to underdeveloped countries.

N. S. Khrushchev's tours of South-East Asia and France, as well as his visit last year to the United States, helped to spread a correct understanding of the policy of the socialist countries, to clear the international atmosphere, to expose the insidious designs of imperialism, and they created a favourable climate for a summit meeting.

But the strengthening of the cause of peace went against the grain in imperialist circles, who abhor a development of international relations which is favourable to the people. Under the pressure of monopolies, which are making enormous profits out of the arms race, the United States government adopted the path of direct provocations against our country, against the cause of peace. American air pirates intruded into the Soviet skies and Eisenhower and the American government cynically proclaimed their " right " to violate our sovereignty, allegedly for the purpose of ensuring their " security."

By sending espionage planes over our country and refusing to plead guilty honestly to these acts of brigandage, the United States government torpedoed the summit meeting. By impermissible delays, by their refusal to conduct serious negotiations on disarmament the western powers made the further participation of socialist countries in the 10-power committee impossible. The imperialists provoked a new flare-up of the "cold war" in order to give another push to the arms race, to feverish military preparations.

But such a line in international relations bodes no good for the imperialists. . . .

We offer to the western powers to conduct honest international negotiations on the outstanding questions of international relations and we consider that this is the most rational way for reducing international tension.

Some western leaders, and in particular the British Prime Minister, Mr. Macmillan, have more than once spoken in favour of such negotiations. The latest steps of the British government, however, compel us to question seriously the sincerity of Mr. Macmillan's statements about the striving of the British government to reduce international tension. Only a few days ago Mr. Macmillan announced to Parliament the conclusion of an agreement between Britain and the United States, under which the American Navy will get a base in Scotland near Glasgow, Britain's second biggest city, [sic] for submarines armed with missiles and nuclear weapons. . . .

It is worth noting that Mr. Macmillan negotiated the establishment of this base during his stay in the United States at the 15th session of the United Nations General Assembly, which has been discussing disarmament as one of the main items.

With the Americans he discussed the question of the base. And with the Soviet delegation Mr. Macmillan discussed the question of the need for negotiations to solve international problems ripe for settlement. Apparently the British government is trying to move simultaneously in two diametrically opposite directions. . . .

Comrades, of the greatest importance for the historical destinies of the peoples is the immediate abolition of the remnants of colonialism which are still strangling tens of millions of human beings. We can no longer resign ourselves to this disgrace.

The Soviet government's proposal that the United Nations should adopt a declaration on the granting of independence to colonial peoples and countries is a vital demand of our time, the voice of mankind's conscience. Some prominent leaders of imperialist states, attempting to minimise the tremendous impression produced by this Soviet proposal upon world opinion, attempting to minimise the tremendous force of attraction of the declaration for the peoples of colonial and dependent countries, allege that the declaration contains nothing but "incitement to rebellion" in the colonies.

Such a police yardstick suits only very narrow-minded and embittered persons who refuse to notice the tremendous changes which are occurring in the world and recognise only their profits, their "right" to plunder other peoples. But no such right exists. This is not a "right" but an iniquity and the peoples reject it.

By its proposals in favour of peace the Soviet government has given an impetus to the struggle for the peaceful solution of most acute international problems and has considerably widened the front of that struggle. Today people in all parts of the world see more clearly the path of the peoples to decide their own destinies.

The vigorous foreign policy of the U.S.S.R., of all the socialist countries, and the successes of the peace movement have already yielded tangible results. The imperialist policy is in the throes of a deep crisis. The moral and political isolation of American imperialism—the mainstay of the militarism and colonialism which are loathed by the peoples—is increasing each day. This is confirmed by the overthrow of the bloody Syngman Rhee régime in South Korea, the fall of the openly pro-American Bayar-Menderes régime in Turkey, the indignation which the American-Japanese military alliance aroused among the Japanese people, and the mounting tide of the national liberation movement of African peoples.

The peoples of Latin America, inspired by the example of heroic Cuba, are intensifying their struggle. All this means that the positions of imperialism continue to grow weaker while the positions of the fighters for peace, for the national independence of the peoples, for socialism, grow ever stronger.

Comrades, the most important prerequisite to ensure lasting peace on earth and new victories of the working people in the struggle against the imperialists is the unity of the countries and peoples of the great socialist camp, the unity of all Communist and Workers' Parties. Our party and our people are sparing no efforts to strengthen this unity.

Armed with Marxist-Leninist theory, communists are guided by Lenin's thesis that " only knowledge of the fundamental features of a given epoch can serve as a basis for taking into account the more detailed traits of some particular country." These remarkable words of Lenin serve as a foundation for the understanding and correct correlation of the international and national tasks of each detachment of the international communist movement. Communists are the most consistent fighters for the fundamental national interests of their peoples. At the same time they express the common interests and aims of all toiling mankind.

Loyalty to the principles of creative Marxism, the ability to understand Leninism correctly and apply it in new historical conditions, international solidarity—therein lies the great strength of the international communist and labour movement.

The fraternal cohesion of the Communist and Workers' Parties and the friendship and mutual assistance of the socialist states constitute the source of the invincibility of the countries of the socialist camp, a guarantee of their successful advance to socialism and communism.

Faithful to Marxism-Leninism, the Communist Party of the Soviet Union, our government, the working people of our country will firmly and consistently strengthen the unity and might of the socialist camp, the unity of the international communist and labour movement and will steadily pursue the Leninist policy of the peaceful co-existence of states with different social systems and strengthen the friendship of all peoples. . . .

[From text in *Soviet News* (London: Soviet Embassy), No. 4371, November 7, 1960.]

✳

" Give Full Play to the Revolutionary Spirit of the 1957 Moscow Declarations "

The development of the situation in the past three years demonstrates that the forces of socialism have further surpassed the forces of imperialism, the forces of national liberation have further surpassed the forces of colonialism, the forces of the people have further surpassed the forces of reaction and the forces of peace have further surpassed the forces of war. This shows that the famous dictum made by Comrade Mao Tse-tung three years ago, that " the east wind has prevailed over the west wind," is perfectly correct.

In a word, the entire situation is highly favourable to the peoples of the world and unfavourable to imperialism and all reactionaries. Any view that overestimates the strength of imperialism and underestimates the strength of the people is contrary to the Moscow Declaration and is completely incorrect. . . .

This is to say, peace can be effectively safeguarded only by incessantly strengthening the socialist camp, the national liberation movement, the people's struggles in the capitalist countries, the forces of all peace-loving people and the unity of all these forces and by waging a joint struggle. The broader and stronger this united front of the peace forces against imperialism unleashing wars and the more extensive and intensive its struggles the firmer will be the guarantee for world peace.

The might and solidarity of the countries of the socialist camp, headed by the Soviet Union, is the main force in opposing imperialism and defending world peace. At the same time, the movement for defending world peace and the revolutionary struggles of the various peoples for national liberation, democracy, freedom and socialism are inter-connected, mutually consistent and complementary to each other. The development of the liberation movement of the oppressed nations and peoples of the world and the victories of their revolutionary struggles constitute a mighty force for preventing imperialism from unleashing war and defending world peace.

After the end of the Second World War, U.S. imperialism, by using the Chiang Kai-shek reactionaries to wage a civil war, tried to wipe out the Chinese people's revolutionary force and to turn China into its colony and military base for attacking the Soviet Union and carrying out aggression against Asia. But the Chinese people, compelled to fight a patriotic revolutionary war in self-defence, finally defeated the attack of the Chiang Kai-shek reactionaries and smashed the U.S. imperialists' rabid schemes of aggression against China. The victory of the Chinese people's revolution has greatly increased the forces defending world peace. The same point is proved by the development and victories of the people's revolutionary movements in the many Asian, African and Latin American countries. Those views which oppose the revolutionary struggles of the various peoples to the struggles for defending world peace are, therefore, very wrong. . . .

The entire theory of Marxism-Leninism is in the service of the world proletariat and the revolution of the various peoples. The revolutionary spirit is the soul of Marxism-Leninism. The combination of a strict scientific spirit and high revolutionary spirit is the inherent characteristic of the Marxist-Leninist theory. If we want to uphold the theoretical positions of Marxism-Leninism and the banners of the Moscow Declaration, then we must defend and give full play to this scientific and revolutionary spirit. New historical developments and new experiences in class struggle constantly demand that we, basing ourselves on the fundamental principles and methods of Marxism-Leninism and on scientific analysis of objective things, make new summations to guide revolutionary struggles and enrich the contents of Marxism-Leninism. But, in the course of studying new situations and new experiences, we should, under no circumstances, depart from the fundamental principles and methods of Marxism-Leninism and disregard the facts. Otherwise, it would be a fundamental violation of Marxism-Leninism.

The Moscow Declaration points to " the necessity of resolutely overcoming revision and dogmatism in the ranks of the Communist and Workers' Parties." It also clearly points out that " the main danger at present is revisionism." The characteristic of revisionism is to emasculate the revolutionary spirit of the theory of Marxism-Leninism. Imperialism and the reactionaries of various countries, in order to save themselves from their fate of decline, are always exerting ceaselessly an influence on the working class. The revisionists of different hues always make use of a certain new situation to distort and adulterate the Marxist-Leninist revolutionary theory so as to lure the working class away from the correct path of revolutionary class struggle, to meet the needs of imperialism and the reactionaries of various countries. . . .

[*People's Daily* editorial, November 21, 1960. From text released by NCNA the same day.]

" Unity under the Banner of Marxism-Leninism "

The Bucharest conference proclaimed that all the conclusions of the Declaration and the Peace Manifesto concerning the peaceful co-existence of countries with different social systems, the possibility of preventing wars in the present period, the need for the peoples to maintain vigilance with regard to the danger of war, the struggle for peace as the paramount task, and the forms of transition of different countries from capitalism to socialism can be fully applied in the present situation too.

At the July plenary meeting of the central committee of the Communist Party of the Soviet Union, our party completely and fully approved the political line and the activity of its delegation, headed by N. S. Khrushchov, at the meeting in Bucharest and also the communiqué issued by this meeting. The C.P.S.U. unanimously stated that it was true to the principles of the Declaration and the Peace Manifesto, which had been tested by experience and fully retained their force under present-day conditions.

The Communist Party of the Soviet Union has always regarded the Leninist principle of the peaceful co-existence of states with different social systems as the general line of the Soviet Union's foreign policy. This principle does not deny the struggle of classes, nor does it mean the reconciliation of socialism with capitalism. Rather, it presupposes an intensification in the struggle for the triumph of socialist ideas, for the complete victory of socialism.

This principle, advanced by V. I. Lenin and further developed in the decisions of the 20th and 21st Congresses of the C.P.S.U., the documents of other Communist and Workers' Parties, and the Declaration and the Peace Manifesto, is the only correct principle for international relations when the world is divided into two systems—the socialist and the capitalist systems.

The C.P.S.U. firmly upholds the principles of creative Marxism-Leninism. Guided by these principles it drew major theoretical conclusions and made generalisations at its 20th and 21st Congresses. . . .

[*Pravda* editorial, November 23, 1960. From text in *Soviet News* (London: Soviet Embassy), No. 4382, November 25, 1960.]

8. The 1960 Moscow Statement

The deliberations in Moscow lasted some three weeks. The delegates of 81 Communist parties had taken part, representing the vast majority of the Communist movement which, according to the final Statement, was now active in 87 countries and embraced over 36 million members. The document that emerged, signed by all, expressed essentially the Soviet views on the major points that had been in dispute, but contained a number of concessions to the Chinese. These concessions meant in effect that Peking could interpret the Statement in such a way as to permit her to continue to pursue her more intransigent line in world affairs without laying herself open to charges of breach of faith from Moscow.[22]

The first section of the Statement defines the major features of the present epoch, a question dealt with at some length in the 1957 Declaration and " Long Live Leninism! " Here the major contention of the document is that: " It is the principal characteristic of our time that the world socialist system is becoming the decisive factor in the development of society." It adds that " Whatever efforts imperialism makes it cannot stop the advance of history. . . . The complete triumph of socialism is inevitable." The corollary of these assertions is that " A new stage has begun in the development of the general crisis of capitalism."

This analysis went a great deal further than the 1957 Declaration when it was claimed only that " the world socialist system, which is growing and becoming stronger, is exerting ever greater influence upon the international situation in the interests of peace and progress and the freedom of the peoples " and that imperialism was " heading towards decline."

The discussion in "Long Live Leninism! " of the present epoch was mainly aimed at refuting the idea that the advent of nuclear weapons had changed its nature. In that article, the Chinese contended that despite the increased strength of the *bloc,* lack of vigilance and a failure to struggle against imperialism would allow imperialism to be able to do as it pleased.

The importance of these semantic differences in practice is that the expression of greater confidence in the 1960 Statement means that the

---

[22] According to Crankshaw, *Observer,* Feb. 19, the document was signed in the interests of unity and Liu Shao-ch'i said he disagreed with some of its provisions.

Communist *bloc* does not have to pursue its aims with as great urgency and, therefore, militancy. If the Communist *bloc* is becoming the decisive factor in world affairs, if victory is inevitable, then there is room for manoeuvre and setbacks can be accepted as temporary and minor and nothing to worry about in the long run.

This overall confidence is reflected in the particular conclusions reached in the document. Section two deals with the Communist *bloc* and asserts that:

> Today the restoration of capitalism has been made socially and economically impossible not only in the Soviet Union, but in the other socialist countries as well. The combined forces of the socialist camp reliably safeguard every socialist country against encroachments by imperialist reaction.

This can be interpreted as an assertion that even if a country like Poland seeks American aid and permits a certain westernisation of its intellectual life, this will not lead to the Americanisation of the country which the Chinese have so strongly condemned in Yugoslavia, much less to Poland being lost to the *bloc*.

Section three deals with the problem of war and peace. Here the tone and some of the language is sternly Chinese. "U.S. imperialism" had already been described as the "chief bulwark of world reaction and an international gendarme" in the first section; here it is described as the "main force of aggression and war." The optimistic and relatively mild language of the Warsaw Pact declaration has completely disappeared.

Nevertheless the theoretical analyses of the inevitability of war made by Khrushchev at the *Twentieth* and *Twenty-first* Congresses of the CPSU are both included, this being the first occasion the Chinese had subscribed to the latter. The devastation that a nuclear war would entail is spelled out in terms never used by the Chinese, who had previously expressed contempt for American nuclear weapons.[23] The "democratic and peace forces" are said to have "*no tasks more pressing* than that of safeguarding humanity against a global thermonuclear disaster" (emphasis added).

The confident tone of the Statement is seen when one compares the assertion in it that "the time is past when the imperialists could decide at will whether there should or should not be war" with that in "Long Live Leninism!" that "whether or not the imperialists will unleash a war is not determined by us." But the Statement does, of course, admit the possibility of war, asserting in Chinese tones that "should the imperialist maniacs start war, the peoples will sweep capitalism out of existence and bury it."

[23] See "Long Live Leninism!" above pp. 92–94.

Not unexpectedly, the Statement is somewhat ambiguous on the importance of the "national liberation movement" in preventing war. On the one hand it lists that movement as one of the forces which could help to prevent war; on the other hand, the Statement does not list *encouraging* the movement as one of the tasks when describing what the fight for peace means. This represents a definite rejection of the Chinese view as expressed by Yü Chao-li quoted on p. 81. One might argue, therefore, that all Communists accept the value to their cause of such movements as the Algerian rebellion, but they have agreed, at least on the surface, that they will not commit themselves to encouraging such movements (by, say, arms deliveries) because, presumably, such actions would increase East-West tension and so the danger of world war.

The ambiguity is increased in section four which is devoted to national liberation movements and the problems of revolution in underdeveloped countries. The national liberation movement is said to receive " powerful support " from the Communist movement, but whether this support is to be moral or concrete is unspecified and therefore presumably left to individual Communist parties to interpret. But the assertion that

> The existence of the world socialist system and the weakening of the positions of imperialism have provided the oppressed peoples with new opportunities of winning independence

seems to suggest that it is sufficient for the Communist *bloc* to help the national liberation movement simply by existing.

There is further ambiguity in the discussion of how national liberation movements achieve success. The Statement mentions both armed struggle and non-military methods; yet it also asserts that the colonial powers never leave of their own free will, the kind of contention which the Chinese had normally used to justify the need for violence.

This section also includes a definition of what are called " independent national democracies "—broadly speaking, successor states to colonial régimes which are acceptable to the *bloc*. Space is devoted to the problem of the " national bourgeois " leadership in those countries, and it is asserted, in keeping with Chinese beliefs, that it has a tendency to compromise more and more with domestic reaction and imperialism. Local Communist parties are said to oppose such compromises; but there is no assertion of the kind Peking would probably have liked to the effect that the Communst *bloc* should give more than moral support where, as in the U.A.R., the local Communists are imprisoned.

In fact it is explicitly stated that Communist states reject " on principle any interference in the internal affairs of young national states ";

the subsequent assertion that Communist states also consider it their internationalist duty to help the peoples in strengthening their independence is designed to justify the substantial Soviet economic aid to non-Communist under-developed countries not in the Western camp.

A strict definition would appear to exclude the U.A.R. and Iraq from the list of independent national democracies though both are wooed by Moscow. But who is to do the defining, and what is the sanction to be imposed by the *bloc* on a state which drifts out of the category?

But perhaps the most important aspect of this section is an omission. There is no mention of the methods or even the need for Communist parties to *obtain power* in such countries. Clearly the Soviet view that the most important thing in the case of neutral countries is to keep them neutral won the day.

In contrast, the following section, devoted primarily to the problems of Communist parties in capitalist countries, does discuss the problem of achieving power. The possibility of " peaceful transition " without civil war is said to exist in a number of countries (another Soviet victory), though it is added that the possibility of non-peaceful transition must be borne in mind (a Chinese codicil?).

Great stress is laid on the need for united fronts with Social Democratic parties, primarily to struggle against atomic weapons and foreign bases. Significantly, Communist parties in deciding on their revolutionary tasks have to pay " due regard to the international situation " which is presumably a euphemism for the subordination of Western Communist parties' programmes to the needs of Soviet foreign policy.

The final section deals with the affairs of the Communist movement. Revisionism " remains " the main danger, but dogmatism is criticised at greater length. Significantly, the Soviet Communist Party is referred to only as the vanguard and not as the leader of the world movement.[24]

The 1960 Moscow Statement

REPRESENTATIVES of the Communist and Workers' Parties have discussed at this Meeting urgent problems of the present international situation and of the further struggle for peace, national independence, democracy and socialism.

The Meeting has shown unity of views among the participants on the issues discussed. The Communist and Workers' Parties have unanimously reaffirmed their allegiance to the Declaration and Peace Manifesto adopted in 1957. These programme documents of creative Marxism-Leninism determined the fundamental positions of the international Communist movement on the more important issues of our time and contributed in great measure toward uniting the efforts of the Communist and Workers' Parties

[24] For a discussion of the significance of this development, see above, pp. 29–32.

in the struggle to achieve common goals. They remain the banner and guide to action for the whole of the international Communist movement.

The course of events in the past three years has demonstrated the correctness of the analysis of the international situation and the outlook for world development as given in the Declaration and Peace Manifesto, and the great scientific force and effective role of creative Marxism-Leninism.

The chief result of these years is the rapid growth of the might and international influence of the world socialist system, the vigorous process of disintegration of the colonial system under the impact of the national-liberation movement, the intensification of class struggles in the capitalist world, and the continued decline and decay of the world capitalist system. The superiority of the forces of socialism over those of imperialism, of the forces of peace over those of war, is becoming ever more marked in the world arena.

Nevertheless, imperialism, which is intent on maintaining its positions, sabotages disarmament, seeks to prolong the cold war and aggravate it to the utmost, and persists in preparing a new world war. This situation demands ever closer joint efforts and resolute actions on the part of the socialist countries, the international working class, the national anti-imperialist movement, all peace-loving countries and all peace champions to prevent war and assure a peaceful life for people. It demands the further consolidation of all revolutionary forces in the fight against imperialism, for national independence and for socialism.

I

Our time, whose main content is the transition from capitalism to socialism initiated by the Great October Socialist Revolution, is a time of struggle between the two opposing social systems, a time of socialist revolutions and national-liberation revolutions, a time of the breakdown of imperialism, of the abolition of the colonial system, a time of transition of more peoples to the socialist path, of the triumph of socialism and communism on a world-wide scale.

It is the principal characteristic of our time that the world socialist system is becoming the decisive factor in the development of society.

The strength and invincibility of socialism have been demonstrated in recent decades in titanic battles between the new and old worlds. Attempts by the imperialists and their shock force—fascism—to check the course of historical development by force of arms ended in failure. Imperialism proved powerless to stop the socialist revolutions in Europe and Asia. Socialism became a world system. The imperialists tried to hamper the economic progress of the socialist countries, but their schemes were foiled. The imperialists did all in their power to preserve the system of colonial slavery, but that system is falling apart. As the world socialist system grows stronger, the international situation changes more and more in favour of the peoples fighting for independence, democracy and social progress.

Today it is the world socialist system and the forces fighting against imperialism, for a socialist transformation of society, that determine the main content, main trend and main features of the historical development of society. Whatever efforts imperialism makes, it cannot stop the advance of history. A reliable basis has been provided for further decisive victories for socialism. The complete triumph of socialism is inevitable.

The course of social development proves right Lenin's prediction that the countries of victorious socialism would influence the development of world revolution chiefly by their economic construction. Socialism has made unprecedented constructive progress in production, science and technology and in the establishment of a new, free community of people, in which their material and spiritual requirements are increasingly satisfied. The time is not far off when socialism's share of world production will be greater than that of capitalism. Capitalism will be defeated in the decisive sphere of human endeavour, the sphere of material production.

The consolidation and development of the socialist system exert an ever-increasing influence on the struggle of the peoples in the capitalist countries. By the force of its example, the world socialist system is revolutionising the thinking of the working people in the capitalist countries; it is inspiring them to fight against capitalism, and is greatly facilitating that fight. In the capitalist countries the forces fighting for peace and national independence and for the triumph of democracy and the victory of socialism are gaining in numbers and strength.

The world capitalist system is going through an intense process of disintegration and decay. Its contradictions have accelerated the development of monopoly capitalism into state-monopoly capitalism. By tightening the monopolies' grip on the life of the nation, state-monopoly capitalism closely combines the power of the monopolies with that of the state with the aim of saving the capitalist system and increasing the profits of the imperialist bourgeosie to the utmost by exploiting the working class and plundering large sections of the population.

But no matter what methods it resorts to the monopoly bourgeoisie cannot rescue capitalism. The interests of a handful of monopolies are in irreconcilable contradiction to the interest of the entire nation. The class and national antagonisms, and the internal and external contradictions of capitalist society, have sharpened greatly. Attempts to prop the decayed pillars of capitalism by militarism are aggravating these contradictions still further.

Never has the conflict between the productive forces and relations of production in the capitalist countries been so acute. Capitalism impedes more and more the use of the achievements of modern science and technology in the interests of social progress. It turns the discoveries of human genius against mankind itself by converting them into formidable means of destructive warfare.

The instability of capitalist economy is growing. Although production in some capitalist countries is increasing to some degree or other, the contradictions of capitalism are becoming more acute on a national as well as international scale. Some capitalist countries are faced with the threat of new economic upheavals while still grappling with the consequences of the recent economic crisis. The anarchical nature of capitalist production is becoming more marked. Capitalist concentration is assuming unprecedented dimensions, and monopoly profits and superprofits are growing. Monopoly capital has greatly intensified the exploitation of the working class in new forms, above all through intensification of labour. Automation and "rationalisation" under capitalism bring the working people further calamities. Only by a stubborn struggle has the working class in some countries succeeded in winning a number of its pressing demands. In many capitalist countries, however, the standard of life is still below pre-war.

Despite the promises made by the bourgeoisie, full employment was provided only in some of the capitalist countries, and only temporarily. The domination of the monopolies is causing increasing harm to the interests of the broad peasant masses and large sections of the small and middle bourgeoisie. In the capitalist countries, including some of the more developed, economically underdeveloped areas still exist where the poverty of the masses is appalling, and which, moreover, continue to expand.

These facts once again refute the lies which bourgeois ideologists and revisionists spread to the effect that modern capitalism has become " people's capitalism ", that it has established a so-called " welfare state " capable of overcoming the anarchy of production and economic crises and assuring well-being for all working people.

The uneven course of development of capitalism is continuously changing the balance of forces between the imperialist countries. The narrower the sphere of imperialist domination, the stronger the antagonisms between the imperialist powers. The problem of markets has become more acute than ever. The new inter-state organisations which are established under the slogan of " integration " actually lead to increased antagonisms and struggle between the imperialist countries. They are new forms of division of the world capitalist market among the biggest capitalist combines, of penetration by stronger imperialist states of the economy of their weaker partners.

The decay of capitalism is particularly marked in the United States of America, the chief imperialist country of today. U.S. monopoly capital is clearly unable to use all the productive forces at its command. The richest of the developed capitalist countries of the world—the United States of America—has become a land of especially big chronic unemployment. Increasing under-capacity operation in industry has become permanent in that country. Despite the enormous increase in military appropriations, which is achieved at the expense of the standard of life of the working people, the rate of growth of production has been declining in the post-war years and has been barely above the growth of population. Over-production crises have become more frequent. The most developed capitalist country has become a country of the most distorted, militarised economy. More than any other capitalist country, the United States drains Asia, and especially Latin America, of their riches, holding up their progress. U.S. capitalist penetration into Africa is increasing. *U.S. imperialism has become the biggest international exploiter.*

The U.S. imperialists seek to bring many states under their control, by resorting chiefly to the policy of military blocs and economic " aid ". They violate the sovereignty of developed capitalist countries as well. The dominant monopoly bourgeoisie in the more developed capitalist countries, which has allied itself with U.S. imperialism, sacrifices the sovereignty of their countries, hoping with support from the U.S. imperialists to crush the revolutionary liberation forces, deprive the working people of democratic freedoms and impede the struggle of the masses for social progress. U.S. imperialism involves those countries in the arms race, in a policy of preparing a new war of aggression and carrying on subversive activities against socialist and neutral countries.

The pillars of the capitalist system have become so decayed that the ruling imperialist bourgeoisie in many countries can no longer resist on its own the forces of democracy and progress which are gaining in scope and strength. The imperialists form military-political alliances under U.S. leadership to fight in common against the socialist camp and to strangle the national-liberation, working-class and socialist movements. *International developments in recent years have furnished many new proofs of the fact that U.S. imperialism is the chief bulwark of world reaction and an international gendarme, that it has become an enemy of the peoples of the whole world.*

The system of military blocs set up by the United States is being weakened both by the struggle going on between their members and as a result of the struggle which the people are waging for the abolition of these blocs. The U.S. imperialists seek to strengthen aggressive blocs, which causes increased resistance on the part of the people. The United States remains the main economic, financial and military force of modern imperialism, although its share in capitalist economy is diminishing. The British and French imperialists are making stubborn efforts to uphold their positions. The monopolies of West Germany and Japan, which have recovered their might and which are closely linked with the U.S. monopolies, are stepping up expansion. The West German monopolies, in pursuing their imperialist policy, seek more and more to exploit the underdeveloped countries.

The peoples are rising with growing determination to fight imperialism. A great struggle is getting under way between the forces of labour and capital, of democracy and reaction, of freedom and colonialism. The victory of the popular revolution in Cuba has become a splendid example for the peoples of Latin America. An anti-colonial movement for freedom and national independence is expanding irresistibly in Africa. The anti-imperialist national uprising in Iraq has been crowned with success. A powerful movement of the people against the Japanese-U.S. military alliance, for peace, democracy and national independence, is under way in Japan. Vigorous actions by the masses in Italy in defence of democracy show the militant resolve of the working people. The struggle for democracy, against the reactionary régime of personal power, is gathering momentum in France. There have been big working-class strikes in the U.S.A., Argentina, Uruguay, Chile, India, Britain, Canada, Belgium and other capitalist countries. The actions of the Negro people in the United States for their fundamental rights are assuming a mass character. There is a growing desire to unite the national forces against the fascist dictatorships in Spain and Portugal, and the democratic movement is gaining strength in Greece. Tyrannical military régimes have been overthrown in Colombia and Venezuela, a blow has been dealt to frankly pro-American puppet governments in South Korea and Turkey. A national-democratic movement, directed against the U.S. imperialists and their flunkeys, is developing in South Viet-Nam and Laos. The Indonesian people are doing away with the economic positions the imperialists still retain in that country, particularly the positions held by the Dutch colonialists. The mass movement in defence of peace is gaining ground in all continents. All this is graphic evidence that the tide of anti-imperialist, national-liberation, anti-war and class struggles is rising ever higher.

A new stage has begun in the development of the general crisis of capitalism. This is shown by the triumph of socialism in a large group of European and Asian countries embracing one-third of mankind, the powerful growth of the forces fighting for socialism throughout the world and the steady weakening of the imperialists' positions in the economic competition with socialism; the tremendous new upsurge of the national-liberation struggle and the mounting disintegration of the colonial system; the growing instability of the entire world economic system of capitalism; the sharpening contradictions of capitalism resulting from the growth of state-monopoly capitalism and militarism; the increasing contradictions between monopolies and the interests of the nation as a whole; the curtailment of bourgeois democracy and the tendency to adopt autocratic and fascist methods of government; and a profound crisis in bourgeois politics and ideology. This stage is distinguished by the fact that it has set in not as a result of the world war, but in the conditions of competition and struggle between the two systems, an increasing change in the balance of forces in favour of socialism, and a marked aggravation of all the contradictions of imperialism. It has taken place at a time when a successful struggle by the peace-loving forces to bring about and promote peaceful coexistence has prevented the imperialists from undermining world peace by their aggressive actions, and in an atmosphere of growing struggle by the broad masses of the people for democracy, national liberation and socialism.

All the revolutionary forces are rallying against imperialist oppression and exploitation. The peoples who are building socialism and communism, the revolutionary movement of the working class in the capitalist countries, the national-liberation struggle of the oppressed peoples and the general democratic movement—these great forces of our time are merging into one powerful current that undermines and destroys the world imperialist system. The central factors of our day are the international working class and its chief creation, the world socialist system. They are an earnest of victory in the struggle for peace, democracy, national liberation, socialism and human progress.

II

A new stage has begun in the development of the world socialist system. The Soviet Union is successfully carrying on the full-scale construction of a communist society. Other countries of the socialist camp are successfully laying the foundations of socialism, and some of them have already entered the period of construction of a developed socialist society.

The socialist system as a whole has scored decisive victories. These victories signify the triumph of Marxism-Leninism; they show clearly to all the peoples who are under the domination of capital that a society based on this doctrine opens up immense opportunities for the fullest development of economy and culture, for the provision of a high standard of living and a peaceful and happy life for people.

The Soviet people, successfully carrying out the Seven-Year Economic Development Plan, are rapidly building up a material and technical basis for communism. Soviet science has ushered in what is virtually a new era in the development of world civilisation; it has initiated the exploration of outer space, furnishing impressive evidence of the economic and technical might of the socialist camp. The Soviet Union is the first country in history to be blazing a trail to communism for all mankind. It is the most striking example and most powerful bulwark for the people of the world in their struggle for peace, democratic freedoms, national independence and social progress.

The people's revolution in China dealt a crushing blow at the positions of imperialism in Asia and contributed in great measure to the balance of the world forces changing in favour of socialism. By giving a further powerful impetus to the national-liberation movement, it exerted tremendous influence on the peoples, especially those of Asia, Africa and Latin America.

The people's democratic republics of Albania, Bulgaria, Hungary, the German Democratic Republic, the Democratic Republic of Viet-Nam, China, the Korean People's Democratic Republic, Mongolia, Poland, Roumania and the Czechoslovak Socialist Republic, which, together with the great Soviet Union, form the mighty socialist camp, have within a historically short period made remarkable progress in socialist construction.

People's government in these countries has proved its unshakable solidity. Socialist relations of production predominate in the national economy; the exploitation of man by man has been abolished for ever, or is successfully being liquidated. The success of the policy of socialist industrialisation has led to a great economic upsurge in the socialist countries, which are developing their economy much faster than the capitalist countries. All these countries have established a developed industry; agrarian in the past, they have become, or are becoming, industrial-agrarian countries.

In recent years all the People's Democracies have solved, or have been successfully solving, the most difficult problem of socialist construction, that of transferring the peasantry, on a voluntary basis, from the road of small private farming to the road of large-scale co-operative farming on socialist lines. Lenin's co-operative plan has proved its great vitality both for countries where the peasant's attachment to private land ownership was a long-standing tradition and for countries that have recently put an end to feudal relations. The fraternal alliance of workers and peasants, which is led by the working class, and the maintenance and consolidation of which is, as Lenin taught, a supreme principle of the dictatorship of the proletariat, has grown stronger. In the course of socialist construction this alliance of two classes of working people, which constitutes the political foundation of the socialist system, develops continuously, and further strengthens people's rule under the leadership of the working class and promotes the socialist reorganisation of agriculture in accordance with the Leninist principle of voluntary co-operation of the peasantry.

Historic changes have taken place in the social structure of society. The classes of landlords and capitalists no longer exist in the People's Democracies. The working class has become the main force of society; its ranks are growing; its political consciousness and maturity have increased. Socialism has delivered the peasantry from age-long poverty and has made it an active force in social progress. A new, socialist intelligentsia, flesh of the flesh of the working people, is arising. All citizens have free access to knowledge and culture. Socialism has thus created not only political but material conditions for the cultural development of society, for the all-round and complete development of the gifts and abilities of man. The standard of life of the people is improving steadily thanks to economic progress.

An unbreakable alliance of the working people of all nationalities has formed and has been consolidated in multi-national socialist states. The triumph of Marxist-Leninist national policy in the socialist countries, genuine equality of nationalities, and their economic and cultural progress serve as an inspiring example for the peoples fighting against national oppression.

In the People's Democracies, socialist ideology has achieved notable successes in its struggle against bourgeois ideology. It is a long struggle that will go on until the complete emancipation of the minds of people from the survivals of bourgeois ideology.

The moral and political unity of society, which for the first time in history has come into existence and firmly established itself in the Soviet Union, is growing now in the other socialist countries as well. This makes it possible to use the creative energy of free workers most effectively for promoting the growth of the productive forces and the prosperity of socialist society.

Socialist society is improving steadily and becoming more and more mature; day after day it gives rise to a Communist attitude to labour and other elements of the future Communist society. The methods of socialist economic management and economic planning are steadily improving. Socialist democracy continues to develop; the masses are playing an increasing role in directing economic and cultural development; certain functions of the state are being gradually transferred to public organisations.

Today the restoration of capitalism has been made socially and economically impossible not only in the Soviet Union, but in the other socialist countries as well. The combined forces of the socialist camp reliably safeguard every socialist country against encroachments by imperialist reaction. Thus the rallying of the socialist states in one camp and the growing unity and steadily increasing strength of this camp ensure complete victory for socialism within the entire system.

Thanks to the heroic effort of the working class and the peasantry and to the tremendous work of the Communist and Workers' Parties, most favourable objective opportunities have been provided in the past years for the further rapid development of the productive forces, for gaining the maximum time and achieving victory for the socialist countries in peaceful economic competition with capitalism. The Marxist-Leninist Parties heading the socialist countries consider it their duty to make proper use of these opportunities.

Having achieved major victories and withstood serious tests, the Communist Parties have gained ample and varied experience in directing socialist construction. The socialist countries and the socialist camp as a whole owe their achievements to the proper application of the general objective laws governing socialist construction, with due regard to the historical peculiarities of each country and to the interests of the entire socialist system; they owe them to the efforts of the peoples of those countries, to their close fraternal co-operation and mutual internationalist assistance, and above all, to the fraternal, internationalist assistance from the Soviet Union.

The experience of development of the socialist countries is added evidence that mutual assistance and support, and utilisation of all the advantages of unity and solidarity among the countries of the socialist camp, are a primary international condition for their achievements and successes. Imperialist, renegade and revisionist hopes of a split within the socialist camp are built on sand and doomed to failure. All the socialist countries cherish the unity of the socialist camp like the apple of their eye.

The world economic system of socialism is united by common socialist relations of production and is developing in accordance with the economic laws of socialism. Its successful development requires consistent application, in socialist construction, of the law of planned, proportionate development; encouragement of the creative initiative of the people; continuous improvement of the system of international division of labour through the co-ordination of national economic plans, specialisation and co-operation in production within the world socialist system on the basis of voluntary participation, mutual benefit and vigorous improvement of the scientific and technological standard. It requires study of collective experience; extended co-operation and fraternal mutual assistance; gradual elimination, along these lines, of historical differences in the levels of economic development, and the provision of a material basis for a more or less simultaneous transition of all the peoples of the socialist system to communism.

Socialist construction in the various countries is a source of collective experience for the socialist camp as a whole. A thorough study of this experience by the fraternal parties, and its proper utilisation and elaboration with due regard to specific conditions and national peculiarities are an immutable law of the development of every socialist country.

In developing industrial and agricultural production in their countries at a high rate in keeping with the possibilities they have, the Communist and Workers' Parties of the socialist countries consider it their internationalist duty to make full use of all the advantages of the socialist system and the internal resources of every country to carry out, by joint effort and as speedily as possible, the historic task of surpassing the world capitalist system in overall industrial and agricultural production and then outstrip the economically most developed capitalist countries in *per capita* output and in the standard of living. To carry out this task, it is necessary steadily to improve political and economic work, continuously to improve the methods of economic management and to run the socialist economy along scientific lines. This calls for higher productivity of labour to be achieved through continuous technical progress, economic planning, strict observance of the Leninist principle of providing material incentives and moral stimuli to work for the good of society by heightening the political consciousness of the people, and for control over the measure of labour and consumption.

To provide a material basis for the transition of the socialist countries to communism, it is indispensable to achieve a high level of production through the use of the latest techniques, electrification of the national economy, and mechanisation and automation of production, without which it is impossible to provide the abundance of consumer goods required by a communist society. On this basis, it is necessary to develop communist social relations, vigorously promote the political consciousness of the people and educate the members of the new, communist society.

The socialist camp is a social, economic and political community of free and sovereign peoples united by the close bonds of international socialist solidarity; by common interests and objectives, and following the path of socialism and communism. It is an inviolable law of the mutual relations between socialist countries strictly to adhere to the principles of Marxism-Leninism and socialist internationalism. Every country in the socialist camp is ensured genuinely equal rights and independence. Guided by the principles of complete equality, mutual advantage and comradely mutual assistance, the socialist states improve their all-round economic, political and cultural co-operation, which meets both the interests of each socialist country and those of the socialist camp as a whole.

One of the greatest achievements of the world socialist system is the practical confirmation of the Marxist-Leninist thesis that national antagonisms diminish with the decline of class antagonisms. In contrast to the laws of the capitalist system, which is characterised by antagonistic contradictions between classes, nations and states leading to armed conflicts, there are no objective causes in the nature of the socialist system for contradictions and conflicts between the peoples and states belonging to it. Its development leads to greater unity among the states and nations and to the consolidation of all the forms of co-operation between them. Under socialism, the development of national economy, culture and statehood goes hand in hand with the strengthening and development of the entire world socialist system, and with an ever greater consolidation of the unity of nations. The interests of the socialist system as a whole and national interests are harmoniously combined. It is on this basis that the moral and political unity of all the peoples of the great socialist community has arisen and has been growing. Fraternal friendship and mutual assistance of peoples, born of the socialist system, have superseded the political isolation and national egoism typical of capitalism.

The common interests of the peoples of the socialist countries and the interests of peace and socialism demand the proper combination of the principles of socialist internationalism and socialist patriotism in politics. Every Communist Party which has become the ruling party in the state, bears historical responsibility for the destinies of both its country and the entire socialist camp.

The Declaration of 1957 points out quite correctly that undue emphasis on the role of national peculiarities and departure from the universal truth of Marxism-Leninism regarding the socialist revolution and socialist construction prejudice the common cause of socialism. The Declaration also states quite correctly that Marxism-Leninism demands creative application of the general principles of socialist revolution and socialist construction depending on the specific historical conditions in the country concerned, and does not permit of a mechanical copying of the policies and tactics of the Communist Parties of other countries. Disregard of national peculiarities may lead to the party of the proletariat being isolated from reality, from the masses, and may injure the socialist cause.

Manifestations of nationalism and national narrow-mindedness do not disappear automatically with the establishment of the socialist system. If fraternal relations and friendship between the socialist countries are to be strengthened, it is necessary that the Communist and Workers' Parties pursue a Marxist-Leninist internationalist policy, that all working people be educated in a spirit of internationalism and patriotism, and that a resolute struggle be waged to eliminate the survivals of bourgeois nationalism and chauvinism.

The Communist and Workers' Parties tirelessly educate the working people in the spirit of socialist internationalism and intolerance of all manifestations of nationalism and chauvinism. Solid unity of the Communist and Workers' Parties and of the peoples of the socialist countries, and their loyalty to the Marxist-Leninist doctrine are the main source of the strength and invincibility of each socialist country and the socialist camp as a whole.

In blazing a trail to communism, the peoples of the socialist countries are creating a prototype of a new society for all mankind. The working people of the capitalist world are following the constructive effort of the builders of socialism and communism with keen interest. This makes the Marxist-Leninist Parties and the peoples of the socialist countries accountable to the international working-class movement for the successful building of socialism and communism.

The Communist and Workers' Parties see it as their task indefatigably to strengthen the great socialist community of nations, whose international role and influence on the course of world events are growing from year to year.

The time has come when the socialist states have, by forming a world system, become an international force exerting a powerful influence on world development. There are now real opportunities of solving cardinal problems of modern times in a new way, in the interests of peace, democracy and socialism.

III

The problem of war and peace is the most burning problem of our time. War is a constant companion of capitalism. The system of exploitation of man by man and the system of extermination of man by man are two aspects of the capitalist system. Imperialism has already inflicted two devastating world wars on mankind and now threatens to plunge it into an even more terrible catastrophe. Monstrous means of mass annihilation and destruction have been developed which, if used in a new war, can cause unheard-of destruction to entire countries and reduce key centres of world industry and culture to ruins. Such a war would bring death and suffering to hundreds of millions of people, among them people in countries not involved in it. Imperialism spells grave danger to the whole of mankind.

The peoples must now be more vigilant than ever. As long as imperialism exists there will be soil for wars of aggression.

The peoples of all countries know that the danger of a new world war still persists. U.S. imperialism is the main force of aggression and war. Its policy embodies the ideology of militant reaction. The U.S. imperialists, together with the imperialists of Britain, France and West Germany, have drawn many countries into NATO, CENTO, SEATO and other military blocs under the guise of combating the " communist menace "; it has enmeshed the so-called " free world ", that is, capitalist countries which depend on them, in a network of military bases spearheaded first and foremost against the socialist countries. The existence of these blocs and bases endangers universal peace and security and not only encroaches upon the sovereignty but also imperils the very life of those countries which put their territory at the disposal of the U.S. militarists.

The imperialist forces of the U.S.A., Britain and France have made a criminal deal with West-German imperialism. In West Germany militarism has been revived and the restoration is being pushed ahead of a vast regular army under the command of Hitler generals, which the U.S. imperialists are equipping with nuclear and rocket weapons and other modern means of mass annihilation, a fact which draws emphatic protests from the peace-loving peoples. Military bases are being provided for this aggressive army in France and other West-European countries. The threat to peace and the security of the European nations from West-German imperialism is increasing. The West-German revenge-seekers openly declare their intention to revise the borders established after the Second World War. Like the Hitler clique in its day, the West-German militarists are preparing war against the socialist and other countries of Europe, and strive to effect their own aggressive plans. West Berlin has been transformed into a seat of international provocation. The Bonn state has become the chief enemy of peaceful coexistence, disarmament and relaxation of tension in Europe.

The aggressive plans of the West-German imperialists must be opposed by the united might of all the peace-loving countries and nations of Europe. An especially big part in the struggle against the aggressive designs of the West-German militarists is played by the German Democratic Republic. The Meeting regards it as the duty of all the countries of the socialist camp and of all the peace-loving peoples to defend the German Democratic Republic—the outpost of socialism in Western Europe and the true expression of the peace aspirations of the German nation.

The U.S. imperialists are also busy reviving the hotbed of war in the Far East. Trampling upon the national independence of the Japanese people and contrary to their will, they have, in collusion with the Japanese reactionary ruling circles, imposed upon Japan a new military treaty which pursues aggressive aims against the Soviet Union, the Chinese People's Republic and other peace-loving countries. The U.S. invaders have occupied the island of Taiwan, which belongs to the Chinese People's Republic, and South Korea and are interfering more and more in the affairs of South Viet-Nam; they have turned them into hotbeds of dangerous military provocations and gambles. Threatening Cuba with aggression and interfering in the affairs of the peoples of Latin America, Africa and the Middle East, the U.S. imperialists strive to create new seats of war in different parts of the world. They use such forms of regional alliance as, for example, the Organisation of American States, to retain their economic and political control and to involve the peoples of Latin America in the realisation of their aggressive schemes.

The U.S. imperialists have set up a huge war machinery and refuse to allow its reduction. The imperialists frustrate all constructive disarmament proposals by the Soviet Union and other peaceful countries. The arms race is going on. Stockpiles of nuclear weapons are becoming dangerously large. Defying protests from their own people and the peoples of other countries, particularly in the African continent, the French ruling circles are testing and manufacturing atomic weapons. The U.S. militarists are preparing to resume disastrous atomic tests; military provocations that threaten serious international conflicts continue.

The U.S. ruling circles have wrecked the Paris meeting of the Heads of Government of the four Great Powers by their policy of provocations and aggressive acts, and have set out to increase international tension and aggravate the cold war. The war menace has grown.

The imperialist provocations against peace have aroused the indignation and resistance of the peoples. U.S. imperialism has exposed itself still more and its influence in the world has sustained fresh and telling blows.

The aggressive nature of imperialism has not changed. But real forces have appeared that are capable of foiling its plans of aggression. War is not fatally inevitable. Had the imperialists been able to do what they wanted, they would already have plunged mankind into the abyss of the calamities and horrors of a new world war. But the time is past when the imperialists could decide at will whether there should or should not be war. More than once in the past years the imperialists have brought mankind to the brink of world catastrophe by starting local wars. The resolute stand of the Soviet Union, of the other socialist states and of all the peaceful forces put an end to the Anglo-Franco-Israeli intervention in Egypt, and averted a military invasion of Syria, Iraq and some other countries by the imperialists. The heroic people of Algeria continue their valiant battle for independence and freedom. The peoples of the Congo and Laos are resisting the criminal acts of the imperialists with increasing firmness. Experience shows that it is possible to combat effectively the local wars started by the imperialists, and to stamp out successfully the hotbeds of such wars.

The time has come when the attempts of the imperialist aggressors to start a world war can be curbed. World war can be prevented by the joint efforts of the world socialist camp, the international working class, the national-liberation movement, all the countries opposing war and all peace-loving forces.

The development of international relations in our day is determined by the struggle of the two social systems—the struggle of the forces of socialism, peace and democracy against the forces of imperialism, reaction and aggression—a struggle in which the superiority of the forces of socialism, peace and democracy is becoming increasingly obvious.

For the first time in history, war is opposed by great and organised forces: the mighty Soviet Union, which now leads the world in the decisive branches of science and technology; the entire socialist camp, which has placed its great material and political might at the service of peace; a growing number of peace-loving countries of Asia, Africa and Latin America, which have a vital interest in preserving peace; the international working class and its organisations, above all the Communist Parties; the national-liberation movement of the peoples of the colonies and dependent countries; the world peace movement; and the neutral countries which want no share in the imperialist policy of war and advocate peaceful coexistence. The policy of peaceful coexistence is also favoured by a definite section of the bourgeoisie of the developed capitalist countries, which takes a sober view of the relationship of forces and of the dire consequences of a modern war. The broadest possible united front of peace supporters, fighters against the imperialist policy of aggression and war inspired by U.S. imperialism, is essential to preserve world peace. Concerted and vigorous actions of all the forces of peace can safeguard the peace and prevent a new war.

The democratic and peace forces today have no task more pressing than that of safeguarding humanity against a global thermo-nuclear disaster. The unprecedented destructive power of modern means of warfare demands that the main actions of the anti-war and peace-loving forces be directed towards preventing war. The struggle against war cannot be put off until war breaks out, for then it may prove too late for many areas of the globe and for their population to combat it. *The struggle against the threat of a new world war must be waged now and not when atom and hydrogen bombs begin to fall, and it must gain in strength from day to day. The important thing is to curb the aggressors in good time, to prevent war, and not to let it break out.*

To fight for peace today means to maintain the greatest vigilance, indefatigably to lay bare the policy of the imperialists, to keep a watchful eye on the intrigues and manoeuvres of the warmongers, arouse the righteous indignation of the peoples against those who are heading for war, organise the peace forces still better, continuously intensify mass actions for peace, and promote co-operation with all countries which have no interest in new wars. In the countries where the imperialists have established war bases, it is necessary to step up the struggle for their abolition, which is an important factor for fortifying national independence, defending sovereignty, and preventing war. The struggle of the peoples against the militarisation of their countries should be combined with the struggle against the capitalist monopolies connected with the U.S. imperialists. Today as never before, it is important to fight perseveringly in all countries to make the peace movement thrive and extend to towns and villages, factories and offices.

The peace movement is the broadest movement of our time, involving people of diverse political and religious creeds, of diverse classes of society, who are all united by the noble urge to prevent new wars and to secure enduring peace.

Further consolidation of the world socialist system will be of prime importance in preserving durable peace. So long as there is no disarmament, the socialist countries must maintain their defence potential at an adequate level.

In the opinion of Communists the tasks which must be accomplished first of all if peace is to be safeguarded are to stop the arms race, ban nuclear weapons, their tests and production, dismantle foreign war bases and withdraw foreign troops from other countries, disband military blocs, conclude a peace treaty with Germany, turn West Berlin into a demilitarised free city, thwart the aggressive designs of the West-German revanchists, and prevent the revival of Japanese militarism.

History has placed a great responsibility for warding off a new world war first and foremost on the international working class. The imperialists plot and join forces to start a thermo-nuclear war. The international working class must close its ranks to save mankind from the disaster of a new world war. *No political, religious or other differences should be an obstacle to all the forces of the working class uniting against the war danger. The hour has struck to counter the forces of war by the mighty will and joint action of all the contingents and organisations of the world proletariat, to unite its forces to avert world war and safeguard peace.*

The Communist Parties regard the fight for peace as their prime task. They call on the working class, trade unions, co-operatives, women's and youth leagues and organisations, on all working people, irrespective of their political and religious convictions, firmly to repulse by mass struggles all acts of aggression on the part of the imperialists.

But should the imperialist maniacs start war, the peoples will sweep capitalism out of existence and bury it.

The foreign policy of the socialist countries rests on the firm foundation of the Leninist principle of peaceful coexistence and economic competition between the socialist and capitalist countries. In conditions of peace, the socialist system increasingly reveals its advantages over the capitalist system in all fields of economy, culture, science and technology. The near future will bring the forces of peace and socialism new successes. The U.S.S.R. will become the leading industrial power of the world. China will become a mighty industrial state. The socialist system will be turning out more than half the world industrial product. The peace zone will expand. The working-class movement in the capitalist countries and the national-liberation movement in the colonies and dependencies will achieve new victories. The disintegration of the colonial system will become completed. The superiority of the forces of socialism and peace will be absolute. *In these conditions a real possibility will have arisen to exclude world war from the life of society even before socialism achieves complete victory on earth, with capitalism still existing in a part of the world.* The victory of socialism all over the world will completely remove the social and national causes of wars.

The Communists of all the world uphold peaceful coexistence unanimously and consistently, and battle resolutely for the prevention of war. The Communists must work untiringly among the masses to prevent underestimation of the possibility of averting a world war, underestimation of the possibility of peaceful coexistence and, at the same time, underestimation of the danger of war.

In a world divided into two systems, the only correct and reasonable principle of international relations is the principle of peaceful coexistence of states with different social systems advanced by Lenin and further elaborated in the Moscow Declaration and the Peace Manifesto of 1957, in the decisions of the 20th and 21st Congresses of the C.P.S.U., and in the documents of other Communist and Workers' Parties.

The Five Principles jointly advanced by the Chinese People's Republic and the Republic of India, and the propositions adopted at the Bandung Conference accord with the interests of peace and the peace-loving peoples.

Peaceful coexistence of countries with different systems or destructive war —this is the alternative today. There is no other choice. Communists emphatically reject the U.S. doctrine of "cold war" and "brinkmanship", for it is a policy leading to thermo-nuclear catastrophe. By upholding the principle of peaceful coexistence, Communists fight for the complete cessation of the cold war, disbandment of military blocs, and dismantling of military bases, for general and complete disarmament under international control, the settlement of international disputes through negotiation, respect for the equality of states and their territorial integrity, independence and sovereignty, non-interference in each other's internal affairs, extensive development of trade, cultural and scientific ties between nations.

The policy of peaceful coexistence meets the basic interests of all peoples, of all who want no new cruel wars and seek durable peace. This policy strengthens the positions of socialism, enhances the prestige and international influence of the socialist countries and promotes the prestige and influence of the Communist Parties in the capitalist countries. Peace is a loyal ally of socialism, for time is working for socialism against capitalism.

The policy of peaceful coexistence meets the basic interests of all peoples, launching vigorous action against the enemies of peace. Peaceful coexistence of states does not imply renunciation of the class struggle as the revisionists claim. The coexistence of states with different social systems is a form of class struggle between socialism and capitalism. In conditions of peaceful coexistence favourable opportunities are provided for the development of the class struggle in the capitalist countries and the national-liberation movement of the peoples of the colonial and dependent countries. In their turn, the successes of the revolutionary class and national-liberation struggle promote peaceful coexistence. The Communists consider it their duty to fortify the faith of the people in the possibility of furthering peaceful coexistence, their determination to prevent world war. They will do their utmost for the people to weaken imperialism and limit its sphere of action by an active struggle for peace, democracy and national liberation.

Peaceful coexistence of countries with different social systems does not mean conciliation of the socialist and bourgeois ideologies. On the contrary, it implies intensification of the struggle of the working class, of all the Communist Parties, for the triumph of socialist ideas. But ideological and political disputes between states must not be settled through war.

The meeting considers that the implementation of the programme for general and complete disarmament put forward by the Soviet Union would be of historic importance for the destinies of mankind. To realise this programme means to eliminate the very possibility of waging wars between countries. It is not easy to realise owing to the stubborn resistance of the imperialists. Hence it is essential to wage an active and determined struggle against the aggressive imperialist forces with the aim of carrying this programme into practice. It is necessary to wage this struggle on an increasing scale and to strive perseveringly to achieve tangible results—the banning of the testing and manufacture of nuclear weapons, the abolition of military blocs and war bases on foreign soil and a substantial reduction of armed forces and armaments, all of which should pave the way to general disarmament. Through an active, determined struggle by the socialist and other peace-loving countries, by the international working class and the broad masses in all countries, it is possible to isolate the aggressive circles, foil the arms race and war preparations, and force the imperialists into an agreement on general disarmament.

The arms race is not a war-deterrent, nor does it make for a high degree of employment and well-being of the population. It leads to war. Only a handful of monopolies and war speculators are interested in the arms race. In the capitalist countries, the people constantly demand that military expenditures be reduced and the funds thus released be used to improve the living conditions of the masses. In each country, it is necessary to promote a broad mass movement, for the use of the funds and resources to be released through disarmament for the needs of civilian production, housing, health, public education, social security, scientific research, etc. Disarmament has now become a fighting slogan of the masses, a pressing historical necessity. By an active and resolute struggle the imperialists must be made to meet this demand of the peoples.

The Communist and Workers' Parties of the socialist countries will go on consistently pursuing the policy of peaceful coexistence of states with different social systems and doing their utmost to spare the peoples the horrors and calamities of a new war. They will display the greatest vigilance towards imperialism, vigorously strengthen the might and defensive capacity of the entire socialist camp and take every step to safeguard the security of the peoples and preserve peace.

The Communists regard it as their historical mission not only to abolish exploitation and poverty on a world scale and rule out for all time the possibility of any kind of war in the life of human society, but also to deliver mankind from the nightmare of a new world war already in our time. The Communist Parties will devote all their strength and energy to this great historical mission.

IV

National-liberation revolutions have triumphed in vast areas of the world. About forty new sovereign states have arisen in Asia and Africa in the fifteen post-war years. The victory of the Cuban revolution has powerfully stimulated the struggle of the Latin-American peoples for complete national independence. A new historical period has set in in the life of mankind: the peoples of Asia, Africa and Latin America that have won their freedom have begun to take an active part in world politics.

The complete collapse of colonialism is imminent. The breakdown of the system of colonial slavery under the impact of the national-liberation movement is a development ranking second in historic importance only to the formation of the world socialist system.

The Great October Socialist Revolution aroused the East and drew the colonial peoples into the common current of the world-wide revolutionary movement. This development was greatly facilitated by the Soviet Union's victory in the Second World War, the establishment of people's democracy

in a number of European and Asian countries, the triumph of the socialist revolution in China, and the formation of the world socialist system. The forces of world socialism contributed decisively to the struggle of the colonial and dependent peoples for liberation from imperialist oppression. The socialist system has become a reliable shield for the independent national development of the peoples who have won freedom. The national-liberation movement receives powerful support from the international working-class movement.

The face of Asia has changed radically. The colonial order is collapsing in Africa. A front of active struggle against imperialism has opened in Latin America. Hundreds of millions of people in Asia, Africa and other parts of the world have won their independence in hard-fought battles with imperialism. Communists have always recognised the progressive, revolutionary significance of national-liberation wars; they are the most active champions of national independence. The existence of the world socialist system and the weakening of the positions of imperialism have provided the oppressed peoples with new opportunities of winning independence.

The peoples of the colonial countries win their independence both through armed struggle and by non-military methods, depending on the specific conditions in the country concerned. They secure durable victory through a powerful national-liberation movement. The colonial powers never bestow freedom on the colonial peoples and never leave of their own free will the countries they are exploiting.

The United States is the mainstay of colonialism today. The imperialists, headed by the U.S.A., make desperate efforts to preserve colonial exploitation of the peoples of the former colonies by new methods and in new forms. The monopolies try to retain their hold on the levers of economic control and political influence in Asian, African and Latin American countries. These efforts are aimed at preserving their positions in the economy of the countries which have gained freedom, and at capturing new positions under the guise of economic " aid," drawing them into military blocs, implanting military dictatorships and setting up war bases there. The imperialists endeavour to emasculate and undermine the national sovereignty of the newly-free countries, to misrepresent the principle of self-determination of nations, to impose new forms of colonial domination under the spurious slogan of " inter-dependence," to put their puppets in power in these countries and bribe a section of the bourgeoisie. They resort to the poisoned weapon of national strife to undermine the young states that are not yet strong enough. They make ample use of aggressive military blocs and bilateral aggressive military alliances to achieve these ends. The imperialists' accomplices are the most reactionary sections of the local exploiting classes.

The urgent tasks of national rebirth facing the countries that have shaken off the colonial yoke cannot be effectively accomplished unless a determined struggle is waged against imperialism and the remnants of feudalism by all the patriotic forces of the nations united in a single national-democratic front. The national democratic tasks on the basis of which the progressive forces of the nation can and do unite in the countries which have won their freedom, are: the consolidation of political independence, the carrying out of agrarian reforms in the interest of the peasantry, elimination of the survivals of feudalism, the uprooting of imperialist economic domination, the restriction of foreign monopolies and their expulsion from the national economy, the creation and development of a national industry, improvement

of the living standard, the democratisation of social life, the pursuance of an independent and peaceful foreign policy, and the development of economic and cultural co-operation with the socialist and other friendly countries.

The working class, which has played an outstanding role in the fight for national liberation, demands the complete and consistent accomplishment of the tasks of the national, anti-imperialist, democratic revolution, and resists reactionary attempts to check social progress.

The solution of the peasant problem, which directly affects the interests of the vast majority of the population, is of the utmost importance to these countries. Without radical agrarian reforms it is impossible to solve the food problem and sweep away the remnants of medievalism which fetter the development of the productive forces in agriculture and industry. The creation and extension on a democratic basis of the state sector in the national economy, particularly in industry—a sector independent from foreign monopolies and gradually becoming a determining factor in the country's economy—is of great importance in these countries.

The alliance of the working class and the peasantry is the most important force in winning and defending national independence, accomplishing far-reaching democratic transformations and ensuring social progress. This alliance forms the basis of a broad national front. The extent to which the national bourgeoisie participates in the liberation struggle also depends to no small degree upon its strength and stability. A big role can be played by the national-patriotic forces, by all elements of the nation prepared to fight for national independence, against imperialism.

In present conditions, the national bourgeoisie of the colonial and dependent countries unconnected with imperialist circles, is objectively interested in the accomplishment of the principal tasks of anti-imperialist, anti-feudal revolution, and therefore can participate in the revolutionary struggle against imperialism and feudalism. In that sense it is progressive. But it is unstable; though progressive, it is inclined to compromise with imperialism and feudalism. Owing to its dual nature, the extent to which the national bourgeoisie participates in revolution differs from country to country. This depends on concrete conditions, on changes in the relationship of class forces, on the sharpness of the contradictions between imperialism, feudalism and the people, and of the contradictions between imperialism, feudalism and the national bourgeoisie.

After winning political independence the peoples seek solutions to the social problems raised by life and to the problems of reinforcing national independence. Different classes and parties offer different solutions. Which course of development to choose is the internal affair of the peoples themselves. As social contradictions grow the national bourgeoisie inclines more and more to compromising with domestic reaction and imperialism. The people, however, begin to see that the best way to abolish age-long backwardness and improve their living standard is that of non-capitalist development. Only thus can the peoples free themselves from exploitation, poverty and hunger. The working class and the broad peasant masses will play the leading part in solving this basic social problem.

In the present situation, favourable domestic and international conditions arise in many countries for the establishment of an independent national democracy, that is, a state which consistently upholds its political and economic independence, fights against imperialism and its military blocs, against military bases on its territory; a state which fights against the new

forms of colonialism and the penetration of imperialist capital; a state which rejects dictatorial and despotic methods of government; a state in which the people are ensured broad democratic rights and freedoms (freedom of speech, press, assembly, demonstrations, establishment of political parties and social organisations), the opportunity to work for the enactment of an agrarian reform and other domestic and social changes, and for participation in shaping government policy. The formation and consolidation of national democracies enables the countries concerned to make rapid social progress and play an active part in the people's struggle for peace, against the aggressive policies of the imperialist camp, for the complete abolition of colonial oppression.

The Communist Parties are working actively for a consistent completion of the anti-imperialist, anti-feudal, democratic revolution, for the establishment of national democracies, for a radical improvement in the living standard of the people. They support those actions of national governments leading to the consolidation of the gains achieved and undermining the imperialists' positions. At the same time they firmly oppose anti-democratic, anti-popular acts and those measures of the ruling circles which endanger national independence. Communists expose attempts by the reactionary section of the bourgeoisie to represent its selfish, narrow class interests as those of the entire nation. They expose the demagogic use by bourgeois politicians of socialist slogans for the same purpose. They work for a genuine democratisation of social life and rally all the progressive forces to combat despotic régimes or to curb tendencies towards setting up such régimes.

The aims of the Communists accord with the supreme interests of the nation. The reactionaries' effort to break up the national front under the slogan of "anti-communism" and isolate the Communists, the foremost contingent of the liberation movement, weakens the national movement. It is contrary to the national interests of the people and threatens the loss of national gains.

The socialist countries are true and sincere friends of the peoples fighting for liberation and of those who have thrown off the imperialist yoke. While rejecting on principle any interference in the internal affairs of young national states, they consider it their internationalist duty to help the peoples in strengthening their independence. They help and support these countries generously in achieving progress, creating a national industry, developing and consolidating the national economy and training national personnel. They co-operate with them in the struggle for world peace and against imperialist aggression.

The class-conscious workers of the colonial powers, who realised that " no nation can be free if it oppresses other nations," fought consistently for the self-determination of the nations oppressed by the imperialists. Now that these nations are taking the path of national independence, it is the internationalist duty of the workers and all democratic forces in the industrially developed capitalist countries to assist them vigorously in their struggle against the imperialists. It is their duty to assist them in their struggle for national independence and its consolidation, and in effectively solving the problems of their economic and cultural rebirth. In so doing, the workers defend the interests of the people of their own countries.

The entire course of the world history of recent decades shows the need for the complete and final abolition of the colonial system in all its forms

and manifestations. All the peoples still languishing in colonial bondage must be given every support in winning their national independence. All forms of colonial oppression must be abolished. The abolition of colonialism will also be of great importance in easing international tension and consolidating universal peace. This Meeting expresses solidarity with all the peoples of Asia, Africa, Latin America and Oceania who are carrying on an heroic struggle against imperialism. The Meeting hails the peoples of the young states of Africa who have achieved political independence—an important step towards complete emancipation. The Meeting extends heartfelt greetings and support to the heroic Algerian people fighting for freedom and national independence, and demands an immediate cessation of the aggressive war against Algeria. It indignantly condemns the inhuman system of racial persecution and tyranny in the Union of South Africa (apartheid) and urges democrats throughout the world actively to support the peoples of South Africa in their struggle for freedom and equality. The Meeting demands non-interference in the sovereign rights of the peoples of Cuba, the Congo and all the other countries that have won their freedom.

All the socialist countries and the international working-class and Communist movement recognise their duty to render the fullest moral and material assistance to the peoples fighting to free themselves from imperialist and colonial tyranny.

V

The new balance of world forces offers the Communist and Workers' Parties new opportunities of carrying out the historic tasks they face in the struggle for peace, national independence, democracy and socialism.

The Communist Parties decide on the prospects and tasks of revolution according to the concrete historical and social conditions in their respective countries and with due regard to the international situation. They are waging a selfless struggle, doing everything already in present conditions, without waiting until socialism triumphs, to defend the interests of the working class and the people, improve their living conditions and extend the democratic rights and freedoms of the people. Knowing that the brunt of the struggle for the liberation of its people from capitalist oppression rests upon it, the working class and its revolutionary vanguard will with increasing energy press forward its offensive against the domination of oppressors and exploiters in every field of political, economic and ideological activity in each country. In the process of this struggle, the people are prepared and conditions arise for decisive battles for the overthrow of capitalism, for the victory of socialist revolution.

The main blow in present conditions is directed with growing force at the capitalist monopolies, which are chiefly responsible for the arms race and which constitute the bulwark of reaction and aggression. It is directed at the whole system of state-monopoly capitalism, which defends monopoly interests.

In some non-European developed capitalist countries which are under the political, economic and military domination of U.S. imperialism, the working class and the people direct the main blow against U.S. imperialist domination, and also against monopoly capital and other domestic reactionary forces that betray the interests of the nation. In the course of this struggle all the democratic, patriotic forces of the nation come together in a united front fighting

for the victory of a revolution aimed at achieving genuine national independence and democracy, which create conditions for passing on to the tasks of socialist revolution.

The big monopolies encroach on the interests of the working class and the people in general all along the line. The exploitation of working people is gaining in intensity; so is the process in which the broad peasant masses are being ruined. At the same time, the difficulties experienced by the small and middle urban bourgeoisie are growing more acute. The oppression of the big monopolies is becoming increasingly heavier for all sections of the nation. As a result, the contradiction between the handful of monopoly capitalists and all sections of the people is now growing more pronounced, along with the sharpening of the basic class contraction of bourgeois society—that between labour and capital.

The monopolies seek to abolish, or cut down to a bare minimum, the democratic rights of the masses. The reign of open fascist terror continues in some countries. In a number of countries, fascisation is developing in new forms: dictatorial methods of government are combined with fictitious parliamentary practices, stripped of democratic content and purely formal in character. Many democratic organisations are outlawed and are compelled to go underground, while thousands of fighters for the working-class cause and champions of peace are in prison.

On behalf of all the Communists of the world, this Meeting expresses proletarian solidarity with the courageous sons and daughters of the working class and the fighters for democracy languishing behind prison bars in the U.S.A., Spain, Portugal, Japan, West Germany, Greece, Iran, Pakistan, the United Arab Republic, Jordan, Iraq, Argentina, Paraguay, the Dominican Republic, Mexico, the Union of South Africa, the Sudan and other countries. The Meeting urges launching a powerful world-wide campaign to secure the release of these champions of peace, national independence and democracy.

The working class, peasantry, intellectuals and the petty and middle urban bourgeoisie are vitally interested in the abolition of monopoly domination. Hence there are favourable conditions for rallying these forces.

Communists hold that this unity can be achieved on the basis of the struggle for peace, national independence, the protection and extension of democracy, nationalisation of the key branches of economy and democratisation of their management, the use of the entire economy for peaceful purposes in order to satisfy the needs of the population, implementation of radical agrarian reforms, improvement of the living conditions of the working people, protection of the interests of the peasantry and the small and middle urban bourgeoisie against the tyranny of the monopolies.

These measures would be an important step along the path of social progress and would meet the interests of the majority of the nation. All these measures are democratic by nature. They do not eliminate the exploitation of man by man. But if realised, they would limit the power of the monopolies, enhance the prestige and political weight of the working class in the country's affairs, help to isolate the most reactionary forces and facilitate the unification of all the progressive forces. As they participate in the fight for democratic reforms, large sections of the population come to realise the necessity of unity of action with the working class and become more active politically. It is the primary duty of the working class and its Communist vanguard to head the economic and political struggle of the people for democratic reforms and the overthrow of the power of the monopolies, and assure its success.

Communists advocate general democratisation of the economic and social scene and of all the administrative, political and cultural organisations and institutions.

Communists regard the struggle for democracy as part of the struggle for socialism. In this struggle they continuously strengthen their bonds with the working people, increase their political consciousness, help them understand the tasks of the socialist revolution and realise the necessity of accomplishing it. This sets the Marxist-Leninist Parties completely apart from the reformists, who consider reforms within the framework of the capitalist system as the ultimate goal and deny the necessity of socialist revolution. Marxists-Leninists are firmly convinced that the peoples in the capitalist countries will in the course of their daily struggle ultimately come to understand that socialism alone is a real way out for them.

Now that more sections of the population are joining in an active class struggle, it is of the utmost importance that Communists should extend their work in trade unions and co-operatives, among the peasantry, the youth, the women, in sports organisations, and the unorganised sections of the population. There are new opportunities now to draw the younger generation into the struggle for peace and democracy, and for the great ideals of communism. Lenin's great behest—to go deeper among the masses, to work wherever there are masses, to strengthen the ties with the masses in order to lead them—must become a major task for every Communist Party.

The restoration of unity in the trade-union movement in countries where it is split, as well as on the international scale, is essential for increasing the role of the working class in political life and for the successful defence of its interests. The working people may belong to different trade unions, but they have common interests. Whenever different trade-union associations fought in common in the greatest class battles of recent years, they usually succeeded, precisely because of their unity, in winning the demands of the working people. The Communist Parties believe that there are real prerequisites for re-establishing trade-union unity, and will work perseveringly to bring it about. In those countries where no trade-union democracy exists in practice, the struggle for trade-union unity calls for continuous efforts aimed at achieving trade-union independence and recognition and observance of the trade-union rights of all working people without political or any other discrimination.

It is also essential to peace and social progress that the national and international unity of all the other mass democratic movements be restored Unity among the mass organisations may be achieved through joint action in the struggle for peace, national independence, the preservation and extension of democratic rights, the improvement of living conditions and the extension of the working people's social rights.

The decisive role in the struggle of the people of capitalist countries for the accomplishment of their tasks is played by the alliance of the working class and the working peasantry, which represents the main motive force of social revolution.

The split in the ranks of the working class, which the ruling classes, the Right-wing Social-Democratic leadership and reactionary trade-union leaders are interested to maintain on a national and international scale, remains the principal obstacle to the achievement of the aims of the working class. Communists work resolutely to eliminate this split.

The imperialists and reactionaries in various countries resort, along with means of suppression, to methods of deception and bribery in order to divide and disrupt the solidarity of the working class. The events of the last few years have again confirmed that this division undermines the positions of the working class and is advantageous only to imperialist reaction.

Some Right-wing Social-Democratic leaders have openly adopted imperialist views, defend the capitalist system and divide the working class. Owing to their hostility to communism and their fear of the mounting influence of socialism in world affairs, they are capitulating to the reactionary, conservative forces. In some countries the Right-wing leadership has succeeded in making the Social-Democratic Parties adopt programmes in which they openly disowned Marxism, the class struggle and the traditional socialist slogans. Thereby they have again done a service to the bourgeoisie. Resistance to this policy of the Right-wing leaders is mounting in the Social-Democratic Parties. The opposition also includes a section of the Social-Democratic Party functionaries. The forces favouring joint action by the working class and other working people in the struggle for peace, democracy and social progress are growing. The overwhelming majority of the Social-Democratic Parties, particularly the workers, are friends of peace and social progress.

Communists will continue to criticise the ideological positions and Right-wing opportunist practices of the Social-Democrats. They will continue working to induce the Social-Democratic masses to adopt positions of consistent class struggle against capitalism, for the triumph of socialism. The Communists are firmly convinced that the ideological differences which exist between themselves and the Social-Democrats must not hinder exchanges of opinion on the pressing problems of the working-class movement and the joint struggle, especially against the war danger.

Communists regard Social-Democrats among the working people as their class brothers. They often work together in trade unions and other organisations, and fight jointly for the interests of the working class and the people as a whole.

The urgent interests of the working-class movement demand that the Communist and Social-Democratic Parties take joint action on a national and international scale to bring about the immediate prohibition of the manufacture, testing and use of nuclear weapons, the establishment of atom-free zones, general and complete disarmament under international control, the abolition of military bases on foreign soil and the withdrawal of foreign troops, to assist the national-liberation movement of the peoples of colonial and dependent countries, to safeguard national sovereignty, promote democracy and resist the fascist menace, improve the living standards of the working people, secure a shorter working week without wage cuts, etc. Millions of Social-Democrats and some Social-Democratic Parties have already in some form or another come out in favour of solving these problems. It is safe to say that *on overcoming the split in its ranks, on achieving unity of action of all its contingents, the working class of many capitalist countries could deliver a heavy blow to the policy of the ruling circles in the capitalist countries. It could make them stop preparing a new war, repel the offensive of monopoly capital, and have its daily vital and democratic demands met.*

199

In the struggle for the improvement of the living conditions of working people, the extension and preservation of their democratic rights, the achievement and defence of national independence, for peace among nations, and also in the struggle to win power and build socialism, the Communist Parties advocate co-operation with the Socialist Parties. The Communists have the great theory of Marxism-Leninism—a theory that is consistent, scientifically substantiated and borne out by life—and rich international experience in socialist construction. They are prepared to hold discussions with Social-Democrats, for they are certain that this is the best way to compare views, ideas and experience with the aim of removing deep-rooted prejudices and the division among the working people, and of establishing co-operation.

The imperialist reactionaries, who try to arouse distrust for the Communist movement and its ideology, continue to intimidate the people by alleging that the Communists need wars between states to overthrow the capitalist system and establish a socialist system. The Communist Parties emphatically reject this slander. The fact that both world wars, which were started by the imperialists, ended in socialist revolutions by no means implies that the way to social revolution is necessarily through world war, especially now that there exists a powerful world system of socialism. Marxists-Leninists have never considered that the way to social revolution lies through wars between states.

The choice of social system is the inalienable right of the people of each country. Socialist revolution cannot be imported, nor imposed from without. It is a result of the internal development of the country concerned, of the utmost sharpening of social contradictions in it. *The Communist Parties, which guide themselves by the Marxist-Leninist doctrine, have always been against the export of revolution. At the same time they fight resolutely against imperialist export of counter-revolution. They consider it their internationalist duty to call on the peoples of all countries to unite, to rally all their internal forces, to act vigorously and, relying on the might of the world socialist system, to prevent or firmly resist imperialist interference in the affairs of any people who have risen in revolution.*

The Marxist-Leninist Parties head the struggle of the working class and the working people, for the accomplishment of the socialist revolution and the establishment of the dictatorship of the proletariat in one form or another. The forms and course of development of the socialist revolution will depend on the specific balance of the class forces in the country concerned, on the organisation and maturity of the working class and its vanguard, and on the extent of the resistance put up by the ruling classes. Whatever form of dictatorship of the proletariat is established, it will always signify an extension of democracy, a transition from formal, bourgeois democracy to genuine democracy, to democracy for the working people.

The Communist Parties reaffirm the propositions put forward by the Declaration of 1957 on the forms of transition of different countries from capitalism to socialism.

The Declaration points out that the working class and its vanguard—the Marxist-Leninist Party—seek to achieve the socialist revolution by peaceful means. This would accord with the interests of the working class and the people as a whole, with the national interests of the country.

Today in a number of capitalist countries the working class, headed by its vanguard, has the opportunity, given a united working-class and popular front or other workable forms of agreement and political co-operation between the different parties and public organisations, to unite a majority of the people, win state power without civil war and ensure the transfer of the basic means of production to the hands of the people. Relying on the majority of the people and resolutely rebuffing the opportunist elements incapable of relinquishing the policy of compromise with the capitalists and landlords, the working class can defeat the reactionary, anti-popular forces, secure a firm majority in parliament, transform parliament from an instrument serving the class interests of the bourgeoisie into an instrument serving the working people, launch an extra-parliamentary mass struggle, smash the resistance of the reactionary forces and create the necessary conditions for peaceful realisation of the socialist revolution. All this will be possible only by broad and ceaseless development of the class struggle of the workers, peasant masses and the urban middle strata against big monopoly capital, against reaction, for profound social reforms, for peace and socialism.

In the event of the exploiting classes resorting to violence against the people, the possibility of non-peaceful transition to socialism should be borne in mind. Leninism teaches, and experience confirms, that the ruling classes never relinquish power voluntarily. In this case the degree of bitterness and the forms of the class struggle will depend not so much on the proletariat as on the resistance put up by the reactionary circles to the will of the overwhelming majority of the people, on these circles using force at one or other stage of the struggle for socialism.

The actual possibility of the one or the other way of transition to socialism in each individual country depends on the concrete historical conditions.

In our time, when communism is not only the most advanced doctrine but a social system which actually exists and which has proved its superiority over capitalism, conditions are particularly favourable for expanding the influence of the Communist Parties, and vigorously exposing anti-communism—a slogan under which the capitalist class wages its struggle against the proletariat—and for winning the broadest sections of the working people for Communist ideas.

Anti-communism arose at the dawn of the working-class movement as the principal ideological weapon of the capitalist class in its struggle against the proletariat and Marxist ideology. As the class struggle grew in intensity, particularly with the formation of the world socialist system, anti-communism became more vicious and insidious. Anti-communism, which is indicative of the extreme decline of bourgeois ideology and of its deep ideological crisis, resorts to monstrous distortions of Marxist doctrine and crude slander against the socialist social system, presents Communist policies and objectives in a false light, and carries on a witch-hunt against the democratic peaceful forces and organisations.

Effectively to defend the interests of the working people, maintain peace and realise the socialist ideals of the working class, a resolute struggle must be waged against anti-communism—that poisoned weapon which the bourgeoisie uses to fence off the masses from socialism. A greater effort is required to explain the ideas of socialism to the working peoples, to educate them in a revolutionary spirit, and to develop their revolutionary class consciousness. It is necessary to show all working people the superiority of socialist society by referring to the experience of the countries of the world socialist system, demonstrating in concrete form the benefits which socialism will actually give to workers, peasants and other sections of the population in each country.

Communism assures people freedom from fear of war; it brings lasting peace, freedom from imperialist oppression and exploitation, and from unemployment and poverty. It leads to general prosperity and a high standard of living; freedom from fear of economic crises, and a rapid growth of the productive forces for the benefit of society as a whole. It frees the individual from the tyranny of the moneybag, and leads to the all-round spiritual development of man, the fullest development of talent and the unlimited scientific and cultural progress of society. All the sections of the population, with the exception of a handful of exploiters, stand to gain from the victory of the new social system, and this must be brought home to millions of people in the capitalist countries.

VI

The world Communist movement has become the most influential political force of our time, a most important factor in social progress. As it fights bitterly against imperialist reaction, for the interests of the working class and all working people, for peace, national independence, democracy and socialism, the Communist movement is making steady headway, is becoming consolidated and tempered.

There are now Communist Parties active in 87 countries of the world. Their total membership exceeds 36,000,000. This is a signal victory for Marxism-Leninism and a tremendous achievement of the working class. Like-minded Marxists are rallying in the countries which have shaken off colonial tyranny and taken the path of independent development. Communist Parties consider it their internationalist duty to promote friendship and solidarity between the working class of their countries and the working-class movement of the countries which have won their freedom in the common struggle against imperialism.

The growth of the Communist Parties and their organisational consolidation, the victories of the Communist Parties in a number of countries in the struggle against deviations, elimination of the harmful consequences of the personality cult, and the greater influence of the world Communist movement open new prospects for the successful accomplishment of the tasks facing the Communist Parties.

Marxist-Leninist Parties regard it as a law of their activity strictly to observe the Leninist standards of Party life in keeping with the principle of democratic centralism, and to cherish Party unity like the apple of their eye. They strictly adhere to the principle of Party democracy and collective leadership, for they attach, in keeping with the organisational principles of Leninism, great importance to the role of the leading party bodies in the life of the Party. They work indefatigably for the strengthening of their bonds with the Party membership and with the broad masses of the working people, and do not allow the cult of the individual, which shackles creative thought and initiative of Communists. They vigorously promote the activity of Communists, and encourage criticism and self-criticism in their ranks.

The Communist Parties have ideologically defeated the revisionists in their ranks who sought to divert them from the Marxist-Leninist path. Each Communist Party and the international Communist movement as a whole have become still stronger, ideologically and organisationally, in the struggle against revisionism, Right-wing opportunism.

The Communist Parties have unanimously condemned the Yugoslav variety of international opportunism, a variety of modern revisionist

" theories " in concentrated form. After betraying Marxism-Leninism, which they termed obsolete, the leaders of the League of Communists of Yugoslavia opposed their anti-Leninist revisionist programme to the Declaration of 1957; they set the L.C.Y. against the international Communist movement as a whole, severed their country from the socialist camp, made it dependent on so-called " aid " from U.S. and other imperialists, and thereby exposed the Yugoslav people to the danger of losing the revolutionary gains achieved through a heroic struggle. The Yugoslav revisionists carry on subversive work against the socialist camp and the world Communist movement. Under the pretext of being outside blocs, they engage in activities which prejudice the unity of all the peace-loving forces and countries. Further exposure of the leaders of Yugoslav revisionists and active struggle to safeguard the Communist movement and the working-class movement from the anti-Leninist ideas of the Yugoslav revisionists, remain an essential task of the Marxist-Leninist Parties.

The practical struggles of the working class and the entire course of social development have furnished a brilliant new proof of the great all-conquering power and vitality of Marxism-Leninism, and have thoroughly refuted all modern revisionist " theories."

The further development of the Communist and working-class movement calls as stated in the Moscow Declaration of 1957, for continuing a deter-mined struggle on two fronts—against revisionism, which remains the main danger, and against dogmatism and sectarianism.

Revisionism, Right-wing opportunism, which mirrors bourgeois ideology in theory and practice, distorts Marxism-Leninism, robs it of its revolu-tionary spirit, and thereby paralyses the revolutionary will of the working class. It disarms and demobilises the workers and all working people, in their struggle against oppression by imperialists and exploiters, for peace, democracy and national-liberation, for the triumph of socialism.

Dogmatism and sectarianism in theory and practice can also become the main danger at some stage of development of individual parties, unless com-bated unrelentingly. They rob revolutionary parties of the ability to develop Marxism-Leninism through scientific analysis and apply it creatively accord-ing to the specific conditions. They isolate Communists from the broad masses of the working people, doom them to passive expectation or Leftist, adven-turist actions in the revolutionary struggle. They prevent the Communist Parties from making a timely and correct estimate of the changing situation and of new experience and using all opportunities to bring about the victory of the working class and all democratic forces in the struggle against imperialism, reaction and the war danger. Thereby they prevent the peoples from achieving victory in their just struggle.

At a time when imperialist reaction is joining forces to fight communism it is particularly necessary to consolidate the world Communist movement. Unity and solidarity redouble the strength of our movement and provide a reliable guarantee that the great cause of communism will make victorious progress and all enemy attacks will be effectively repelled.

Communists throughout the world are united by the great doctrine of Marxism-Leninism and by the joint struggle for its realisation. The interests of the Communist movement require solidarity by every Communist Party in the observance of the estimates and conclusions on the common tasks in the struggle against imperialism, for peace, democracy and socialism, jointly reached by the fraternal Parties at their meetings.

The interests of the struggle for the working-class cause demand of each Communist Party and of the great army of Communists of all countries ever-closer unity of will and action. It is the supreme internationalist duty of every Marxist-Leninist Party to work continuously for greater unity in the world Communist movement.

A resolute defence of the unity of the world Communist movement on the principles of Marxism-Leninism and proletarian internationalism, and the prevention of any actions which may undermine that unity, are a necessary condition for victory in the struggle for national independence, democracy and peace, for the successful accomplishment of the tasks of the socialist revolution and of the building of socialism and communism. Violation of these principles would impair the forces of communism.

All the Marxist-Leninist Parties are independent and have equal rights; they shape their policies according to the specific conditions in their respective countries and in keeping with Marxist-Leninist principles, and support each other. The success of the working-class cause in any country is unthinkable without the internationalist solidarity of all Marxist-Leninist parties. Every party is responsible to the working class, to the working people of its country, to the international working-class and Communist movement as a whole.

The Communist and Workers' Parties hold meetings whenever necessary to discuss urgent problems, to share experiences, acquaint themselves with each other's views and positions, work out common views through consultations and co-ordinate joint actions in the struggle for common goals.

Whenever a Party wants to clear up questions relating to the activities of another fraternal Party, its leadership approaches the leadership of the Party concerned; if necessary, they hold meetings and consultations.

The experience and results of the meetings of representatives of the Communist Parties held in recent years, particularly the results of the two major meetings—that of November 1957 and this Meeting—show that in present-day conditions such meetings are an effective form of exchanging views and experience, enriching Marxist-Leninist theory by collective effort and elaborating a common attitude in the struggle for common objectives.

The Communist and Workers' Parties unanimously declare that the Communist Party of the Soviet Union has been, and remains, the universally recognised vanguard of the world Communist movement, being the most experienced and steeled contingent of the international Communist movement. The experience which the C.P.S.U. has gained in the struggle for the victory of the working class, in socialist construction and in the full-scale construction of communism, is of fundamental significance for the whole of the world Communist movement. The example of the C.P.S.U. and its fraternal solidarity inspire all the Communist Parties in their struggle for peace and socialism, and represent the revolutionary principles of proletarian internationalism applied in practice. The historic decisions of the 20th Congress of the C.P.S.U. are not only of great importance for the C.P.S.U. and communist construction in the U.S.S.R., but have initiated a new stage in the world Communist movement, and have promoted its development on the basis of Marxism-Leninism.

All Communist and Workers' Parties contribute to the development of the great theory of Marxism-Leninism. Mutual assistance and support in relations between all the fraternal Marxist-Leninist Parties embody the revolutionary principles of proletarian internationalism applied in practice.

Ideological issues are of especial significance today. The exploiting class tries to counteract the achievements of socialism by exerting ever greater ideological pressure on the people as it seeks to keep them in spiritual bondage to bourgeois ideology. Communists regard it as their task to launch a determined offensive on the ideological front, to work to free the people from the shackles of all types and forms of bourgeois ideology, including the pernicious influence of reformism, and to disseminate among the people progressive ideas making for social advancement, the ideas of democracy and freedom, the ideology of scientific socialism.

Historical experience shows that the survivals of capitalism in the minds of people persist over a long period even after the establishment of a socialist system. This demands extensive work by the Party for the Communist education of the people and a better Marxist-Leninist training of Party and government cadres.

Marxism-Leninism is a great integral revolutionary doctrine, the guiding light of the working class and working people of the whole world at all stages of their great battle for peace, freedom and a better life, for the establishment of the most just society, communism. Its great creative, revolutionising power lies in its unbreakable link with life, in its continuous enrichment through a comprehensive analysis of reality. On the basis of Marxism-Leninism, the community of socialist countries and the international Communist, working-class and liberation movements have achieved great historic successes, and it is only on its basis that all the tasks facing the Communist and Workers' Parties can be effectively accomplished.

The meeting sees the further consolidation of the Communist Parties on the basis of Marxism-Leninism, of proletarian internationalism, as a primary condition for the unification of all working-class, democratic and progressive forces, as a guarantee of new victories in the great struggle waged by the world Communist and working-class movement for a happy future for the whole of mankind, for the triumph of the cause of peace and socialism.

[Text as published in *World Marxist Review*, December 1960.]

9. Soviet and Chinese Interpretations of the Statement

ON the conclusion of the Moscow conference, Liu Shao-ch'i and some members of the Chinese delegation made a short good-will tour of the Soviet Union, going to Minsk and Kiev. The tour underlined the fact that the major agreement reached at the Moscow conference was on the continuing imperative need for unity between the major powers of the Communist *bloc*. Both Mr. Khrushchev in his report on the conference and the Chinese central committee in its resolution on it went out of their way to stress the strength of Sino-Soviet friendship, providing a classic case of protesting too much.[25]

Mr. Khrushchev's report was far longer and more informative than the Chinese resolution. He elaborated on a number of points on which the Russians had got their way in Moscow. He spelled out the meaning of a nuclear disaster, using estimates of casualties made by Dr. Linus Pauling which, though he did not admit this, referred to the Soviet Union as well as to America and the West. He went into greater detail than the declaration in asserting that war was unnecessary for the spread of Communism, rejecting the idea that because the First and Second World Wars led to the spread of Communism world war was an indispensable condition for Communist success. This might well have been a rejoinder to Mao's publicly expressed belief, not that world war was indispensable to the spread of Communism, but that just as the First and Second World Wars had led to the spread of Communism, so a third world war would contribute even more to its final triumph.[26]

Mr. Khrushchev's modification of the virulent anti-Americanism of the Statement has been described above.[27] Suffice it to add that his reassertion of the existence of " saner " *representatives* of the Western *ruling*

---

[25] Mr. Khrushchev admitted the existence of " some shortcomings and rough edges " in intra-*bloc* relations.

[26] Mao Tse-tung, " On the Correct Handling of Contradictions among the People," *Jen-min Shou-ts'e* (*People's Handbook*), *1958* (Peking: *Ta Kung Pao*), p. 19. In the Statement, the Russians subscribed to the ritual assertion that if imperialism launched a new war it would be wiped out, but to my knowledge they have not in recent years inferred the probable results of a third world war from those of World Wars One and Two in Mao's complacent manner. Khrushchev repeated this ritual assertion but added significantly that the working class would be the first to suffer in the event of war. According to Crankshaw's account, the Chinese argued in Moscow that war was necessary: (*Observer*, February 12).

[27] See above, p. 33.

classes with whom peaceful coexistence could be agreed was a justification for negotiation with the new American administration far clearer than the Statement's admission that "a definite section of the bourgeoisie" in the West feared war; the latter analysis could be taken to refer to the people at large and not to their leaders.

The importance of Mr. Khrushchev's elaboration of the concept of wars of national liberation has also been discussed above.[28] It should be added that Mr. Khrushchev did not mention the national liberation movement when stating why world war could now be prevented, though in the section on the movement he described it as "strengthening peace." Mr. Khrushchev justifies at some length his aid to the non-Communist leaderships of newly independent countries on the grounds that combination with all possible allies "no matter if inconsistent, shaky and unstable" is essential in the anti-imperialist struggle.[29]

The Chinese resolution emphasises all the strongest anti-imperialist points in the Statement, repeating the description of America as the "world gendarme" which Khrushchev had omitted. It listed the national liberation movement as one of the forces helping to prevent war. There is no mention of "saner" representatives or even sections of the bourgeoisie. Nor does the resolution repeat Khrushchev's *Twenty-first* Congress formulation on the prevention of world war, albeit the Chinese delegation had subscribed to it in the Statement.

The conclusion to be reached on the basis of these interpretations of the Statement is that there is no *documentary* evidence so far that the Moscow conference solved the basic disagreements between Russia and China. Both sides, it seems, will interpret the Statement in accordance with their previous policy predilections rather than on the basis of a new global policy hammered out in conclave.

Khrushchev's Report on the Moscow Conference

Now that a socialist world system has taken shape and with anti-imperialist, national-liberation revolutions in full flood, it is necessary to determine the further course and perspective of world development. This cannot be done without a profound understanding of the essence, content and nature of the decisive tasks of the present epoch.

The question of the character of the epoch is not an abstract, purely theoretical question. Inseparably linked with it are the general strategy and tactics of world communism and of each communist party. . . .

The statement adopted by the meeting defines the epoch in these terms:

" Our times, the basic content of which is the transition from capitalism to socialism initiated by the great October Socialist Revolution, are times of struggle between the two opposed social systems, times of socialist revolutions and national-liberation revolutions, of the breakdown of imperialism, of the

---

[28] pp. 33–34.
[29] For a discussion of other aspects of Mr. Khrushchev's report, see above, pp. 33–34.

abolition of the colonial system, times of the transition of more peoples to the socialist path, of the triumph of socialism and communism on a world-wide scale."

This definition of the character of the present epoch can be regarded as an example of a creative, genuinely scientific solution of an important and responsible task. . . .

In defining the essence and character of the present epoch as a whole, it is absolutely essential that we should be clear about the main peculiarities and distinguishing features of its present stage. The post-October period, seen from the point of view of it basic motive forces, is clearly divided into two stages. One of these began with the victory of the October Revolution. It was, to use Lenin's phrase, the period of establishing and developing the national dictatorship of the proletariat, that is, the dictatorship of the proletariat within the national bounds of Russia alone.

Although right from its inception the Soviet Union began to exert a very great influence on international affairs, imperialism had largely determined the course and character of international relations. But even in those early days it proved incapable of crushing the Soviet Union, of preventing it from becoming a mighty industrial power, the bulwark of progress and civilisation a centre of attraction for all the forces fighting against imperialist oppression and fascist enslavement.

The second stage in the development of the contemporary epoch dates from the rise of the socialist world system. This was a revolutionary process of historic significance. The October Revolution broke the first link in the imperialist chain. After this the chain was broken in a number of places. In the past we used to speak about the breaking of one or more links in the imperialist chain, but at present an all-embracing chain of imperialism no longer exists. The dictatorship of the working class has emerged beyond the confines of one country and become an international force. Imperialism has lost not only the countries where socialism has triumphed, it is rapidly losing nearly all its colonies. Naturally, as a result of these blows and losses, the general crisis of capitalism has become much more acute, and the balance of force in the world has changed radically in favour of socialism.

The main distinguishing feature of our time is the fact that the socialist world system is becoming the decisive factor in the development of human society. This finds direct expression also in the sphere of international relations. In the conditions of today socialism is in a position to determine, in growing measure, the character, methods and trends of international relations. This does not mean that imperialism is an " insignificant factor " which can be ignored. Not at all. Imperialism is still very strong. It controls a powerful military machine.

Now in peacetime imperialism has created a gigantic war machine and a ramified system of military blocs and has subordinated its economy to the arms drive. The U.S. imperialists, bent on bringing the whole world under their sway, are threatening mankind with missile-nuclear war. Modern imperialism is increasingly marked by decay and parasitism. In their evaluation of the prospects of international development, Marxist-Leninists do not, and must not, have any illusions with regard to imperialism.

The facts of the barefaced provocations and aggression on the part of the imperialists are countless. There is nothing new in this. What is new is that all the imperialist probings, in addition to being conclusively exposed, are firmly repelled, and the attempts made by the imperialists to start local wars are being thwarted.

The present balance of world forces enables the socialist camp and the other peace forces for the first time in history to set themselves the entirely realistic task of forcing the imperialists to refrain, for fear of seeing their system destroyed, from starting a world war.

In connection with the possibility of preventing a world war, I should like to deal with the prospects of the further development of the general crisis of capitalism. It is common knowledge that both the First and Second World Wars greatly influenced the rise and aggravation of the general crisis of capitalism. Can it be inferred from this that world war is an indispensable condition for the further intensification of the general crisis of capitalism? Such an inference would be absolutely wrong, because it distorts the Marxist-Leninist theory of socialist revolution and inverts the true causes of revolution. A proletarian revolution is not caused solely by military cataclysms; first and foremost it is the result of the development of the class struggle and of the internal contradictions of capitalism. . . .

Having profoundly analysed the international situation as a whole, the meeting reached a conclusion of very great theoretical and political significance, namely that " *a new stage has begun in the development of the general crisis of capitalism.*" The feature of this new stage is that it originated, not in the conditions of a world war, but in the circumstances of competition and struggle between the two systems, of the ever-growing changes in the balance of forces in favour of socialism, and of pronounced aggravation of all the contradictions of imperialism, in the circumstances when the successful struggle of the peace supporters for peaceful co-existence has prevented the imperialists from wrecking world peace by their aggressive actions, in an atmosphere of rising struggle for democracy, national liberation and socialism by the masses. All this speaks of the further aggravation of the general crisis of capitalism.

Our militant comrades in the communist parties in the capitalist countries take cognisance of this when defining their further tactical line in the struggle for the working-class cause. And we can confidently say that the immediate future harbours new successes for the combined forces of world socialism, the working class and the national-liberation movement. . . .

Prospects for the World Socialist System

The countries of the socialist world system are drawing closer to each other; their co-operation in all fields of endeavour is growing. This is a natural development. There are no insoluble contradictions between the socialist countries. The more developed and economically stronger are rendering disinterested fraternal aid to those less developed. For instance, some 500 industrial enterprises and installations have been built in the fraternal socialist countries with Soviet help. Our loans and credits to these countries amount to 7,800 million roubles in the new currency. At the same time we are bound to acknowledge that the fraternal socialist countries are aiding in the development of the Soviet economy. . . .

The consolidation of the common economic base of the socialist world system and the creation of the material base for the more or less simultaneous transition of all the peoples of the socialist system to communism will be accelerated to the extent that the internal resources of each of the countries and the advantages of the socialist international division of labour are fully utilised; this will result in evening up the various levels of economic development. . . .

The Communist and workers' parties have correctly defined in the spirit of Marxism-Leninism and proletarian internationalism, the principles governing the relations among the socialist countries and nations. It stands to reason that some shortcomings and rough edges are bound to appear in such a momentous undertaking. But the socialist community is characterised, not by incidental shortcomings, but by the essentially international nature of socialism, by the international policy of the fraternal parties and countries and the epoch-making successes achieved thanks to this policy. As to the shortcomings, we must remove them, guided by the principles of Marxism-Leninism, of international solidarity and fraternal friendship, seeing our main aim in consolidating the socialist camp. The Soviet Union has always sacredly fulfilled its international duty, putting the interests of the unity of the socialist countries and of the international Communist movement first. Our party will steadfastly adhere to this policy. . . .

Prevention of War is the Question of Questions

Wars arose with the division of society into classes. This means that the breeding ground of war will be completely abolished only when society will no longer be divided into hostile, antagonistic classes. With the victory of the working class throughout the world, with the triumph of socialism, which will destroy all the social and national causes giving rise to wars, mankind will be able to rid itself of this dreadful scourge.

In the present conditions we must distinguish the following kinds of war: world wars, local wars, and wars of liberation or popular uprisings. This is necessary in order to work out correct tactics in regard to each.

Let us begin with the problem of *world wars*. The Communists are the most resolute opponents of world wars, as they are of wars between countries in general. Only the imperialists need these wars in order to seize foreign territories and to enslave and plunder the peoples. Prior to the rise of the socialist world camp, the working class was unable to exert a decisive influence on the decision of the question whether there would or would not be a world war. In those circumstances the finest representatives of the working class advanced the slogan of turning an imperialist war into a civil war, that is, of the working class and all working people using the situation created by the war to take power. A situation of this kind set in during the First World War, and it was used in classical fashion by Lenin and the Bolshevik Party.

In our time the conditions are different. The socialist world camp with its powerful economy and armed forces exerts an ever-growing influence on the decision of questions of war and peace. To be sure, acute contradictions and antagonisms between the imperialist countries and the urge to profit at the expense of the weaker still exist. However, the imperialists are compelled to heed the Soviet Union and the entire socialist camp, and fear to start a war between themselves. They are trying to tone down their differences. They have formed military *blocs* and have entangled many capitalist countries in them. And although these *blocs* are torn by internal conflicts, their members are united, as they themselves admit, by their hatred of communism and, naturally, by the common nature and aspirations of the imperialists.

save the main productive force of society—the worker—we shall get everything back, but, should we fail to save him, we are lost. . . ." (*Collected Works*, Russ. ed., Vol. 29, pp. 334–335.)

There exists in the world today, not just one country of workers and peasants, but a whole system of socialist countries. It is our duty to safeguard peace and ensure the peaceful development of this grand creation of the international working class, to protect the peoples of all countries from a new war of annihilation. The victory of socialism on a world scale, inevitable by virtue of the laws of history, is no longer far off. War between countries is not needed for this victory.

A sober consideration of what a nuclear war implies is indispensable if we are to pursue a consistent policy of averting war and of mobilising the masses for the purpose of doing so. For the realisation by the masses of what a nuclear war means strengthens their resolve to fight against war. It is necessary, therefore, to warn the masses about the deadly consequences of a new world war and arouse their righteous wrath against those who are plotting this crime. The possibility of averting war is not a gift from heaven. Peace cannot be had by request. It can be secured only by an active, purposeful struggle. That is why we have been waging this struggle, and will continue to do so. . . .

Peaceful Coexistence

The policy of peaceful co-existence is, then, as far as its social content is concerned, a form of intense economic, political and ideological struggle between the proletariat and the aggressive forces of imperialism in the world arena.

The struggle against imperialism can succeed only if its aggressive actions are firmly resisted. Scolding will not halt the imperialist adventurers. There is only one way in which they can be curbed: steady strengthening of the economic, political and military power of the socialist countries, vigorous consolidation and reinforcement of the world revolutionary movement, mobilisation of the people for the struggle to avert war. . . .

When we call for a world without arms and without wars, we take into account, of course, that in the conditions of today, with two differing world social systems, there are forces in the imperialist camp, and fairly strong forces at that, who not only refuse to support this call, but who are waging a struggle against it.

The question of the struggle for communism is a class question. In the case of the struggle for peace, this is a question the solution of which can unite not only the working class, the peasantry and the petty bourgeoisie, but also that part of the bourgeoisie which sees the real danger of a thermonuclear war. . . .

Two trends can be observed in the policy of the capitalist camp in relation to the socialist countries—one bellicose and aggressive, the other moderate and sober. Lenin pointed to the need of establishing contacts with those circles of the bourgeoisie which gravitate towards pacifism, " be it even of the palest hue " (*Collected Works*, Russ. ed., Vol. 33, p. 236). In the struggle for peace, he said, we should not overlook also the saner representatives of the bourgeoisie.

The soundness of these words is confirmed by current events as well. Fear for the future of capitalism haunts the ruling classes of the imperialist

In the conditions of today the likelihood is that there will not be wars between the capitalist, imperialist countries, although this eventuality cannot be ruled out. The imperialists are preparing war chiefly against the socialist countries, above all against the Soviet Union, the most powerful of the socialist countries. They would like to sap our might and by so doing restore the one-time rule of monopoly capital.

The task is to raise insurmountable obstacles to the unleashing of war by the imperialists. Our possibilities for putting roadblocks in the way of the warmongers are growing, so much so that we can avert a world war. It stands to reason that we cannot completely exclude the possibility of war, since imperialist countries continue to exist, but it is now much more difficult for the imperialists to start a war than was the case heretofore, prior to the rise of the powerful socialist camp. The imperialists can start a war, but they cannot do so without giving thought to the consequences.

I have had occasion to say that if even Hitler had had an inkling that his reckless gamble would end in the way it did and that he would be forced to commit suicide, then in all probability he would have thought twice before starting the war against the Soviet Union. But at that time there were but two socialist countries—the Soviet Union and the Mongolian People's Republic. Yet we smashed the aggressors, and in doing so we made use also of the contradictions between the imperialist states.

Today the situation is entirely different. At present the imperialist camp is opposed by the socialist countries, and they are a mighty force. It would be wrong to underestimate the strength of the socialist camp, its influence on world developments and, consequently, on deciding the question whether there is to be war or not. Now that there is a mighty socialist camp with powerful armed forces, the peoples can undoubtedly prevent war and thus ensure peaceful co-existence provided they rally all their forces for active struggle against the bellicose imperialists.

Local Wars

Now about *local wars*. There is much talk in the imperialist camp today about local wars, and the imperialists are even making small-calibre atomic weapons to be used in such wars. There is even a special theory on local wars. Is this mere chance? Not at all. Some of the imperialist groups fear that a world war might end in complete destruction of capitalism, and for this reason they are banking on local wars.

There have been local wars in the past and they may break out again. But the chances of starting wars even of this kind are dwindling. A small-scale imperialist war, no matter which of the imperialists starts it, may develop into a world thermonuclear and missile war. We must, therefore, fight against both world war and against local wars.

An example of a local war started by the imperialists was the aggression of Britain, France and Israel against Egypt. They wanted to strangle Egypt and intimidate the other Arab countries fighting for their independence, to scare the peoples of Asia and Africa. When we were in London, British statesmen, Mr. Eden included, spoke to us quite frankly about their desire to settle accounts with Egypt. We told them plainly: " If you start a war, you will lose it, we will not be neutral." Eventually, when the war did break out, the United Nations formally condemned it, but this did not upset the aggressors; they went ahead with their dirty business and thought they would soon reach their goal. The Soviet Union, and the socialist camp as a whole, came to the defence of Egypt. The stern warning which the Soviet Government gave to Eden and Guy Mollet stopped the war. A local war, the gamble in Egypt failed ignominiously.

That was in 1956 when the balance of forces between the socialist and imperialist countries was not quite as favourable to us as it is now. At that time we were not as powerful as we are today. Moreover, the rulers of Britain, France and Israel banked on profiting from the difficulties that had arisen in Hungary and Poland. Representatives of the imperialist countries whispered to us, " You have your difficulties in Hungary, we have ours in Egypt, so don't meddle in our affairs." But we told the whisperers what we thought of them. We refused to shut our eyes to their knavish acts. We intervened, and we frustrated their aggression.

There you have an example of how a local war, started by the imperialists, was nipped in the bud by the intervention of the Soviet Union and the entire socialist camp.

I have said that local wars may recur. It is our task, therefore, always to be on the alert, to summon to action the forces of the socialist camp, the people of the other countries and all peace-loving forces, in order to prevent wars of aggression. If the people of all countries are united and rallied, if they fight indefatigably and combine their forces both in each country and on an international scale, wars can be prevented.

National-Liberation Wars

Now about *national-liberation wars*. Recent examples of wars of this kind are the armed struggle waged by the people of Viet Nam or the present war of the Algerian people, which is now in its seventh year.

These wars, which began as uprisings of colonial peoples against their oppressors, developed into guerrilla wars.

There will be liberation wars as long as imperialism exists, as long as colonialism exists. Wars of this kind are revolutionary wars. Such wars are not only justified, they are inevitable, for the colonialists do not freely bestow independence on the peoples. The peoples win freedom and independence only through struggle, including armed struggle.

Why was it that the U.S. imperialists, who were eager to help the French colonialists, did not venture directly to intervene in the war in Viet Nam? They did not do so because they knew that if they gave France armed assistance, Viet Nam would receive the same kind of assistance from China, the Soviet Union and the other socialist countries, and that the fighting could develop into a world war. The outcome of the war is known—North Viet Nam won.

A similar war is being waged today in Algeria. What kind of a war is it? It is an uprising of Arab people against French colonialists. It has assumed the form of a guerrilla war. The imperialists of the U.S.A. and Britain are helping their French allies with arms. Moreover, they have allowed France, a party to N.A.T.O., to transfer troops from Europe to fight against the Algerian people. The people of Algeria, too, get help from neighbouring countries and others sympathising with their love of freedom. But this is a liberation war, a war of independence waged by the people. It is a sacred war. We recognise such wars; we have helped and shall continue to help peoples fighting for their freedom.

Or take Cuba. A war was fought there too. It began as an upr against a tyrannical régime, backed by U.S. imperialism. Batista w puppet of the United States and the United States helped him actively. H ever, the U.S.A. did not directly intervene with its armed forces in Cuban war. Led by Fidel Castro, the people of Cuba won.

Is there the likelihood of such wars recurring? Yes, there is. uprisings of this kind likely to recur? Yes, they are. But wars of this l are popular uprisings. Is there the likelihood of conditions in other count reaching the point where the cup of the popular patience overflows and t take to arms? Yes, there is such a likelihood. What is the attitude of Marxists to such uprisings? A most favourable attitude. These uprisi cannot be identified with wars between countries, with local wars, because insurgent people are fighting for the right of self-determination, for tl social and independent national development; these uprisings are direc against the corrupt reactionary regimes, against the colonialists. The Co munists support just wars of this kind wholeheartedly and without res vations and they march in the van of the peoples fighting for liberation.

Comrades, mankind has arrived at the stage in history when it is in position to solve problems that were too much for the previous generatio This applies also to the problem of all problems, that of preventing world w

The working class, which today rules over a vast area of the world a in time will rule over all the world, cannot allow the forces doomed history to bring down hundreds of millions into the grave with them. F a world war in the conditions of today would be waged with missiles ai nuclear weapons, that is, it would be the most destructive war in all histor

Among the H-bombs already tested there are bombs each of which several times more powerful than all the explosives used in the Second Wor War and, indeed, ever since man appeared on earth. Scientists have est mated that the explosion of a single H-bomb in an industrial area would ki up to 1,500,000 outright and bring death to another 400,000 through radia tion. Even a medium hydrogen bomb would be enough to wipe out a larg city. According to British scientists four megaton bombs, one each fo London, Birmingham, Lancashire and Yorkshire, would kill at least 2 million. According to data supplied by U.S. experts to the Senate, th anticipated casualties in the United States in twenty-four hours of nuclea war would range from 50 to 75 million people. The American physicis Linus Pauling says that the areas likely to receive powerful nuclear blow are inhabited by a total of about a thousand million people and that 500 to 750 million people would be likely to perish within sixty days of a nuclear blow. Nor would nuclear war spare the people in the countries not directly subjected to the bombing; in particular, millions would die as a result of radiation.

We know that if the imperialist madmen were to begin a world war, the peoples would wipe out capitalism. But we are resolutely opposed to war, because we are concerned for the destinies of mankind, its present and its future. We know that the first to suffer in the event of war would be the working people and their vanguard—the working class.

We remember how Lenin put the question of the destiny of the working class. Just after the revolution, when the first country of the workers and peasants found itself besieged, he said, " If we can save the working man, camp. The more reactionary circles are displaying a growing nervousness and tendency towards reckless practices and aggression, by means of which they hope to mend their fences. At the same time, there are also among the ruling circles of these countries those who know the danger of a new war to capitalism. Hence the two trends: one leaning towards war, the other towards accepting, in one way or another, the idea of peaceful co-existence.

The socialist countries take both of these trends into account in their policy. They work for negotiations and agreements with the capitalist countries on the basis of constructive proposals and promote personal contact between statesmen of the socialist and capitalist countries. Every opportunity should be used as before to expose the cold-war men, those who want to keep up the arms drive, and to convince the masses that the socialist countries really mean what they say in working to safeguard world peace. . . .

Abolition of Colonialism and the Newly-Independent Countries

We were glad to welcome at the Moscow meeting representatives from the fraternal Communist parties of the Asian, African and Latin American countries, staunch fighters for the independence and free development of the peoples. Today there are Communist parties in more than fifty countries of those continents. This has extended the sphere of influence of the Communist movement, making it truly world-wide. . . .

Lenin saw that task in encouraging the revolutionary urge of the working masses for activity and organisation irrespective of the level they had attained, in using Communist theory in the specific conditions of their countries, in merging with the proletarians of other countries in common struggle (*Collected Works*, Russ. Ed., Vol. 30, pp. 137–138).

This task had not yet been realised anywhere when Lenin first set it, and there was no book to tell how it should be carried out. The Communist parties in the countries which are now fighting for national independence or which have already won it, are in an incomparably more favourable position, for there is now a vast store of experience in applying Marxist-Leninist theory in the conditions of countries and areas which capitalism had doomed to age-long backwardness.

This experience gained by the world Communist movement is a great treasure-house for all Communists. Obviously, only the Party operating in the country concerned can make proper use of this experience and correctly shape the policy to be pursued.

These parties are concentrating on the main point of how best to approach their own peoples, how to convince the masses that they cannot win a better future unless they fight against imperialism and the forces of internal reaction, and how to strengthen international solidarity with the socialist countries, with the communist vanguard of the working people of the world.

The renovation of the world on the principles of freedom, democracy and socialism, in which we are now participating, is a great historical process in which different revolutionary and democratic movements unite and co-operate, with socialist revolutions exerting the determining influence. The success of the national-liberation movement, due in large measure to the victories of socialism, in turn strengthen the international positions of socialism in the struggle against imperialism. It is this truly Leninist concept of the historical processes that forms the basis of the Communist parties and socialist countries, a policy aimed at strengthening the close alliance with those people fighting for independence or who have already won it. . . .

The imperialist powers, above all the United States, are doing their utmost to harness the countries that have cast off the colonial yoke to their system and thereby strengthen the positions of world capitalism, to infuse it, as bourgeois ideologists put it, with fresh blood, to rejuvenate and consolidate it. If we look the facts in the face, we shall have to admit that the imperialists have powerful economic levers with which to exert pressure on the newly-independent countries. They still succeed in enmeshing some of the politically-independent countries in the web of economic dependence. Now that it is no longer possible to establish outright colonial régimes, the imperialists resort to disguised forms and methods of enslaving and plundering the countries that have attained freedom. At the same time, the colonial powers back the internal reactionaries in all these countries; they impose on them puppet dictatorial régimes and involve them in aggressive *blocs*. Although there are sharp contradictions between the imperialist countries, they often take joint action against the national-liberation movement.

But if we take account of all the factors shaping the destinies of the peoples that have shaken off colonial rule, we will see that in the final analysis the trends of social progress opposing imperialism are bound to prevail.

But these matters are resolved in bitter struggle within each country. The statement of the meeting contains important propositions on the basic issues of the national-liberation movement. It defines the tasks of the Communist parties and their attitude to the various classes and social groups. In expressing the identity of views of the Marxist-Leninist parties, the statement calls for the maximum utilisation of the revolutionary possibilities of the various classes and social strata and for drawing all allies, no matter if inconsistent, shaky and unstable, into the struggle against imperialism.

The Communists are revolutionaries and it would be a bad thing if they failed to discern the new opportunities, to find the best ways and the best means of reaching the goal. Special note should be taken of the idea set forth in the statement about the formation of national democratic states. The statement outlines the main characteristics of these states and their tasks. It should be stressed that in view of the great variety of conditions in those countries where the peoples, having achieved independence, are now moulding their own way of life, a variety of ways of solving the tasks of social progress is bound to emerge.

The correct application of Marxist-Leninist theory in the newly-independent countries consists precisely in seeking the forms that take cognisance of the peculiarities of the economic, political and cultural life of the peoples to unite all the sound forces of the nation, to ensure the leading role of the working class in the national front, in the struggle completely to eradicate the roots of imperialism and the remnants of feudalism, and to clear the way for the ultimate advance towards socialism.

Today, when imperialist reaction is striving to foist the policy of anti-communism on the young independent states, it is most important to give a truthful explanation of the Communist views and ideals. Communists support the general democratic measures of the national governments. At the same time, they explain to the masses that these measures are far from being socialist.

The aspirations of the peoples now smashing the fetters of colonialism are particularly appreciated and understood best of all by the working people of the socialist countries, by the Communists of the whole world. Our world outlook, the interests of all working people for which we are fighting, impel us to do our best to ensure that the peoples take the right road to progress, to the flowering of their material and spiritual forces. We, by means of our policy, must strengthen the confidence of the peoples in the socialist countries.

The aid extended by the U.S.S.R. and the other socialist states to the countries which have won independence has but one aim—to help strengthen the position of these countries in the struggle against imperialism, to further the development of their national economy and improve the life of their people. Noting that the working class of the advanced countries is vitally interested in " ensuring the independence " of the colonial countries " in the shortest possible period," Engels wrote: " One thing is indisputable: the victorious proletariat cannot impose happiness on another nation without undermining thereby its own victory " (K. Marx and F. Engels, *Works*, Russ. ed., Vol. 27, pp. 238, 239).

The international duty of the victorious working class consists in helping the peoples of the economically underdeveloped countries to smash the last links in the chains of colonial slavery, in rendering them all-round aid in their struggle against imperialism, for the right to self-determination and independent development. However, it does not follow that socialist aid exerts no influence on the prospects of the further development of newly-independent countries.

The Soviet Union has been and is the sincere friend of the colonial peoples; it has always championed their rights, interests and strivings for independence. We shall continue to strengthen and develop our economic and cultural co-operation with countries which have become independent.

The Soviet Union submitted to the Fifteenth Session of the U.N. General Assembly the declaration for granting independence to colonial countries and peoples.

As a result of the bitter political struggle which raged round this proposal both within and without the U.N., the General Assembly adopted the declaration. The basic point in the Soviet Declaration—the need for abolishing colonialism in all its forms and manifestations rapidly and for good—was in the main reflected in the resolution adopted by the United Nations. This was a victory for the progressive forces and all the socialist countries, which are defending the cause of freedom and independent national development of peoples firmly and consistently. . . .

The peoples of the socialist countries, the Communists and progressives all over the world see their duty in abolishing the last remnants of the colonial system of imperialism, in supporting the peoples now liberating themselves from the colonial powers and in helping them to realise their ideals of liberation. . . .

Some Ideological Questions of the Communist Movement

For us Soviet Communists, sons of the October Revolution, recognition of the necessity of the revolutionary transformation of capitalist society into socialist society is axiomatic. The road to socialism lies through the proletarian revolution and the dictatorship of the proletariat. As regards the forms of the transition to socialism, these, as pointed out by the Twentieth

Congress of the C.P.S.U., will become more and more varied. This does not necessarily mean that the transition to socialism will everywhere and in all cases be associated with armed uprising and civil war. Marxism-Leninism starts from the premise that the forms of the transition to socialism may be peaceful and non-peaceful. It is in the interests of the working class, of the masses, that the revolution be carried out in a peaceful way. But in the event of the ruling classes resisting the revolution with violence and refusing to submit to the will of the people, the proletariat will be obliged to crush their resistance and launch a resolute civil war.

We are convinced that with the growth of the might of the socialist world system and the better organisation of the working class in the capitalist countries, increasingly favourable conditions for socialist revolutions will arise. The transition to socialism in countries with developed parliamentary traditions may be effected by utilising parliament and in other countries by utilising institutions conforming to their national traditions. In this case it is a question of using the parliamentary form and not the bourgeois parliament as such in order to place it at the service of the people, and to fill it with new meaning. Thus, it will not be a matter of electoral combinations or simply skirmishes round the polls. The reformists indulge in this sort of thing. Such combinations are alien to us Communists. For us the rallying and consolidation of the revolutionary forces of the working class and of all working people, and the launching of mass revolutionary action are an absolute condition for winning a stable majority in parliament. To win a majority in parliament and transform it into an organ of the people's power, given a powerful revolutionary movement in the country, means smashing the military-bureaucratic machine of the bourgeoisie and setting up a new, proletarian people's state in parliamentary form.

It is quite obvious that in those countries where capitalism is still strong and still commands a huge military and police apparatus, the transition to socialism will inevitably take place in conditions of sharp class struggle. The political leadership of the working class, headed by the Communist vanguard, is the decisive condition no matter what the forms of transition to socialism are. . . .

The struggle against revisionism, against any deviation from Leninism, is as important as ever. It is a struggle aimed at strengthening the socialist camp, at consistently applying the principles of Marxism-Leninism. . . .

The Communist movement faces yet another danger—dogmatism and sectarianism. At present, when all forces must be united to fight imperialism, prevent war and end the omnipotence of the monopolies, dogmatism and sectarianism can do great harm to our cause. Leninism is uncompromising towards dogmatism. Lenin wrote: " . . . It is necessary to grasp the indisputable truth that the Marxist should study life as it is, the precise facts of *reality*, and should not cling to the theory of yesterday which, like any theory, at best can but indicate the basic, the general factors, and can but *draw close* to an understanding of the complexities of life " (*Collected Works*, Russ. ed., Vol. 24, p. 26).

Dogmatism nourishes a sectarian bigotry, which hampers the unity of the working class and of all progressive forces with the Communist parties. Dogmatism and sectarianism are irreconcilably at variance with the creative development of revolutionary theory and its creative application, they lead to the isolation of Communists from the masses of the working people, doom them to passive anticipation or to reckless ultra-leftism in the revolutionary struggle, prevent them from utilising all the opportunities in the interests of the victory of the working class and of all the democratic forces.

The statement stresses that the Communist parties will continue to wage a resolute struggle on two fronts—against revisionism, which is still the main danger, and against dogmatism and sectarianism. Dogmatism and sectarianism may also become the main danger at one or another stage in the development of the various parties unless a consistent struggle is waged against them. . . .

Soviet Leadership of the Communist Camp

It should be noted that at the meeting the delegation of the CPSU expressed its point of view concerning the formula that the Soviet Union stands at the head of the socialist camp and the CPSU at the head of the Communist movement. The delegation declared that this formula was regarded above all as high appreciation of the services rendered by our Party, founded by Lenin, and expressed its heartfelt gratitude to all the fraternal parties for it. Our Party, reared by Lenin, has always seen its first duty in fulfilling its international obligations to the working class of the world. The delegation assured the meeting that the CPSU would continue to hold high the banner of proletarian internationalism and would spare no effort in carrying out its international duties.

Nevertheless the CPSU delegation proposed that that formula be not included in the statement or other documents of the Communist movement.

As to the principles of relations between the fraternal parties, the CPSU very definitely expressed its views on this matter at its Twenty-First Congress. From the rostrum of the Congress, we declared to the whole world that in the Communist movement, as in the socialist camp, there has always been complete equality and solidarity of all the Communist and Workers' parties and socialist countries. The Communist Party of the Soviet Union does not lead other parties. There are no " superior " and " subordinate " parties in the Communist movement. All the Communist parties are equal and independent, all are responsible for the destiny of the Communist movement, for its setbacks and victories. Every Communist and Workers' Party is responsible to the working class, to the working people of its country, to the entire international working-class and Communist movement.

The role of the Soviet Union does not lie in its leading the other socialist countries, but in its being the first to blaze the trail to socialism, in its being the most powerful country in the socialist world system, in its having accumulated vast positive experience in building socialism, and being the first to embark on the full-scale building of communism. It is stressed in the statement that the Communist Party of the Soviet Union has been and remains the universally recognised vanguard of the world Communist movement, being its most experienced and steeled contingent.

At the present time, when there is a large group of socialist countries each facing its own specific tasks, when there are eighty-seven Communist and Workers' parties each with its own tasks, it is impossible to lead all the socialist countries and Communist parties from any single centre. It is both impossible and unnecessary. Tempered Marxist-Leninist cadres capable of leading their parties, their countries, have grown up in the Communist parties.

And, indeed, it is well known that the CPSU does not issue directives to other parties. The fact that we will be called " the head," spells no advantages for our Party or the other parties. Just the reverse. It only creates difficulties.

As is seen from the statement, the fraternal parties agreed with the reasons stated by our delegation. The question may arise: will not our international solidarity be weakened by the fact that this proposition is not written down in the statement? No, it will not. At present there are no rules regulating relations between parties, but we have a common Marxist-Leninist ideology, and loyalty to this ideology is the main condition of our solidarity and unity. It is essential that we guide ourselves consistently by the directions of Marx, Engels and Lenin, that we persistently put into practice the principles of Marxism-Leninism. The international solidarity of the Communist movement will then constantly increase. . . .

Inasmuch as in the socialist countries conditions differ from country to country, it is only natural that each Communist Party applies Marxist-Leninist theory in keeping with the conditions obtaining in its country. For this reason, we must show understanding for this urge of the fraternal parties, which should know the conditions and features of their countries best. . . .

Naturally, one must not inflate the importance of these distinctive features, exaggerate them and overlook the basic general line of socialist construction charted in the doctrine of Marx and Lenin. We have always firmly championed the purity of the great teaching of Marxism-Leninism and the basic principles for its realisation, and will continue to do so.

Representatives of the Communist and Workers' parties exchanged opinions on questions of the current international situation and discussed the pressing problems of the Communist and working-class movement, or, as comrades put it figuratively at the meeting, we set our watches. Indeed, the socialist countries and the Communist parties need to set the time. When someone's watch is fast or slow, it is adjusted, so as to show the right time. The Communist movement, too, needs to set the time, so that our formidable army marches in step and advances with confident stride towards communism. Putting it figuratively Marxism-Leninism, the jointly prepared documents of international Communist meetings, are our time-piece.

Now that all the Communist and Workers' parties have adopted unanimous decisions at the meeting, each Party will strictly and undeviatingly abide by these decisions in everything it does. . . .

The unity of every Communist Party, the unity of all the Communist parties, is what makes up the integral world Communist movement, which is aimed at achieving our common goal, victory for communism throughout the world. The main thing that is required of all the Communist and Workers' parties today, is perseveringly to strengthen to the utmost the unity and cohesion of their ranks. . . .

Our Party will do everything to make the socialist camp and the world Communist front still stronger.

The Communist Party of the Soviet Union is firmly determined to strengthen unity and friendship with all the fraternal parties of the socialist countries, with the Marxist-Leninist parties of all the world. In this connection I want to emphasise our invariable effort to strengthen bonds of fraternal friendship with the Communist Party of China, with the great Chinese people. In its relations with the Communist Party of China our

Party always proceeds from the premise that the friendship of our two great peoples, the unity of our two parties, the biggest parties in the international Communist movement, are of exceptional importance in the struggle for the triumph of our common cause. Our Party has always exerted and will continue to exert every effort to strengthen this great friendship. We have one common goal with People's China, with the Chinese Communists, as with the Communists of all countries—safeguarding peace and the building of communism; common interests—the happiness and wellbeing of the working people: and a firm common basis of principle—Marxism-Leninism. . . .

[At a meeting of party organisations of the Higher Party School, the Academy of Social Sciences, and the Institute of Marxism-Leninism, January 6, 1961. From text in *World Marxist Review*, No. 1, 1961.]

Chinese Communist Party Resolution on the Moscow Conference

The ninth plenary session of the Eighth Central Committee of the Communist Party of China, after hearing a report by Comrade Teng Hsiao-p'ing on the meeting of representatives of Communist and Workers' Parties held in November 1960, expressed satisfaction with the work of the Chinese Communist Party delegation headed by Comrade Liu Shao-ch'i. . . .

The achievements of this meeting have greatly inspired the people of the world, who are striving for world peace, national liberation, democracy and socialism, have dealt heavy blows at the imperialists headed by the United States of America, the reactionaries of all countries and the Yugoslav revisionist clique, and have strengthened the solidarity of the socialist camp and the international communist movement on the new basis. The statement of this meeting reiterated that the 1957 Moscow Declaration and peace manifesto were the fighting banners and guides to action for the whole international communist movement; it enriched the 1957 documents by its correct analysis of the international situation during the past three years and of a series of important problems confronting the international communist movement. The Communist Party of China, always unswervingly upholding Marxism-Leninism and the principle of proletarian internationalism, will defend the statement of this meeting, just as it has defended the Moscow Declaration of 1957, and will resolutely strive for the realization of the common tasks set forth by this document.

As the statement says, our time is a time of struggle between two opposing social systems, a time of socialist revolutions and national-liberation revolutions, a time of the breakdown of imperialism, of the abolition of the colonial system, a time of transition of more peoples to the socialist path, of the triumph of socialism and communism on a world-wide scale. The doom of imperialism and the triumph of socialism are inevitable. The course of social development has once again testified to the great vitality of Marxism-Leninism and has thoroughly refuted all modern revisionist "theories" against Marxism-Leninism.

At present, there is a new upsurge in the struggle of the people thoughout the world against imperialism, for world peace, national liberation, democracy and socialism. The powerful socialist camp is becoming the decisive factor in the development of human society. The rise of the national democratic revolutions is a great development second only to the formation of the world socialist system. The mass political and economic struggles waged by the peoples in the developed capitalist countries against oppression by domestic and foreign monopoly capital have been gaining momentum. All these forces have merged into a giant torrent battering the world imperialist system. The general crisis of capitalism has reached a new stage of development. The forces of peace have surpassed the forces of war. The progressive forces have surpassed the reactionary forces. The forces of socialism have surpassed the forces of imperialism. A bright prospect for the cause of peace, national liberation, democracy and socialism is unfolding before the people of the world.

The present situation imperatively demands that peoples all over the world further unite and wage an unremitting struggle against the policies of aggression and war of the imperialists headed by the United States. The United States, the chief imperialist country of our time, being the biggest international exploiter, the world gendarme, the chief bulwark of world reaction and modern colonialism and the main force of aggression and war of our time, is the main enemy of the peoples of the whole world. U.S. imperialism, together with other imperialist countries and the reactionaries of all countries, has formed all kinds of military and political alliances and is carrying out with increased intensity criminal activities to oppose the socialist camp and to strangle the national-liberation movement, the revolutionary movement of the working class and democratic movements in general. As a result of its persistence in this reactionary policy, U.S. imperialism has landed itself in unprecedented isolation. With the peoples of the world persevering in a resolute struggle against the forces of reaction and aggression headed by the United States, the peace, national-liberation, democratic and socialist movements are sure to win ever greater victories. Revolution is the affair of the peoples themselves in the various countries. The communists have always been against the export of revolution. They also resolutely oppose imperialist export of counter-revolution, against imperialist interference in the internal affairs of the people of various countries who have risen in revolution. The Communist Party of China and the Chinese people will, as in the past, make unremitting efforts in close unity with the fraternal parties and the revolutionary peoples of various countries to further the cause of the peoples of the world against imperialism and for world peace, national-liberation, democracy and socialism. They deem it their internationalist obligation to support the struggles of oppressed nations and oppressed peoples against imperialism.

The defence of world peace, the realization of peaceful co-existence and peaceful competition among countries of different social systems and the prevention of the new world war which is now being planned by the imperialists constitute the most pressing tasks for the peoples of the world. The imperialists headed by the United States are stubbornly persisting in a " cold war " policy leading to the catastrophe of nuclear war, intensifying the arming of the militarist forces of West Germany and Japan and fanatically engaging in armaments expansion and war preparations. Facts have proved that the aggressive nature of imperialism has not changed. As long as imperialism exists there will be soil for wars of aggression. The danger is not yet over that imperialism will launch a new and unprecedentedly destructive world war. It is more imperative than ever that the peoples should be especially vigilant. However, owing to the fundamental change in the international balance of class forces, a new world war can be prevented by the joint efforts of the powerful forces of our era—the socialist camp, the international working class, the national-liberation movement and all peace-loving countries and peoples. Peace can be effectively safeguarded provided there is reliance on the struggle of the masses of the people and provided a broad united front is established and expanded against the policies of aggression and war of the imperialists headed by the United States. Marxist-Leninists have never held that the way to socialist revolution necessarily lies through wars between states. The socialist countries have always persisted in the policy of peaceful co-existence and peaceful competition with the capitalist countries, advocated the settlement of international disputes through negotiation, advocated disarmament, the banning of nuclear weapons, the disbandment of military *blocs*, the dismantling of military bases in foreign territory, and the prevention of the revival of the militarist forces in West Germany and Japan. The peace proposals put forward by the socialist countries, and first of all by the Soviet Union, have won warm endorsement and support from people the world over. The Communist Party and the people of China have always regarded the safeguarding of world peace, the realization of peaceful co-existence and the prevention of another world war as their most urgent tasks in the international struggle. During the past year, our country concluded treaties of friendship and mutual non-aggression or treaties of peace and friendship with Burma, Nepal, Afghanistan, Guinea and Cambodia, a boundary treaty with Burma, an agreement on the boundary question with Nepal and an arrangement for the implementation of the treaty concerning the question of dual nationality with Indonesia. The conclusion of these treaties, this agreement and this arrangement has borne out the inexhaustible vitality of the five principles of peaceful co-existence and has made important contributions to the cause of safeguarding world peace. In the future, we shall continue to stand by the other socialist countries and all peace-loving countries and peoples in tenacious struggles to defend world peace and prevent world war.

The solidarity of the socialist camp and of the international communist movement is the most important guarantee for victory in the struggle of all peoples for world peace, national liberation, democracy and socialism. This great solidarity is forged by common ideals and the common cause and has been developed and consolidated in the common struggle against the common enemy. It is based on Marxism-Leninism and the principle of proletarian internationalism. The Communist Party of China, in accordance with the principle of proletarian internationalism, has consistently striven to safeguard this great solidarity.

The socialist countries carry on political, economic and cultural co-operation in accordance with the principles of complete equality, mutual respect for independence and sovereignty, mutual non-interference in internal affairs, mutual benefit and comradely mutual assistance. The Communist Parties of all countries are independent and equal and at the same time, in the spirit of proletarian internationalism, they must adhere to the common stand on the struggle against imperialism and for peace, national liberation, democracy and socialism as jointly adopted at meetings of the fraternal parties and must unite as one and support each other in their common cause. The statement of this meeting pointed out that the Communist and Workers' Parties should hold meetings whenever necessary to discuss urgent problems, acquaint themselves with each other's views and positions, work out common views through consultations and co-ordinate joint actions in the struggle for common goals. This is entirely necessary for the strengthening of solidarity and for victory in the common cause.

The great Marxist-Leninist teachings are the unshakable ideological foundation of the solidarity of the socialist camp and the unity of the international communist movement. In order to safeguard the purity of Marxism-Leninism and its creative application and development, it is necessary firmly to combat revisionism which mirrors bourgeois ideology and departs from and betrays Marxism-Leninism, and especially to combat Yugoslav revisionism. Modern revisionism is still the main danger for the international communist movement. At the same time, the tendencies of dogmatism and sectarianism, which are divorced from reality and from the masses, must also be opposed. The plenary session of the Central Committee of the Communist Party of China held that it is of particular importance at present to continue to carry out the principle of integrating the universal truth of Marxism-Leninism with the specific practice of China's revolution and construction, and to raise the level of Marxism-Leninism of the cadres of the Party and the state.

The unity between China and the Soviet Union and between the Chinese and the Soviet Parties is of particularly great significance. In the international communist movement, the great Communist Party of the Soviet Union is the vanguard with the longest history and richest experience. The great Soviet Union is the most advanced and most powerful country in the socialist camp. The Communist Party of China has consistently striven to maintain and strengthen the unity between the Chinese and the Soviet Parties and between the two countries, holding that this is in the fundamental interests of the peoples of China and the Soviet Union and also of the peoples of the whole world. The imperialists will never succeed in their hopeless scheme to split the unity between the Chinese and the Soviet Parties and between the two countries. . . .

[Adopted January 18. NCNA, January 20, 1961.]

10. Appendices: "Inside" Reports of the Dispute

The Chinese Position

IF West Bengal's Harekrishna Konar is to be believed, he has been chosen by the Chinese to lead the attack on the Soviet positions in the Communist Party of India. He is reported to have told the Calcutta District Party Council last week how Kerala's Damodaran was snubbed by the Chinese and he himself had long interviews with important leaders. Damodaran and Konar had gone to Hanoi as CPI's fraternal delegates to the Vietnamese Lao Dang Party Conference.

Damodaran's fault was that he stuck to General Secretary Ajoy Ghosh's instructions to keep away from the Chinese and to tell them, if they took the initiative in fraternising, what the CPI feels about the Chinese general political line and particularly about the Chinese attitude towards India.

Chinese views. Konar told the Calcutta District Council that so far, Indian Communists knew only the Soviet point of view but now he was in a position to place the Chinese point of view before them and he considered it his duty to do so even if it amounted to a technical breach of Party forms. He said, the Chinese told him that their differences with the Soviet Party started soon after Stalin's death. They did not like the Soviet leadership's handling of the Beria case. The way the Soviet leadership went about denigrating Stalin was "obnoxious." The Soviet attitude towards Yugoslav revisionism was "cringing" and one of giving concessions. On every occasion the Chinese pointed out the mistakes of the Russians to them but the latter paid no heed. At the time of the Twentieth Congress they did not take account of the Chinese criticism of their "distortions of Marxism." Even at the time of the Hungarian "counter-revolution" the Soviet attitude was "vacillating" and Khrushchev was on the point of withdrawing Soviet armies. It was with great difficulty that the Chinese succeeded in "persuading" the Soviet leaders to take a "firm line" and "go to the defence of Hungarian revolution."

The Chinese complained that even at the time of the Moscow (1957) Conference the Soviet Leaders did not take a firm attitude and were prepared to give more concessions to the Yugoslavs. The Soviet leaders were of the view that revisionism was no longer the main enemy and that under the changed circumstances fire had to be concentrated against dogmatism; it was because the Russians themselves were taking revisionist positions. The Chinese told them, " If you do not fight revisionism we will have to take up the battle single-handed against all distortions of Marxism." It was only then that the Russians agreed to accept the Chinese amendments to the draft declaration on behalf of 12 parties. The Yugoslavs refused to sign the amended declaration. But later the Soviet leaders too went back upon the Declaration.

Complaining bitterly about the unfriendly attitude of the Soviet leaders since then the Chinese held that almost all the Russian technicians had been withdrawn from China even before their term of contract had ended. The Soviet leaders did not like the " political education " of the technicians arranged by the Chinese Party as a gesture of its fraternal feelings for the Russians, the Soviet leaders considered it an interference with their inner-Party affairs—an echo, according to the Chinese, of the complaint of Tito against Stalin in 1948. The Chinese also told Konar that while the American Embassy in Moscow was allowed to bring out its journal in Russian, the paper published by the Chinese was closed down on the plea that it sought to propagate ideas in conflict with the official Soviet line.

Cold War. Coming to the issues round which the Soviet-Chinese controversy centres, the Chinese said that the alternative to peaceful co-existence was not war; it was cold war. By putting forward the thesis that war would break out if the policy of peaceful co-existence was given up, the Soviet leaders, according to the Chinese, were trying to create a scare among the people and deaden the edge of anti-imperialist and anti-war struggles of the people of capitalist and colonial countries. By insisting that peaceful co-existence was possible the Soviet leaders were sowing illusions about imperialism. The Chinese also dismissed the possibility of peaceful transition to socialism. They believe that the Soviet line of peaceful co-existence and peaceful transition arose out of a wrong understanding of the nature of imperialism and the role of working class.

About the approach to the bourgeoisie and the governments of the newly liberated countries, the Chinese said that capitalism in Asia was weak in relation to imperialism and was bound to line up with the latter, whatever might be the attitude adopted by it (capitalism in the newly liberated countries of Asia) earlier as a result of the pressure of the people. There was a swing towards the Right in the government of these countries.

China and India. The Chinese estimate of India is that the Government and Jawaharlal Nehru were now leaning more on imperialism and coming out in their " true reactionary colours in domestic policies." The Chinese assured the Indian listener that they had no intention of crossing the MacMahon Line. Soviet and Indian party leaders should have no fears on this account. According to the Chinese the Government of India came to know of the Ladakh incident from its spies or from Soviet reports and began to make much noise about it. Even if the Ladakh incident had not taken place the Indian government would have cooked up some other issue so that it could divert the attention of the people from its shift in foreign policy and also from its reactionary home policy. . . .

[Report carried in the Indian news magazine *Link*, October 16, 1960.]

The Soviet Position

The Chinese Party has been accused of not accepting the ideas embodied in the 18-Parties Rome Declaration and the 12-Parties Moscow Declaration. The differences seem to have begun soon after the Soviet Party Congress when the Chinese began criticism of the common understanding arrived at between the fraternal delegations of different parties to the Congress. Earlier, in the days of Stalin also, the Chinese had criticised certain Soviet policies but the criticism at that time had acted as a " corrective " while now they took up positions basically opposed to those accepted at international conferences. (Long quotations from the Chinese publication "Long Live Leninism" have been given to show how the Chinese went back upon the declarations and statements they had signed along with other parties.) Moreover, the Chinese resented Soviet criticism of some of their policies such as their Tibet policy, Communes and "Leap Forward" and considered such criticism "unfriendly."

Among the "unfriendly" acts of the Chinese listed is interference in the internal affairs of two East European Parties. Soviet political instructors sent to work among Soviet citizens in China were not allowed to function and attempts were made to subvert the political allegiance of Soviet Communists in China; it was only then that Soviet technicians were withdrawn. The Chinese periodical published from Moscow was stopped for printing articles distorting and attacking Soviet positions; but it was stopped only after the Soviet periodical published from Peking had been closed down. The gravest charges against the Chinese, however, are those which relate to the activities of the Chinese representatives on international mass organisations like the World Federation of Trade Unions, the Women's Organisation and the Peace Movement. The Chinese are accused of attempts to break the unity of these "non-party" mass organisations and to convert them into purely communist organisations contrary to the accepted policy of other Communist Parties. The Chinese who have withdrawn their representative from the World Peace Movement's headquarters wanted Peace Partisans not merely to campaign against the danger of war but also participate in anti-imperialist and anti-capitalist mass actions. . . .

[*Link*, October 30, 1960.]